Make the Cut

Make the Cut

A Guide to Becoming a Successful Assistant Editor in Film and TV

Lori Jane Coleman, A.C.E.
and Diana Friedberg, A.C.E.

ELSEVIER

AMSTERDAM • BOSTON • HEIDELBERG • LONDON • NEW YORK • OXFORD
PARIS • SAN DIEGO • SAN FRANCISCO • SINGAPORE • SYDNEY • TOKYO
Focal Press is an imprint of Elsevier

Focal Press is an imprint of Elsevier
30 Corporate Drive, Suite 400, Burlington, MA 01803, USA
The Boulevard, Langford Lane, Kidlington, Oxford, OX5 1GB, UK

Notices
Knowledge and best practice in this field are constantly changing. As new research and experience broaden
our understanding, changes in research methods, professional practices, or medical treatment may become necessary.

Practitioners and researchers must always rely on their own experience and knowledge in evaluating and
using any information, methods, compounds, or experiments described herein. In using such information or
methods they should be mindful of their own safety and the safety of others, including parties for whom they
have a professional responsibility.

To the fullest extent of the law, neither the Publisher nor the authors, contributors, or editors, assume any liability
for any injury and/or damage to persons or property as a matter of products liability, negligence or otherwise, or
from any use or operation of any methods, products, instructions, or ideas contained in the material herein.

Library of Congress Cataloging-in-Publication Data
Friedberg, Diana.
   Make the cut : a guide to becoming a successful assistant editor in film and tv / Diana Friedberg.
      p. cm.
   Includes bibliographical references and index.
   ISBN 978-0-240-81398-1
   1. Motion pictures—Editing. 2. Television—Production and direction.   I. Title.
TR899.F85 2010
778.5'35—dc22   2010008982

British Library Cataloguing-in-Publication Data
A catalogue record for this book is available from the British Library.

ISBN: 978-0-240-81398-1

For information on all Focal Press publications
visit our website at www.elsevierdirect.com

10 11 12 13 14   5 4 3 2 1

Printed in the United States of America

**Working together to grow
libraries in developing countries**

www.elsevier.com | www.bookaid.org | www.sabre.org

ELSEVIER   BOOK AID
International   Sabre Foundation

Contents

Contents

Dedications

For my Mom, Bebe Yuni Kranze, whose heart and soul enters each phrase of encouragement in this book, and for my Dad, Don Kranze, whose wisdom and work ethics are the construct of *Make the Cut*. Thank you. You were my first and best mentors.

For my amazing daughters, Deirdre and Allison, thank you for all your inspiration. And for their Dad, Charley Coleman, who taught me how to change the block on my very first coding machine.

For my better half, Scott Gordon, thank you for your support through all my absences.

For my assistant editors who guided me through the transition from film to current technology, Daniel Valverde and Jan Northrop, thank you for all that you have taught me.

Last, but not least, this book is dedicated to all the ACE internship applicants from around the world. This book is the internship program in a nutshell, and I hope it helps you on your journey.

Lori Jane Coleman

For my beloved husband Lionel, who has shared my passion for filmmaking and has been a constant inspiration during all our cinematic collaborations over the past 40 years. We dreamed the dream and crossed continents to make Hollywood a reality. Thank you for sharing the journey. It has been awesome and a privilege.

For my wonderful children, David and Amanda-Mae, thank you for playing such a vital role in my life and being my dearest companions. I will forever cherish happy memories of your participation in many of my film adventures. For Robby, I treasure your friendship and support.

Thank you to all the mentors in my life. Particularly Jackie le Cordeur in South Africa, who offered to train me as an assistant editor when I completed my university studies in Cape Town. Thank you for waiting. You ignited the fire, which is still burning brightly.

For all you aspiring assistants, to whom we hand down the flame of our experiences, you can make the cut.

Diana Friedberg

Acknowledgments

We would like to extend our appreciation to American Cinema Editors (ACE) for providing the opportunity and support for the internship program upon which this book is based. Bill Gordean, A.C.E. began this mentorship program in the early 1990s, and we have been at the helm for nearly two decades—expanding, teaching, and encouraging with renewed annual vigor. Many thanks go to Jenni McCormick and the tireless ACE staff for their dedication and time.

Special thanks to Alan Heim, A.C.E., Sabrina Plisco, A.C.E., Matt Chesse, A.C.E., Mark Helfrich, A.C.E., Troy Takaki, A.C.E., and Stephen Lovejoy, A.C.E. for allowing us to include their words from the 2009 lecture series. The advice you shared helps pave the way for the next generation.

Others have been leaned on for advice and expertise. Many thanks to Lauren Pendergrass for editing our chapter on getting ready to online. Our deepest gratitude goes to Marissa Mueller and Jered Zalman for their insight on assisting in reality television. A special nod of appreciation to Carsten Kurpanek for creating templates of paperwork necessary for the cutting room. Daniel Nussbaum, Jered Zalman, Addison Donnell, Dillon Thomas, and Ashley Miller meticulously helped with transcriptions. Much gratitude goes to Larry Jordan for his technical advice.

We offer our deepest thanks to Tina Hirsch, A.C.E., Chris Cooke, A.C.E., and to so many other fellow editors and assistants who have participated in the internship program. Their loyalty to the endeavor of embracing the newly arrived assistant editors goes beyond the call of duty.

And last but not least, to our editor, Dennis McGonagle, thank you for your faith in our book, *Make the Cut*, and for paving our virginal journey into the world of publishing. It has been a seamless enterprise.

Preface

Twenty years from now you will be more disappointed by the things you didn't do than by the ones you did do. So throw off the bowlines. Sail away from the safe harbor. Catch the trade winds in your sails. Explore. Dream. Discover.

Mark Twain

Choose a job you love and you'll never have to work a day in your life.

Confucius

If you are passionately in love with the art of editing and have dreamed of making it your professional career, there is little doubt in our mind that you *can* make the cut. We would like to share with you our strategies on how to navigate your career in the film industry from your first step as an assistant film editor to the ultimate goal—becoming a film editor.

There are many ladders that can be climbed in the world of filmmaking. Some departments have well-trodden paths that cultivate the initiate. This is particularly true in the world of editing. In postproduction, there are entry-level jobs that include postproduction assistant, shipping and receiving clerk at post facilities, apprentice editor, and eventually an assistant editor. These jobs will lead toward a career as a picture editor. Though there is no *guarantee* that you will move up to an editing seat, we believe that you *can* and *will* if you pursue your dream tenaciously. There are hurdles—they can be overcome. There are personal shortcomings—they are surmountable. Your journey to success should be paved with *energy*, *skill*, and *tunnel vision*.

Becoming an assistant editor has its heartaches and rewards. There are long hours, social politics to navigate, career decisions to be made, and jobs to be won or lost. After dealing with all the doors that deny entry and celebrating those that allow access, the goals attained will ultimately be wholly satisfying. You just have to *stay your course*.

The assistant editor is the heart of the cutting room and is responsible for the body of work that is completed each day. The cutting rooms cannot function smoothly without the *consummate* assistant editor. During the course of the day, the editor will ask the assistant to deal with computer crashes, help find great stock shots, and watch and critique a scene. The editor needs you to be a loyal confidante and trustworthy partner for the duration of the film.

In *Make the Cut* we have encapsulated many of the attributes—social as well as technical—that are long-time industry standards. These attributes are still held in high esteem in professional editing rooms around the world. When applied, they will lead you to stand out amongst the throngs and **shine**.

You can do it, too.

You just have to make the cut.

Part 1

Getting Started

Chapter 1

On Your Way

The moment you cross the threshold of a cutting room, you enter the magical film world of storytelling. It is the last frontier where the original script can be reconceived and reconciled with the film that has been shot. It is the room in which the final rewrite occurs. The editing process provides countless hours of creativity and personal satisfaction to the editor and the editing crew.

To become an editor, you first have to be an assistant. American Cinema Editors (ACE) offers an internship program that is designed to train interns to become consummate assistant editors. The mission statement for the internship is:

> On a social level, you will cultivate a relationship with your Editor, and an entire postproduction and production crew. You have to know how to handle stress, high stakes, and mistakes. Trust and honesty are essential. There is the possibility of taking jobs with odd hours, traveling far from home and learning networking protocols. With our guidelines, you will begin to enjoy the challenges of postproduction and develop the skills necessary to succeed. Editorial differs dramatically from production in that we are some-what of a standalone island. We are entrusted with the keys to the kingdom. Errors in workflow design and execution have implications that are far-reaching and expensive. Taking personal responsibility is paramount for every individual on the editorial team. Technically, you will be responsible for paperwork systems, project settings and organization, digitizing, import/export/file transfer procedures, logging, media storage, backup technologies and procedures. You will need to understand how you handle stock footage, sound effects (SFX), music (MX), visual effects (VFX or VIZFX), automatic dialog replacement (ADR), onlining, protecting network/studio assets and even organizing the office space. On larger VFX shows you may need to demonstrate your database design and concepts for VFX tracking.

To further your career quickly and advance to the level of editor, you have to be the *best* assistant you can possibly be. There are a variety of venues—from television to features, from trailers to documentaries, from pilots to reality TV—and though there are many similarities, there are also many differences in the daily work flow. When you've learned the basics of assisting, you will be able to adapt your skills to any production. If you go above and beyond the basic skills, you will **shine** and be in high demand.

DOI: 10.1016/B978-0-240-81398-1.00001-8

The length of each project will vary widely. Features may take longer than a year or be as short as 3 months. Television seasons last from 3 to 10 months. Some projects require weekend work and 15-hour days, and some shows demand only 40- to 50-hour weeks. Some shows are shot on location and allow the editorial staff to remain on home turf, and some request the editorial crew to be on-site. All projects are finite, so you will have to look for a job each time a show ends. If you are the *best* assistant in town, the search for a new gig is hampered only by the need to decide which job to accept. However, there will always be *down* time in-between movies. We suggest you look for your next job while you are still employed and budget for the weeks of unemployment that occur periodically.

Getting your first job is the hardest step, just like making your first cut in a scene. One of the first tactics on your journey toward employment is to find your way into a cutting room. This way you will be able to observe the work flow and witness how the assistant editor handles the real world of day-to-day chores.

1.1 Find an Assistant

Assistant editors can be your best allies. They are doing the job you want to do. They are assisting the editor you would dearly love to have as your mentor, so they must be doing something right. They have been in your position as a newly arrived assistant editor and know the pitfalls and lessons of the editing rooms. They are often offered jobs for which they are not available and will recommend *someone* for it. If all goes well, and you prove yourself to them, perhaps you will be the one they recommend.

When you get an invitation to visit an editing room, know that this opportunity is rare and should be cherished. It is exactly what you are looking for—an editing venue where you are allowed to learn, help, contribute, and observe the *assistant* at work. Here is our suggested short list of what to observe when you are there:

- Look at his paperwork.
- How does he organize the lined script?
- What does he digitize first?
- How does he arrange the Scene bins for his editor?
- Does he use group clips?
- How has the project been set up?
- Does he color code his time line?
- What does his continuity look like?

- How has he prepared the notebooks for incoming paperwork (sound reports, camera reports, telecine logs)?
- How does he prepare for an output?
- What sort of title card does he use, and what information does he have on it?
- Does he put black between acts, and if so, how much?
- How does he prepare for a sound effects and music spotting session?
- What paperwork needs to be distributed at his spotting sessions?
- Does he have ADR lists with master timecodes?
- Does he have photocopies of the scripts prepared?
- Have the audio lists gone to the online session?
- How has he prepared the tracks for online?
- Has he separated out the dialog, SFX, and MX to the specified channels?
- Has he put the stereo pairs in for the music editor?
- Has he prepared the chase cassette for the online?
- Has he prepared a list of the needle drops used in the show with their durations, artists' names, and song titles?

These are a few of the points of interest to touch on when given the opportunity to visit a cutting room. See if the assistant has templates for all of his paperwork, and check to see how they differ from the ones provided in this book. Ask if he will share and allow you to copy them. See if he has a checklist for preparing dailies, outputting, and onlining. These are valuable lists that have been prepared through the years and have suffered the consequences of past errors and are now nearly perfect. Every editing room varies, and there is always some new technique or method that organizes the room better. Steal all these good ideas.

When visiting friends or family, it is always appreciated when you arrive with a plate of sweets or flowers to grace their house. To show your appreciation to the assistant editor for the privilege of entering his cutting room, we suggest you bring donuts (or something equally sweet and kind) as an offering.

After you have visited the editing room, remember to write a thank-you note. Emails are acceptable, but there is something wonderful about a written note.

Keep all names, phone numbers, email addresses, and cutting room contact numbers on a list for future reference. Buy yourself a special notebook into which you will write these contacts and note all personal information as well—names of spouses and children and birthdays.

If you have done well during your visit and are pleasant to have in the cutting room, you might be rewarded with an invitation to return or maybe a recommendation for a job. Stay in touch with all the folks you can, letting them know when you have landed a job and that you are deeply appreciative of their help.

When you are allowed entree into an editing room, the temptation will be to watch the editor work. It is fun and will give you lasting editing insights. However, the relationship you need to pursue is with the assistant editor. It is he who will turn you on to assisting jobs if he likes you, and will be in your network of colleagues who can talk you through problems that will arise on your first gig. It is he who will share with you his paperwork templates and knowledge of shortcuts and systems about which you need to learn, and will determine whether you will be welcomed back in the cutting room.

The relationship between the editor and the assistant is a finely tuned balance of boss–employee, mentor–student, and mutual protector. When you visit their editing suite, you might be tipping this balance as you sit with the editor. It is a highly coveted privilege to watch an editor cut, one that the assistant longs for but the workload prevents. Be sensitive to whatever toes you might tread upon when you enter their space.

A good job is not good enough in this business. You have to be great in so many different areas. You have to excel technically; have people skills; know how to take care of your editor, producer, and director; and interface with the rest of the crew. The editor wants everyone that comes in contact with the cutting room to go away thinking, "What a great bunch of people." That means the assistant has to help create that impression. What you have to be is someone who editors and producers want to hire again and recommend to colleagues. The recommendation needs to be stellar, and you have to *earn* it. One of the worst things that can happen is when your former editor or producer gives a reference saying, "Well…he did a good enough job." This euphemism suggests that you were mediocre, lackluster, and eminently not a good hire.

It's great to be an assistant editor—you are part of the creative process in which the editor crafts the film from dailies to the final cut. During the course of the day you will decipher reams of paperwork provided to you by the camera department, sound department, script supervisor, and telecine house as you import and digitize dailies into your editing system. You will determine whether a scene has been completed by production, and if not, what coverage is missing. You will decide which scene should be digitized first so that your editor will be able to start cutting as soon as possible. The editor should never be *down*—without dailies to cut. You must organize the bins differently for each editor you work with to satisfy his inherently unique style. These are just a few of the myriad tasks that you will perform daily. It might seem overwhelming at first, but when you have completed an entire show, it will become as automatic as riding a bicycle.

Stay your course, and with Lady Luck smiling *down* upon you, you will be the most sought after assistant in the business. When this has been accomplished, you will have your pick of editors to assist. This will place you amidst the best editing teams and creative talents working in the industry.

1.2 Know Your Tools

Make sure you know your tools. Film and digital are the two sources of media with which you will work. Most editing rooms around the world are digital, requiring the knowledge of various systems—Avid (Meridian, Adrenaline, Nitris DS, Red Camera and Final Cut Pro are the most widely used in Hollywood. A firm grasp of Mac and PC platforms, Adobe After Effects, Photoshop, etc. will be a great contribution to the editing process.

When we first began our editing careers as assistants, it was mostly film, and we learned the machines for that medium. Now the majority of all movies, even when photographed on film, get transferred to hard drives or telecined to tape. The majority of movies are edited digitally. Keep abreast of all new technologies and their programs. You must have this knowledge to apply for a job. Remember, competition for an assistant editor's seat is fierce.

It is best to arrive in the workplace with a firm knowledge of all current editing systems. There are books, film schools, and training programs throughout the world that offer this education. There are traditionally two types of training courses—one to be an assistant and the other to be an editor. Take both courses because the skills learned are remarkably different. During your training, compare the skill sets so that you are able to contribute that much more to the editing process.

Along with your courses, hone your skills with many hours of practice. The more familiar you are with the processes involved in editing, the better you will be able to anticipate the questions and requests made by your editor.

1.3 Basic Setups

On your first job, regardless of which system you have—Avid or Final Cut Pro (FCP)—you will find that there are commonalities in their functions and setups. You should be familiar with all the basics to be found in the editing rooms of both the editor and the assistant.

You will have source, record, and playback monitors that need to be set up properly (picture tuned, sizes adjusted); you will have a DVD–CD player (DVCAM, Beta, DVD, or miniDVCAM) with which you digitize that needs to be tested before you can input your first dailies; and you need to know how much RAM you should have installed by the technicians (techs) to maximize the speed with which you can work. You must know how to check the default settings and video settings on the editing system to ensure that the rate of the sound is in synchronization (sync) with the specifications (specs) laid out for you by your post producer (the coproducer or associate producer who is the head of the post department); you will be asked to record temporary (temp) ADR (also referred to as *looping*) in the cutting room. Make sure you have a microphone that works and you know which buttons on your soundboard need to be engaged or disengaged to record. Know how to finalize, change formats from 4:3 to 16:9 to HD letterbox, and how to add visible timecode. Also know all the format necessities for a successful output. Test the machines on your first day. It is not a given that the tech has set up a system that satisfies all your needs. Digitize some media, do an output, and record some dialog.

You must be able to troubleshoot the error messages and circumnavigate the problems that arise with your machine. You will often have tech support, but this can be very frustrating when they have no solutions and tell you to redo your user settings. While learning about Avid or FCP, make sure you familiarize yourself with these tasks and you are able to execute them. Always have your user manuals available—you will need them. The more you know about your tools, the less stress you will have on your first day of work. After you have worked a few years, you will be familiar with most of the error messages and will know instinctively how to fix the newest problem.

You will also have your favorite *go to* friends in the industry with whom you can confer in times of emergencies. They will guide you through dailies and difficulties via the phone and Internet when you are in a bind.

Back in the 1970s, when I was an assistant, my friend Paul Rubell, A.C.E. got his first job on a film with little knowledge of how to sync dailies. Through his first few days on the job, I would tell him how to pop the tracks, put an X on the sync point for the slate, put it in his synchronizer, line it up with the picture, and splice it to the next take to build his first reel of dailies. Steven Spielberg and his editor, Michael Kahn, A.C.E., Quentin Tarantino and his editor, Sally Menke, A.C.E., are some of the last holdouts in America to cut or screen film. Today, we receive our dailies on tape or a hard drive. A colleague talks an inexperienced assistant through the process of digitizing, setting tone, checking the blacks, double-checking audio timecode, or even how to apply music codes.

—ljc

A network of colleagues will help you in times of trouble, but you still have to apply for your first job with a basic foundation of technical knowledge, an understanding of your tools, the confidence to accomplish the tasks at hand, and the ability to troubleshoot whatever emergencies arise.

1.4 Bank It

At the beginning of all journeys, you must start with a passport, a goal in mind, and money to support yourself. The same rules apply to starting your editing career. Your passport is your degree in filmmaking or technical training. Your goal is to be an editor, which dictates that you place yourself in the city with the largest pool of available jobs. To support your dream, you need a nest egg or ancillary financial resources. With these three important factors in place, you are most likely to succeed.

In America, Hollywood offers the greatest amount of opportunities in the film industry. There are multiple alternatives—New York City, Atlanta, Chicago—but most features and television shows are produced in Los Angeles.

It is important to have enough money in the bank to support yourself during the search for a position as an assistant editor. There are often times when you will have to work for free to make your first contacts in the film industry. It will most likely take a while to find your first paid job. There are also many times when you will be in between jobs because this is a freelance career.

> One of the common threads in editors' descriptions of their first year in the industry is that they have all worked for free. My gratis stint was for Michael Berman, A.C.E., editor on *McCloud* at Universal Studios. I learned all I could from his assistant editor, Gene Ranney, before being offered my first assistant editing gig on a nonunion feature. I was lucky—some people have to work for free multiple times at the beginning of their careers. I still do pro bono work to help a friend or lay the groundwork for a future gig.
>
> —ljc

> In the late 1960s, producer–director Ashley Lazarus from Cape Town, South Africa organized with the British Guild of Editors an unpaid internship for me at Pinewood Studios in England. I crossed the sea on an ocean liner from Cape Town to London and was placed on a movie of the week (MOW) for Universal Studios with director Boris Sagal. As a result of this experience, I was able to catapult my editorial career upon my return to South Africa, and I worked on 19 feature films and countless hours of episodic television.
>
> —df

Without a monetary nest egg, these opportunities would have been untenable. If you want to get your career started, you must have the freedom to accept and pursue jobs that will help you stay your course—regardless of pay. Let your head and heart guide you—not your bankbook. Many opportunities to be involved in a project that would be fantastic for your resume, or are subject matters that are important to you, will not have to be passed up due to finances. You will encounter this dilemma throughout your career. If you amortize your earnings and are prepared for long hiatuses, you will be able to take your preferred job offers. So, bank it!

1.5 Move to Hollywood

There are many venues for filmmaking around the world. From Rome to New York City, from India to Sydney and Auckland, and from China to Sweden, the world has small communities of filmmakers who need editors and their assistants. However, those seats are predominantly filled with natives of their respective cities, and those communities are difficult to breach. In America, Hollywood provides the best chance of breaking in. Because the largest amount of production is centered in southern California, there are more editorial seats available. Clearly, the greater the amount of production, the more opportunities will present themselves. After you have worked your way into the heart of the film industry in Los Angeles, you can choose to move to the city in which you prefer to live. You can move on to other centers with credits and references—your reputation earned in Hollywood will be respected worldwide. You will, of course, have to spend the time to make new contacts, but that will be easier because you have worked in Hollywood. The competition is still stiff, but you can compete by being the best assistant possible. This is how you will **shine**.

Now that you've begun your training and have a skill set, a nest egg, and you live in Los Angeles, you can further enhance your education as you seek employment. Here is a list of courses and references:

3D Labs
Alan's Tech Page
American Cinema Editors (www.ace-filmeditors.org): Subscribe to
    the *CinemaEditor Magazine*
Apple Pro Training Series, Final Cut Pro for Avid Editors
Avid Knowledgebase
Avid Tips and Techniques
CheckHD
Cinematographer.com
Digidesign User Conference
EditorsNet
Motion Picture Editors Guild (www.editorsguild.com): *Editors Guild*
    Magazine
Moviola
Nonlinear Gear Links
RefDesk
The Art of Avid Editing
Video Symphony

When you have settled in, your next step is to re-create your resume. This is a significant document because it creates the first impression in the interview process. It is your passport to entering the world of editing.

> **TIP**
>
> Take extra classes. They will increase your knowledge and help you to begin networking, which is elemental to your success.

> **TIP**
>
> You will not be able to rely on public transportation for any length of time in Los Angeles. You need to buy a car. Los Angeles is a city that is spread out, with studios up to 60 miles apart—from Hollywood to Santa Monica, downtown Los Angeles to Manhattan Beach, and Culver City to Santa Clarita.

1.6 Create Your Resume

Your resume—its format, contents, and aesthetic appeal—becomes an important factor in the cumulative impression you leave behind. It is your calling card.

You've probably been advised by college books and resume websites about the format for a polished resume. This is a great starting point, but we need to tailor these ideas for the film industry. You must know that you are not the only assistant presenting a document. Your resume must stand out amidst the myriad resumes received by producers and editors. Oftentimes the remembered ones are those that use an italic font or are printed on pink paper! Presentation *does* count. Take the time to choose the amount of information carefully. If it takes too long to read, there is a great possibility that it will be tossed.

Figure 1.1 is an example of a layout we recommend.

RESUME

Jonathan Smith

Assistant Film Editor

(h) 310 555.0199 (c) 818 555.0199 jsmith@gmail.com 55 linden road, los angeles, CA90069

Film Experience – Assistant Film Editor

Mary Moves to L.A.	Editor: John Boss	Director: Mary Sunshine	Jan. 2009
Mary Runs Out of Money	Editor: John Boss	Director: Mary Moonshine	June 2008
Mary Makes Money	Editor: Joe Hunt	Director: Mary Sunshine	Jan. 2008

Skills

PC and Mac Platforms, Avid Media Composer, Meridian, Adrenaline, Final Cut Pro, Adobe After Effects, Adobe Photoshop, DigiDesign ProTools
Bilingual – Spanish

Education

University of Filmland, B.A. Film Studies, Muncie, Indiana 2005–2009
G.P.A. 3.9 Minor in English
University of London, Summer Program, Intern for the BBC 2008

Hobbies

golf, tango, quilting, baking, photography

References

John Boss	310 555.7272	(Film Editor)
Joe Hunt	323 555.7070	(Film Editor)
Mary Sunshine	310 555.2020	(Director)

Figure 1.1 *Resume*

The heading should include your name, your title, and your contact information. As you can see in the template, we have discarded "Objective." Oftentimes we receive resumes of newly graduated film students who put their objective at the top of the resume, such as "Objective—to become an Assistant Editor in Hollywood." Remove it. This will immediately identify you as a novice. You want to present yourself as an already accomplished assistant editor. We know your objective is to be an assistant editor—it is the job for which you are interviewing.

The first information deals with film work or experience. This gets a bit confusing for you right now because you were probably the editor, director, or writer on many of your school films, or conversely you have absolutely no credits. If you've only taken training courses and have yet to edit or assist on a film, we suggest you make a home movie and give yourself a credit! Be creative.

The interviewer is interested in what you have *assisted* on. This is because we are looking for someone who will be able to handle all the assisting contingencies that arise during the course of the day. When you're starting your postproduction career, it's understandable that you would want to include all your previous jobs, including editing, on the resume. Be careful, though, to present yourself as an assistant editor because that is the job for which you are interviewing. You can include some editing credits at the start of your film career (we know these are entry-level credits). Make sure you include and finish with assistant editing credits. We will regard this as a natural progression to a more mainstream production on which you had to go back to assisting to further your career. We are also looking to see if you have worked for the same editor more than once. If you have, this means you are doing something right!

Some of you have edited all of your own films. If you were the editor on the project, you were most likely your own assistant. It is more important to state on your resume that you know how to assist rather than to edit, so make sure you include this project as one you have assisted on as well. Most editors like to hire an assistant who knows how to edit because it is helpful during a crunched schedule. However, there are some editors who want to know that you are focused on one thing—being the best assistant. A potential employer might be concerned that you would be dissatisfied with your position and too anxious to move up to editing. This would be to the detriment of your responsibilities and could be a factor in whether you get hired or not.

Remove the descriptions of the jobs you have had. When you are applying for an assistant editor position, it is superfluous information when your resume says that your tasks involved digitizing, logging, transferring, dubbing, and outputting. We know what an assistant does, so don't waste our time by making us read this. We have too many resumes to read. You must get to the bare bones quickly.

Format your resume by dividing the names of shows, directors, and editors into easy-to-read columns. It is easier on the eye to scan and pick up who you have worked for on multiple projects, as well as identify common friends or colleagues.

In the skills section, remove all adjectives and verbs, such as "highly skilled on the Avid," and "proficient with FCP." Change it to "Avid" and "FCP." The interviewer assumes you are highly skilled and proficient with all programs listed on your resume. When you write how great you are at them, it makes us think you are *not*.

Mention all of the technical skills that pertain to editing and technology—Avid, FCP, Adobe Workshop, After Effects, Unity and SAN, PC and Mac platforms, etc.

For education, include your college degrees and internships that are germane to editing. Do not include high school or camp. It is important to understand that your recent graduation needs to take a backseat to your skills. As you gain more experience as an assistant editor, you will eventually remove references to your alma maters.

Under hobbies, you may add miscellaneous skills like golf, basketball, weaving, or tapestry. These are all good conversation pieces. Be careful to stay away from too many religious or political penchants because they can cause strife. You need to find subjects that unify rather than repel. A colleague shared her story once about an apprentice who included on his resume that he made a fantastic cappuccino. This delighted her so much that he got the job.

The final subject is references. Think of three people (not your mom!) who are willing to speak glowingly about you. Include their contact information. It is not okay to say "references upon request" because that will create more work for the interviewer.

Try to get your resume on one page.

This resume template is a great starting point, but feel free to embellish and personalize it all you want. Keep it simple. Because your resume is your introduction to your prospective employer, it is important to get off to a proper start. Remember, the first impression is the strongest.

> **SHINE NOTE**
>
> Use paper stock that is a cut above the standard typing paper when you mail it or present it in person. This will stand out, and you need to **shine** in the face of all the competition.

If you email your resume, include a cover letter that is brief, friendly, and personalized. Spell the names correctly. Michael Tronick, A.C.E. once intimated that when he receives correspondence with his name spelled incorrectly, he is inclined to read no further.

It is important to know something about the editor—his films and inherent editing styles. Include a brief comment about your favorite part of his film or what affected you most. Find at least one nice thing to say in an introductory email. Make the editor feel singled out and special. Schmoozing is a good thing, especially when done from the heart. Do your homework by looking everyone up on IMDb.com. This way your introductory letter for your resume will invite a positive reaction.

Heads of postproduction, producers, and editors receive countless resumes, and their fate ranges from being thrown in the trash to being filed away. If your resume has made a good impression, you will have a better chance of being selected for an interview or hired.

Whenever it is possible, deliver the resume in person. When you put a face with your name, you become that much more memorable. It provides the opportunity for you to meet the people in charge and begin the networking process.

1.7 Your Favorite Five

One of the best ways to launch your career is to begin networking. This process will continue throughout your career, and it is an essential skill you need to hone. The first step is to identify the editors whose bodies of work have been an inspiration to you. Choose five editors you admire the most. Write to them, ask to meet them, take them out for coffee or stop by their editing room for a brief meeting.

Let's say you choose Anne Coates, A.C.E. (her name appears on most of the fave five lists). Go to IMDb, get the list of her credits, and take a long look at her films. Make sure you are watching the editing styles, not the directing, cinematography, and acting. See if you can glean an overall style of her work. Is it the use of sound, the cadences of her dialog scenes, the cutting patterns for the opening or closing of scenes that has touched you? Do you think she has a certain elegance of storytelling that transcends the individual film and carries throughout her body of work?

In your letter or email, introduce yourself as an assistant film editor who has been affected greatly by her editing and that you would be honored to have the opportunity to meet her. Mention your favorite bits of her films. Be brief. Suggest coffee (your treat!), or even better, ask if you can stop by her editing room to see where she works. That way you will get to meet her assistant editors (key to this plan!) and make friends with them. You want to be especially nice to the assistant because it is he who often determines how much access to the editor will be allowed. It is during your short visit with the editor that you will ask if you could stop by again and spend some time with her assistant. It is important to initiate a relationship with the editing crew because it is the assistant who will remember you, hopefully, and think of you when he is in need of a second assistant editor or apprentice.

Bring donuts! It is always nice to bear gifts. Everyone in the cutting room will appreciate the gesture, and it will make an impression. The donuts will be gone by the time you leave.

You will be able to find your favorite editors' email or mailing addresses at the ACE office in Universal City or the Editors Guild in Hollywood. Sometimes their personal information is unavailable, but both offices will forward mail to the editor or his agent.

Repeat these steps with your other favorite editors. Do not be a feature snob—there are countless editors working in television and cable who are equally talented and willing to open their doors to you. Try to distinguish the stylistic differences amongst the multiple editors on a given show. This might lead to an engaging conversation with one of your fave five, and these first seeds you will plant will one day flower into a possible job opportunity.

1.8 Find the Job

There are several ways to find work. Popular avenues to investigate include websites such as mandy.com, realitystaff.com, indeedjobalert.com, simplyhired.com, and entertainmentcareers.net. Production weekly reports and the trades (*The Hollywood Reporter*, *Variety*) can be found on the Internet. However, the most tried and true way to get a job is through word of mouth. Remember that when a colleague recommends you to a friend, his relationship and reputation is at stake. You must live up to the faith he places in you.

When you have been recommended for a job and begin to prepare for the interview, there are certain protocols and checklists that will help you through the process.

1.9 Prepare for the Interview

As you enter the room for the interview, the first thing that is noticed is your face and body language. Then there is the handshake (always firm and combined with eye contact). The next step is to hand over your resume. Your resume is your calling card. This all takes place in less than a minute, and your resume becomes an integral part of the first impression you have made on your potential employer.

As in all first meetings, there are awkward moments, which is when the interviewer might refer to your resume and ask questions about colleagues you know in common, what it was like working with so-and-so, or even commenting on your education or hobbies. While these pleasantries are being exchanged, he is observing you, clocking you, and wondering…

- Are you responsible?
- Can you handle pressure situations?
- Are you honest?
- Do you have a sense of humor?
- How would it be to work with you 12 hours a day?
- Would it be pleasant to have lunch with you every day?

He is looking beyond your resume and deciding if you are a good fit. It's like editing—you read the expressions, the aversion of the eyes, the details that help fill in the unwritten lines of dialog in the script—all of this informs you about the character (the interviewee).

How you present yourself is the unwritten part of your resume. Dressing is an issue. For guys, no suit and tie—it is too formal. Wear clean jeans (we notice if you are groomed), a clean shirt (ready to work but still presentable), and closed-toe shoes (be prepared for industrial accidents). Do not wear a T-shirt to the interview—you can wear that after you get the gig. For gals, it is a bit harder. Do you wear slacks and a blouse? Maybe a skirt (not too short) or a dress (maybe too formal?). Jeans are always a safe bet (please, no holes). One thing everybody should remember is that you do not want to get a job based on false impressions. Tight clothing, cleavage, lots of bare leg, or a cute butt is the wrong message. Most importantly, you need to make your work ethic and personality the qualities that people respond to as opposed to your physical attributes.

> I got called in for a last-minute interview once and was already dressed to go clubbing. The editor asked me to stop by on my way out, and I agreed to meet him. I got hired, and when I arrived the next week on location, the editor had adjoining rooms for us and suggested we could just leave the door open! Not a fun situation, and it went downhill from there. This became an ill-fated movie for me. It is the only film I have ever quit in 37 years in the industry.
>
> —ljc

Know the address of the interview location and how to get there. Allow double the amount of driving time you think you need, and if possible do a dry run. That way, on the day of the interview you will not get lost or be late. Remember, being on time is critical.

My father, a producer and former assistant director, defines *on time* as 15 minutes early. It still works for me.

—ljc

Bring your resume. It doesn't matter that you emailed it in advance, it has been misplaced already. Go the extra mile and print it on pretty paper.

Do your research. Remember to IMDb everyone who will be at the interview. They will be impressed with your interest in their careers as well as your ability to add to the interview instead of simply responding to questions. This will also give you something to contribute during dialog lapses. Remember, they are trying to get to know you.

1.10 The Interview

Try to relax and relate to the interviewer as you would a respected mentor. Remember: half of the interview is about how well he will get along with you 12 hours a day. He will assume you have the skills.

Avoid asking if there is overtime, how long the days will be, whether you have to work weekends, and what the salary will be. That comes later. These questions are indicative of someone who will be watching the clock and is less likely to perform well under pressure. It makes you seem anxious to leave work as soon as possible and therefore an undesirable hire.

> **SHINE NOTE**
>
> These are the ways you will **shine**. Ask the interviewer what the schedule is like, where the cutting rooms are, whether they are shooting high def, red, 24P, and if you could get a copy of the script, what editing platform you will have, etc. Participate!

Be cheerful, poised, positive, and respectful to everyone and make eye contact.

Fingers crossed, you will get the job. If he goes with someone else and calls to let you know (unfortunately, sometimes you will not be called), remain pleasant and wish him luck on the project. Briefly express the hope to work for him in the future. Get used to rejection and deal with it philosophically. Ask yourself how you can improve on your next interview, and give yourself a good talking to.

Let's assume you do get the assistant editor job, because let's face it—you are skilled, personable, and well-groomed.

There are many ways to be ahead of the game, such as preparation for your first day of work. What follows is a guideline for that.

Chapter 2

Before Your First Day on the Job

There are tasks that can be accomplished in advance of your first day on the job. This preparation will benefit both you and the editor.

Though you are not yet on the clock, all of the charts that you create and the lists of supplies you request are essential for your success during the entire production. You will be ahead of the game on your first day.

2.1 Be Prepared

After you have been offered the assistant editor position, you are a bona fide member of the crew. If this is a first-season television show, movie of the week (MOW), or feature, the startup process is far more intensive. If you are joining a show that has been on the air before your arrival, many of the following tasks will have been addressed. If you are the first assistant, the setup tasks will be your responsibility.

As soon as you are hired, you will have access to the production office. Contact the production coordinator, make friends, and ask for the script. It will either be emailed, photocopied, or snail mailed to you. You will eventually want a hard copy to facilitate the next tasks at hand.

Read the script with paper and pen in hand so that you can begin your *breakdowns*. The first breakdown is a list of sound effects (SFX), music (MX), playback, visual effects (VFX), stock shots, and various elements that are necessary for the edited show. This will become your *script elements* list. Then you can do a *scene breakdown* with the act breaks, inherent scene numbers, and the number of pages in each act. When the shooting schedule is distributed, you will notate on which days the crew will be shooting playback (video and/or music) and add these pertinent dates to the *schedule for elements*. Next, create the *continuity*, which is a list of the scenes with a brief description. Also create a *wall continuity*, which differs from the continuity only in that is created with a larger font size and has four additional columns of information for each scene regarding their length. A *measurement chart* is created and placed on the bulletin board. It reflects the act measurements and total running time of each successive version of the film, from editor's cut to final locked show. Make a list of office supplies and furniture necessary to fill an empty editing room.

2.2 Script Elements

Think about what you should list in your breakdowns as you read the following scene from a film.

DOI: 10.1016/B978-0-240-81398-1.00002-X

17

Excerpt from the Show *The Competition*. Episode 103, "The Surprise Party"

```
Sc. 4 INT. GYMNASIUM - DAY INTERIOR
```

Deirdre joins Ali on the mat and begins stretching. Ali looks exuberant. Deirdre is on edge wondering if Charley has spoken to Ali and told her anything about the surprise party.

DEIRDRE
Hey, I thought you were skipping today's practice.

ALI
No, my Mom said I had to come.

DEIRDRE
Michael is on the warpath today. I swear, if we don't find a new coach soon, I'm going to go crazy.

ALI
I know. And I hate the new music he picked for me. At least you have a good song.

DEIRDRE
I suppose. But I would give anything to have my old music back. I think it was so much more fun.

The coach, Michael, starts the music ("Go for Gold" by the Phantastiks) for Deirdre's floor routine and turns to her to get her attention.

MICHAEL
Deirdre! Let's get to work. Show me your new routine.

Michael turns on his video camera to record her for later viewing and instruction.

DEIRDRE
Okay! I'm coming.

Sc. 5 EXT. GYMNASIUM

The parking lot is beginning to fill. Charley drives in, parks, and walks to Michael's trailer. He removes the note he has written and tapes it to the front door. He is hesitant about leaving it, knowing he will be in a lot of trouble when Michael reads his confession.

DEFINITION	
DX:	Day exterior
FX:	Effects
GFX:	Graphic effects
MX:	Music
NX:	Night exterior
SFX:	Sound effects
VFX:	Visual effects

There are several written and *implied* elements that need to be ordered for the editor before the shoot begins. Even though the production sound mixer is recording the dialog, there will be additional sounds needed to complete the overall ambience of the scene. Though the script might not call for an establishing shot, the editor adds a shot to orient the audience to the location of a scene. The assistant must anticipate these *unwritten* elements for the editor so that they may be included in the first cut. To prepare in advance, this is what you can add to your breakdown:

Script Elements

Stock

- Sc. 04 DX gym
  - Time-lapse night to day

SND FX

- Sc. 04 DX
  - Birds
  - Traffic: Car-bys
  - Dog barking in distance
  - Int. gymnasium presence
  - Laughter
  - Walla (chatter): BG gymnasts and coaches
  - Gymnastics sounds: Feet landing, running, mounting, dismounting, rings, beam footfalls
  - Gymnasium doors opening and closing
  - Boom box button clicks
  - Tape being inserted, rewound, fast forwarded, removed

MX: Needle drops

- Sc. 04 Chosen needle drop: "Go for Gold" by the Phantastiks

You will break down every scene throughout the script, adding the information to your various lists. The production crew will shoot all the coverage and record the dialog, but the illusion of a given location is made in the editing room. We create the ambience with extra sounds to enhance the scene. The assistant editor must be able to envision the scenes and their inherent background sounds (BGs). The ability to anticipate the needs of the editor is a skill that is held in the highest regard.

After you finish reading and breaking the script down, you will have a complete list of all the needle drop MX that you need to order in *advance* of the shoot.

In some scripts, for example, the writer will specify the needle drop they would like you to use. If it is written in the script that Led Zeppelin kicks in as the choreographed dance begins, chances are you will be looking for a replacement cue. The song might not be one that can be licensed, or it might be too expensive.

It is best to have the original version of the song in the Music bin in advance of the shoot date. This way, the editor will be able to cut it in after he has received the dailies. It is also wise to have alternate songs to replace the drop should it be necessary to change it. This

> **DEFINITION**
>
> Needle drop (or *drop*) is music that is bought or licensed for background use in the film. It can be a song with lyrics as well. A score is music written by a composer who is hired specifically for the show.

entails calling the MX supervisor to ask for alternative drops (*alts*) for the scripted needle drop, which he will happily supply to the editorial staff. It is his job to license the music, and he is eager to provide a song that can be licensed and is affordable. The assistant must also create a consummate list of all the playback and VFX that is going to be needed for the show.

2.3 Scene Breakdown

The assistant needs to list which scenes are in which act. It is good to know how many pages there are for each act because this is a way to estimate the length of each scene and act (see Table 2.1).

Table 2.1 *Scene breakdown*

Episode 103 "The Surprise Party"

Acts	Scenes	Pages	Totals
TEASER	SC. 01–06	PG. 01–07	07
ACT 01	SC. 07–15	PG. 08–17	10
ACT 02	SC. 16–A23	PG. 18–23	06
ACT 03	SC. 23–28	PG. 24–32	09
ACT 04	SC. 30–33	PG. 33–39	07
ACT 05	SC. 34–37	PG. 42–48	07
Totals:		48 pages	47 minutes

The page counts are a bit tricky—make a note that you counted the pages inclusively. Because the rule of thumb is 1 minute per page, the minute count is often different than the page count because some script pages are only 1/8 or 1/2 of a page. In approximating the amount of time a page will be on screen, take into account that action scenes described on two lines can turn into a 3-minute sequence or more, and that a 3-page scene describing a party could turn into a 30-second montage. It is not the job of the assistant editor to give an estimated timing of the script—that responsibility belongs to the script supervisor. But it is a great exercise to do a rough estimate of the length of the film and begin to hone your skills. If the editor is aware that the show that is about to be shot is either too short or too long, he can alert the writers or director in advance of the shoot to this important information.

> I edited a miniseries, *The Hades Factor*, by Robert Ludlum and directed by Mick Jackson. Before starting the project, I did a breakdown, and Part Two timed short. During shooting, I kept a watchful eye on the timings of the scenes and continually compared them to my original estimates. Mick was able to ask the writers to beef up certain scenes to get us closer to our projected format footage for that network.
>
> —ljc

2.4 Schedule for Elements

The production office will generate many informative breakdowns with useful information that can be used by postproduction. For example, a shooting schedule will be distributed by the production coordinator, which has the dates for when playback, VFX, and green screen will be shot. These special occurrences and dates affect the assistant and editor and should be added to your schedule for elements (see Table 2.2).

Table 2.2 *Schedule for elements*

Sc.	Stock	VFX	Playback	MX	FX	Shoot date
Sc. 07		Composite BG mountains			Crime scene	5/02
Sc. 25	NX party		Prerecord "Last Night"			5/08

The final list will include all of your breakdown work. By creating this list in advance, you will know what needs to be ordered—stock, VFX, playback, MX, and FX—before the editor begins to cut. You will know the dates by which you need to complete preparations for the playback to a computer monitor or TV set, as well as the MX for playback. You will make sure your editor has the necessary elements to cut the scene on the day that dailies are received. Note the added element of the *shoot date*. This is a projected date that can be altered during the course of the shoot, and the assistant should keep an eye on the shooting schedule updates.

2.5 Continuity

The fourth breakdown that you should have prepared before your first day of dailies is the continuity—a one-line description of each scene.

The first assistant director (1st AD) publishes a *one-liner* before the shooting starts. It also describes each scene in one line (hence the name). You should ask the production coordinator for this paperwork, but it is best to create your own descriptions; they will help you familiarize yourself with the script. When you create the continuity (see Figure 2.1), it helps you understand the script's interwoven themes. This is the beginning of the training you need to make the cut and become a great editor!

The continuity should contain the title of the show, episode number, act number, scene number, whether it is Day 1 (D1) or Night 3 (N3), the location of the scene, the gist of the scene, and the timing of the latest cut of that scene (which is updated on each output). Be careful for the gist of the scene; you might be tempted to write clever summations, with a bit of humor. Because the continuity goes to directors, producers, the studio, and network, it is best to get to the heart of it and leave your emotional reactions out of the description.

After you create the continuity, copy and enlarge it so that a wall continuity can be posted on the bulletin board in your editor's room. It differs in several ways from the continuity that is on 8 1/2 × 11-inch paper for the binder and distribution.

"THE COMPETITION"
EP. 103 – "The Surprise Party"

SC #	D/N		
		RECAP	31:05
SC #	D/N	TEASER	6:09:29
		DX SCHOOL (STOCK, IN HOUSE)	4:04
2	D1	INT. THE SCHOOL – GYM FLOOR: Deirdre enters, sees Ali finishing her routine.	55:17
4	D1	INT. THE SCHOOL – GYM FLOOR: Deirdre and Ali – Coach plays MX for Deirdre's routine MX: "Go for the Gold" THE PHANTASTIKS	31:24
5	D1	EXT. STONE HOUSE – ENGLAND: David drives up to his house	16:28
6	D1	INT. THE SCHOOL – GYM FLOOR: Deirdre finishes routine. Coach is not happy.	58:01
7	D1	EXT. STONE HOUSE – ENGLAND: David enters his house, finds it in disarray. Calls the police.	2:11:26
8	D1	INT. THE SCHOOL – GYM FLOOR: Deirdre and Ali discuss the new music for both routines. Ali realizes that Deirdre doesn't know about her surprise party.	1:16:25
SC #	D/N	ACT 1	8:59:01
		DX SCHOOL (STOCK, IN HOUSE)	4:23
9	D1	INT. THE SCHOOL – COACHES OFFICES: [Fill in description from your script here]	52:02
10	D1	INT. THE SCHOOL – GYM FLOOR – CONTINUOUS:	38:01
11	D1	EXT. THE SCHOOL – CONTINUOUS:	57:04
12	D1	INT. THE SCHOOL – PARENT'S VIEWING AREA – LATER:	21:16
13	D1	INT. THE SCHOOL – GYM FLOOR – CONTINUOUS	1:55:18
13A	D1	INT. THE SCHOOL – BAG PILE – MOMENTS LATER:	41:19
		DX MALL – (STOCK, IN HOUSE)	2:17
14	D1	EXT CAFE – LATER:	3:24:13
SC #	D/N	ACT 2	10:03:24
		DX NEIGHBORHOOD – (STOCK, IN-HOUSE)	3:15
15	D1	INT. SMITH APT. – LATER:	1:22:22
		DX JONES HOUSE – (STOCK, IN HOUSE)	1:26
16	D1	INT. JONES HOUSE – KITCHEN:	1:20:29
17	N1	INT. JACKSON MANSION – DEIRDRE'S ROOM:	1:58:00
		NX SMITH APT. (STOCK, IN HOUSE)	2:06
18	N1	INT. SMITH APT. – SAME TIME:	56:10
		NX SMITH APT (STOCK, IN HOUSE)	2:24
19	N1	INT. SMITH APT. – LATER:	1:57:17
21A	N1	EXT. PARTY – CONTINUOUS:	50:14
		NX RESTAURANT – (STOCK, IN HOUSE)	2:15
22	N1	INT. RESTAURANT:	1:35:14
SC #	D/N	ACT 3	5:25:16
23A	N1	EXT. PARTY – SAME TIME: MX: "Rock On" – 1-69	3:39:11
24	N1	INT. RESTAURANT:	1:46:02

Figure 2.1 *Continuity template* The Competition. *Episode 103, "The Surprise Party"*

SC #	D/N	ACT 4	7:49:06
25	N1	**EXT. PARTY:** MX: "Last Night" – THE BACKWARDS	2:17:08
25A	N1	**EXT. PARTY:** MX: "It Takes Two" - SPEECHES	1:29:01
27	N1	**EXT. PARTY – LATER:**	1:21:10
		NX ROAD – (STOCK, IN HOUSE)	1:26
27A	N1	**INT. DAVID'S CAR – SAME TIME:** ***VFX TO COME: STABILIZATION*** MX: "5 Men" – THE BACKWARDS	42:10
28	N1	**EXT. PARTY/CABIN – A LITTLE LATER:**	1:58:15
SC #	D/N	ACT 5	5:03:19
29	N1	**INT. DAVID'S CAR:**	53:16
		NX SMITH APT. – (STOCK, IN HOUSE)	2:14
29A	N1	**EXT. SMITH APT. – FRONT DOOR:**	1:17:21
		NX JACKSON MANSION – (STOCK, IN-HOUSE)	2:16
30	N1	**INT. JACKSON MANSION – DEIRDRE'S ROOM – LATER THAT NIGHT:** MX: "Follow Your Dreams" – BRAD NEXTOWN (thru scene 31)	1:11:01
31	N1	**INT. CABIN – SAME TIME:**	1:42:22
		*TOTAL RUNNING TIME OVER/UNDER (+/–)	**45:00:06** **+47:26**
		LIFTED SCENES	
1	D1	**EXT. ESSEX, ENGLAND:** A mini drives past a sign: Buckhurst Hill, 12KM	10:16

Figure 2.1 (*Continued*)

2.6 Wall Continuity

Your fifth template to create is the wall continuity (see Figure 2.2). It will be printed with a large font that is easily read from a distance and pinned to the bulletin board. A different template must be made for this because it contains additional information.

The additional columns contain the timings of the scenes. There are columns for the following:

1. The script supervisor's original pretimings of each scene before principal photography begins
2. The on-set scene timing of the scene
3. The scene timing of the edited scene
4. The differential of the cut and the *on-set timing*

(One can choose to use the differential of the cut and the pretiming if the script supervisor has provided the timing for the script.)

Number 4 is the most important column for the editor because after a few days of dailies, one is able to extrapolate how long or short the show may be running. It can be a tremendous help to the director and the

RECAP			31:05	
TEASER	**Orig. Time**	**On Set Time**	**EC w/ frames**	**+/−**
DX SCHOOL (STOCK, IN HOUSE)			4:04	
INT. THE SCHOOL – GYM FLOOR: Deirdre enters, sees Ali finishing her routine.	:45	1:00	55:17	−4:13
INT. THE SCHOOL – GYM FLOOR: Deirdre and Ali – Coach plays MX for Deirdre's routine *MX: "Go for the Gold" THE PHANTASTIKS*	:30	:30	31:24	+1:24
EXT. STONE HOUSE – ENGLAND: David drives up to his house	:20	:25	16:28	−8:02
INT. THE SCHOOL – GYM FLOOR: Deirdre finishes routine. Coach is not happy.	1:00	1:10	58:01	−11:29
EXT. STONE HOUSE – ENGLAND: David enters his house, finds it in disarray. Calls the police.	2:30	2:00	2:11:26	+11:26
INT. THE SCHOOL – GYM FLOOR: Deirdre and Ali discuss the new music for both routines. Ali realizes that Deirdre doesn't know about her surprise party.	1:30	1:25	1:16:25	−8:05
TEASER TOTALS:	**6:35**	**6:30**	**6:09:29**	**−20:01**

ACT 1	**Orig. Time**	**On Set Time**	**EC w/ frames**	**+/−**
DX SCHOOL (STOCK, IN HOUSE)			4:23	
INT. THE SCHOOL – COACHES OFFICES: [Fill in description from your script here]	1:00	1:00	52:02	−7:28
INT. THE SCHOOL – GYM FLOOR – CONTINUOUS:	:45	:40	38:01	−1:29
EXT. THE SCHOOL – CONTINUOUS:	1:00	1:00	57:04	−2.26
INT. THE SCHOOL – PARENT'S VIEWING AREA – LATER:	:30	:25	21:16	−3:14
INT. THE SCHOOL – GYM FLOOR – CONTINUOUS	2:00	1:50	1:55:18	+5:18
INT. THE SCHOOL – BAG PILE – MOMENTS LATER:	:30	:30	41:19	+11:19
DX MALL – (STOCK, IN HOUSE)			2:17	
EXT CAFE – LATER:	3:00	2:50	3:24:13	+34:13
ACT 1 TOTALS:	**8:45**	**8:15**	**8:59:01**	**+44:01**

ACT 2	**Orig. Time**	**On Set Time**	**EC w/ frames**	**+/−**
DX NEIGHBORHOOD – (STOCK, IN-HOUSE)			3:15	
INT. SMITH APT. – LATER:	1:30	1:20	1:22:22	+2:22
DX JONES HOUSE – (STOCK, IN HOUSE)			1:26	
INT. JONES HOUSE – KITCHEN:	1:30	1:30	1:20:29	−9:01
INT. JACKSON MANSION – DEIRDRE'S ROOM:	2:00	1:50	1:58:00	+8:00
NX SMITH APT. (STOCK, IN HOUSE)			2:06	
INT. SMITH APT. – SAME TIME:	1:00	:50	56:10	+6:10
NX SMITH APT (STOCK, IN HOUSE)			2:24	
INT. SMITH APT. – LATER:	2:00	1:50	1:57:17	+7:17
EXT. PARTY – CONTINUOUS:	1:00	:50	50:14	+0:14

Figure 2.2 *Wall continuity template*

24

NX RESTAURANT – (STOCK, IN HOUSE)			2:15	
INT. RESTAURANT:	1:30	1:30	1:35:14	+5:14
DX NEIGHBORHOOD – (STOCK, IN-HOUSE)			3:15	
ACT 2 TOTALS:	**10:30**	**9:40**	**10:03:24**	**+23:24**

ACT 3	Orig. Time	On Set Time	EC w/ frames	+/–
EXT. PARTY – SAME TIME: *MX: "Rock On" – 1-69*	3:00	3:00	3:39:11	+9:11
INT. RESTAURANT:	1:30	1:45	1:46:02	+1:02
ACT 3 TOTALS:	**4:30**	**4:45**	**5:25:16**	**+40:16**

ACT 4	Orig. Time	On Set Time	EC w/ frames	+/–
EXT. PARTY: *MX: "Last Night" – THE BACKWARDS*	2:00	2:00	2:17:08	+17:08
EXT. PARTY: *MX: "It Takes Two" - SPEECHES*	1:30	1:20	1:29:01	+9:01
EXT. PARTY – LATER:	1:00	1:00	1:21:10	+21:10
NX ROAD – (STOCK, IN HOUSE)			1:26	
INT. DAVID'S CAR – SAME TIME: ***VFX TO COME: STABILIZATION*** *MX: "5 Men" – THE BACKWARDS*	:30	:45	42:10	−2:20
EXT. PARTY/CABIN – A LITTLE LATER:	2:00	2:00	1:58:15	−1:15
ACT 4 TOTALS:	**7:00**	**7:05**	**7:49:06**	**+44:06**

ACT 5	Orig. Time	On Set Time	EC w/ frames	+/–
INT. DAVID'S CAR:	1:00	1:00	53:16	−6:14
NX SMITH APT. – (STOCK, IN HOUSE)			2:14	
EXT. SMITH APT. – FRONT DOOR:	1:00	1:00	1:17:21	−17:21
NX JACKSON MANSION – (STOCK, IN-HOUSE)			2:16	
INT. JACKSON MANSION – DEIRDRE'S ROOM– LATER THAT NIGHT: *MX: "Follow Your Dreams" – BRAD NEXTOWN (thru scene 31)*	1:00	1:00	1:11:01	+11:01
INT. CABIN – SAME TIME:	1:30	1:30	1:42:22	+12:22
ACT 5 TOTALS:	**4:30**	**4:30**	**5:03:19**	**+33:19**

TOTAL RUNNING TIME:		40:45	45:00:06	+4:15:06
OVER/UNDER (+/–)				

LIFTED SCENES			
EXT. ESSEX, ENGLAND: A mini drives past a sign: Buckhurst Hill, 12KM			10:16

Figure 2.2 (*Continued*)

producer to know that they are going long and need to consider dropping a scene. Conversely, if the show is running short, it needs to be flagged. The writer can then infuse additional dialog or new scenes before the completion of principal photography.

2.7 Measurement Charts

Another template that you create before your first day is the measurement chart (see Figure 2.3). As the show progresses through editor's cut (EC), director's cut (DC), producer's cut (PC), and studio and/or network's cut (SC or NC), the total footages of each version should be written on the measurement chart. Some editors refer to their first pass as editor's cut, first cut, or assembly. Although the term assembly once meant simply cutting off the slates and stringing the dailies together, the process of putting the movie into its' formative stage has evolved tremendously. Regardless of the nomenclature, the editor's cut is a meticulous and carefully sculpted study of the story, characters and dailies that includes sound effects and music. Prepare this chart and post it on the bulletin board in the editor's cutting room so that it is ready to be filled in when the first assembly is complete. This will track the progression of individual acts and overall footage as it compares to the target time on the format sheet. You will know at all times whether the show is over- or underfootage.

	"THE COMPETITION" EP. 103 – "The Surprise Party"									
Date:										
Day:										
	Assembly	**EC1**	**EC2**	**DC1**	**DC2**	**PC1**	**PC2**	**PC3**	**NC1**	
TEASER	6:20:01	6:09:29								
ACT 1	9:22:24	8:59:01								
ACT 2	10:05:03	10:03:24								
ACT 3	6:30:11	5:25:16								
ACT 4	7:59:21	7:49:06								
ACT 5	5:04:04	5:03:19								
TOTALS:	45:22:04	43:31:07								
FORMAT:	42:15:00	42:15:00								
+/–	+3:07:04	+45:06								

Figure 2.3 *Measurement chart template*

2.8 SFX

As you read the script, you will notate what SFX will be necessary to make the scene fully tracked with BGs (background sounds). It is the assistant editor's job to make sure that the sound effects department has provided all of the SFX the editor will need to cut in. After the picture is locked, the movie will be given to the various departments (sound and music) to replace all of the temp tracks the editor has laid in. During principal photography, the extras in the gym will be silent; they are not paid to talk. If they do talk, the production will have to pay for an upgrade of the actor from extra to day player—very expensive. It is the editor's job to fill in all the supplementary sounds of each location by the time they hand over their editor's cut. If you have a restaurant scene, you will need the sound of the grill, utensils, walla, doors, and cash registers. If you have a stadium scene, you will need the sounds of crowds cheering, clapping, and booing; vendors; planes; helicopters; TV announcers; boom boxes—let your imagination run wild.

You can archive the sound effects from all your past shows and bring them with you because the sound department might not be up and running when you begin a new show. A website from which you can download free sound effects is www.freesound.org. Through the years our collections have grown to include all the necessary sounds for car chases, crime scenes, courtrooms, offices, hospital rooms and surgeries, plus numerous transition sound effects that come in ever so handy—all the toll hits, whooshes, and electronica that can become your emphasis sound in a scene.

When preparing a scene for your editor, pull several choices for each sound from the Internet or your sound effects department. Your editor will have more leeway to create the environment he needs to enrich the scene. You can prepare a list of all the sound effects needed for the entire episode in advance of the first day of shooting. Each production has a sound supervisor to whom you can fax this list, and his department will send what you need. Many times, you will have access to an SFX library from which you can cull the best takes. Through the years, you will build your own library that you can bring with you to each new show. Sometimes your editor will already have his own favorite SFX library on a hard drive. Ask him if you can pick it up so that you might digitize the library on your first day on the job.

When you have compiled various BGs for a specific scene (e.g., a gymnasium), you can blend them together in an artful form and do a mixdown to one track. This way your editor will have to cut in only one piece of media instead of taking the time to lay in each sound himself. One of my assistants, Melissa Brown, did a mixdown of the BGs for me on *Make It or Break It* and saved me so much time.

—ljc

Offer to cut in the SFX too! This is a great way to start cutting for your editor. When you edit anything, it will help stretch your skills and build your confidence. Your editor will give you changes, and this will help you understand his taste. You can apply what you learn from each session to your next bit of cutting. One day you will cut in the sound effects, and your editor will have no notes for you! This will be a wonderful feeling.

2.9 MX: Needle Drops and Score

Not all shows have needle drops. There is an entire world associated with buying music for your film. Many shows have music supervisors who help select songs and are responsible for licensing them. Every show has a MX budget, which should not be exceeded. There are whole libraries of drops that are indies (independent, without a label) and therefore more affordable, and it is the editor's job to stay within the confines of this budget without sacrificing too much quality.

Music is subjective, so many hours are spent selecting the right MX for a scene. You will create an Alt bin where you will keep versions of a scene cut with many different drops. Sometimes the writers and/or producers select a specific drop for a scene, which the MX supervisor will clear (license). When a song title is written into the script, the assistant should download it from iTunes or contact the MX supervisor, who will upload it to his website or send a CD for you to import into your editing system. If production uses a song during shooting, you need to ask for a copy of that playback tape from your post producer as well. Most of the time, you will lay in the highest quality sound possible for the drop. This only differs when you are using a song as playback to which the actor mouths the words. It is *essential* to get this playback from production for sync in your scene.

> **SHINE NOTE**
>
> When multiple tunes have been sent to your editor for song replacement, it helps tremendously to create an Alt bin with a subclip of the scene so that the assistant or editor can cut in the new drops on separate tracks.

Dropping in multiple tunes on different tracks saves your editor so much time, even if he has to slide the music to a different start or end point. This is what the editor will do in preparation for the producer so that he can view and listen to his new choices quickly. Remember that your goal is to make your director's or producer's time in the editing room as streamlined as possible.

A template to keep track of the drops that your editor uses is provided in Figure 2.4. The assistant will send the list to the MX supervisor to keep him apprised and to determine the approximate costs.

The assistant will update this template whenever a tune is replaced and create a final list when the show is locked and ready for air.

> **DEFINITION**
>
> *Locked* means that all picture notes have been completed, the network has signed off, and no further changes are anticipated.

After you lock, there will be two *spotting* sessions. One session will be with your supervising sound editor and his staff, where they will determine what lines of dialog need to be replaced and the sound design for various scenes. Another session will be with the composer and his music editor, during which the director and producers will give notes concerning where the music will be placed, where it will start, when it will end, and what the tone should be. The associate producer (A.P.) is present during these spotting sessions because he is in charge of the final mix. The FX and MX that the editor has cut into the show will serve as a template and is often emulated in the final dub.

"THE COMPETITION"								
EP. 103 "THE SURPRISE PARTY"								
ACT	**SC**	**MASTER TC**	**DUR**	**TITLE**	**ARTIST**	**COST**	**COMMENTS**	
Teaser	04	01:00:00:00	1:23:18	*'Go for the Gold'*	*THE PHANTASTIKS*	Ad Card		
03	23A	01:22:13:04	1:48:13	*'Rock On'*	*1–69*		TBR/w/Score (to be replaced)	
04	25	01:31:01:12	0:17:14	*'Last Night'*	*THE BACKWARDS*		TBR/w/Score	
04	25A	01:34:20:06	2:01:10	*'It Takes Two'*	*SPEECHES*			
05	30–31	01:40:12:24	1:24:02	*'Follow Your Dreams'*	*BRAD NEXTOWN*			
					TOTAL			
					BUDGET	$12,500		

Figure 2.4 *Needle drop template*

When you read the script, keep in mind that scenes will need to be scored with music that underlines the emotions of the scene and that the editor cuts a temporary score (temp) into the film. If there is a composer on the show, then it will help to have an eclectic collection of his past scores available for your editor. If there is specific MX referred to in the script, it is the assistant's job to make sure that the soundtrack from that film is imported into the editing system along with similar soundtracks. Even when there is no mention of music, it is good practice to think about what sort of music might enhance the film—and digitize it!

SHINE NOTE

Many editors and assistants collect feature scores and keep them on a personal hard drive (see Figure 2.5). Be prepared to digitize these on your first day of work, just as you did with SFX. Understand that this is only temp and will be replaced by the composer's score written specifically for this movie. If you arrive with a breakdown of possible MX scores appropriate for your current film and have digitized them for your editor, you will be many steps ahead of the game! Do a printout of the MX and FX libraries that have been digitized for easy reference.

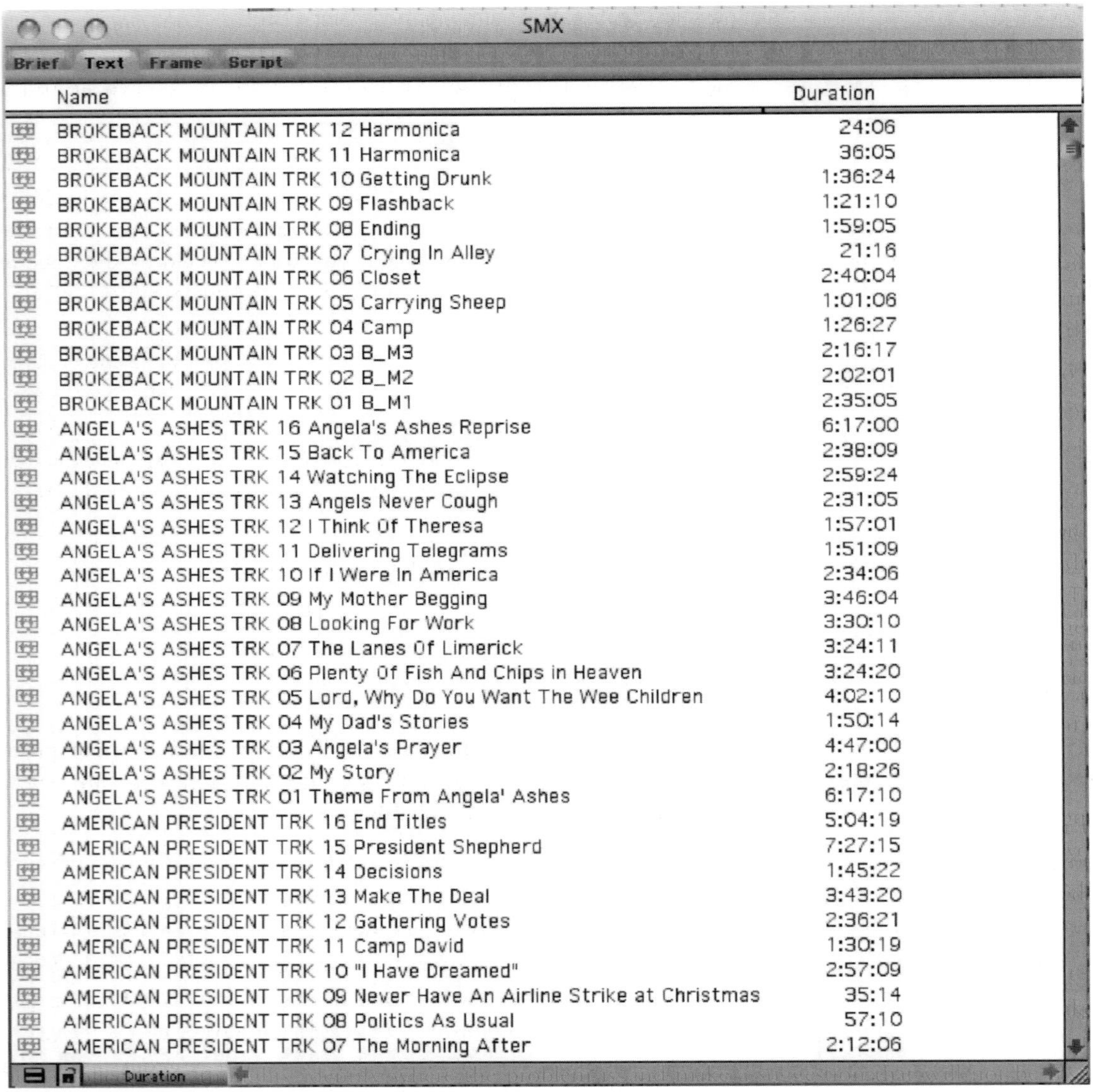

Name	Duration
BROKEBACK MOUNTAIN TRK 12 Harmonica	24:06
BROKEBACK MOUNTAIN TRK 11 Harmonica	36:05
BROKEBACK MOUNTAIN TRK 10 Getting Drunk	1:36:24
BROKEBACK MOUNTAIN TRK 09 Flashback	1:21:10
BROKEBACK MOUNTAIN TRK 08 Ending	1:59:05
BROKEBACK MOUNTAIN TRK 07 Crying In Alley	21:16
BROKEBACK MOUNTAIN TRK 06 Closet	2:40:04
BROKEBACK MOUNTAIN TRK 05 Carrying Sheep	1:01:06
BROKEBACK MOUNTAIN TRK 04 Camp	1:26:27
BROKEBACK MOUNTAIN TRK 03 B_M3	2:16:17
BROKEBACK MOUNTAIN TRK 02 B_M2	2:02:01
BROKEBACK MOUNTAIN TRK 01 B_M1	2:35:05
ANGELA'S ASHES TRK 16 Angela's Ashes Reprise	6:17:00
ANGELA'S ASHES TRK 15 Back To America	2:38:09
ANGELA'S ASHES TRK 14 Watching The Eclipse	2:59:24
ANGELA'S ASHES TRK 13 Angels Never Cough	2:31:05
ANGELA'S ASHES TRK 12 I Think Of Theresa	1:57:01
ANGELA'S ASHES TRK 11 Delivering Telegrams	1:51:09
ANGELA'S ASHES TRK 10 If I Were In America	2:34:06
ANGELA'S ASHES TRK 09 My Mother Begging	3:46:04
ANGELA'S ASHES TRK 08 Looking For Work	3:30:10
ANGELA'S ASHES TRK 07 The Lanes Of Limerick	3:24:11
ANGELA'S ASHES TRK 06 Plenty Of Fish And Chips in Heaven	3:24:20
ANGELA'S ASHES TRK 05 Lord, Why Do You Want The Wee Children	4:02:10
ANGELA'S ASHES TRK 04 My Dad's Stories	1:50:14
ANGELA'S ASHES TRK 03 Angela's Prayer	4:47:00
ANGELA'S ASHES TRK 02 My Story	2:18:26
ANGELA'S ASHES TRK 01 Theme From Angela' Ashes	6:17:10
AMERICAN PRESIDENT TRK 16 End Titles	5:04:19
AMERICAN PRESIDENT TRK 15 President Shepherd	7:27:15
AMERICAN PRESIDENT TRK 14 Decisions	1:45:22
AMERICAN PRESIDENT TRK 13 Make The Deal	3:43:20
AMERICAN PRESIDENT TRK 12 Gathering Votes	2:36:21
AMERICAN PRESIDENT TRK 11 Camp David	1:30:19
AMERICAN PRESIDENT TRK 10 "I Have Dreamed"	2:57:09
AMERICAN PRESIDENT TRK 09 Never Have An Airline Strike at Christmas	35:14
AMERICAN PRESIDENT TRK 08 Politics As Usual	57:10
AMERICAN PRESIDENT TRK 07 The Morning After	2:12:06

Figure 2.5 *Film scores from personal music library*

2.10 Playback: MX and PIX

MX playback is broken down into stages. First, the song is selected by the director, producers, and MX supervisor. It is licensed and cleared for use before any further steps are taken. If the song is to be sung live onstage, a prerecord session is booked, the artist is recorded, and the preferred take is decided upon. The scene is shot using this playback, and the actor can lip sync to it. When dailies arrive the next day, make sure the post facility has telecined the playback tape as well as the production track. When you prepare the Dailies bin (organize it according to the editor's preferences), include the playback song as written in the script, and label it with the title and name of the artist. For example, in our Scene 04 in "The Surprise Party," the song "Going for Gold" by the Phantastiks should be included in the Scene bin.

Picture playback is needed when you shoot a scene in which a television or computer monitor has a moving picture on it. It can also be broken down into stages. First the material needs to be selected by the director and approved by the producers. For example, if you are use stock footage of the Los Angeles riots to play on a background television while a scene is being shot, the post producer must first order the stock from a stock house. Next, the material needs to be digitized, edited, and approved by the director and the producer. After the selected footage has been telecined, the associate producer ships the sequence to a 24-frame playback house to be prepared for the set. If this step is skipped, you will see a black line scrolling on the TV screen or computer monitor. If playback uses an LCD or plasma monitor, there is no need for this process. Now the playback is ready for the shoot. Again, the assistant editor must make sure that the playback material accompanies the dailies.

Playback (MX or picture) is serious business; when it goes wrong on the set, it costs time and money. Make careful note of when scenes containing playback will be shot so that all the prep work *you* are responsible for is done in a timely fashion.

2.11 VFX

The task of temp VFX has fallen largely to the assistant editor. You must be knowledgeable about green screens, 3-D warp, motion effects, titling, and much more. Your VFX skills will save the editor so much time and will be tremendously appreciated. This is one area where you can **shine**.

2.12 Stock

When you are reading the script, you will also make a list of the stock shots that will be needed for the show. These can be ordered from a stock house, and some stock might exist from a previous season of the show you are on. Sometimes a stock shot is not written in the script, but you will have to decide whether one might be needed. Rather be safe than sorry, so add it to your list. Before Sc. 02 in "The Surprise Party," there is no mention of a stock shot. But there is a great chance that an establishing stock shot will be requested by the producers to orient the audience. Make sure you have placed in your Stock bin all the stock shots to establish locations that are used in your show. The gym, school, homes, and restaurants will all need stock shots for DX (day exterior) and NX (night exterior) and should be organized in a Stock bin.

You can order these stock shots from a stock house, or the production company will shoot it for you during the course of your show. But you must make a note of this and be prepared to provide these stock shots for your editor before he starts cutting the scene. Put this on your breakdown under *stock*. You will ask the production office for the shooting schedule before you start work so you will know what day the flagged scenes will be shot. You will also ask to receive the call sheet daily to confirm that the scene has not been rescheduled to another day.

The stock you order has been shot on different formats—16 mm, 35 mm, standard definition (SD), anamorphic, Cinemascope, 16:9, or 4:3. You must import it at its best resolution and alert the post department as soon as the shot has been selected and locked. There has to be adequate time to receive the media and transfer it at the highest resolution in time for the online.

> ### SHINE NOTE
>
> It helps when you know the story inside and out. When discussing a story point, playback date, or stock footage availability, you will have the answers at your fingertips. This will make you **shine**.

You have just finished your first breakdown of the script! You have created the continuity and various templates for your new show. Well done. The information you have culled from the script is immense. Now what you do with what *was not* written is what makes this breakdown so special. Read between the lines; try to guess what sounds or visuals will make the scene play better. Understand that what you bring to the editing room—the information you have gathered from this breakdown—is invaluable to the editing process. It will serve you well when you are discussing the script with your editor, director, writer, or producer.

> Before editing a film, I break down the script for FX, MX, stock, and playback. I find it immensely helpful to also do a *character breakdown* for each of the principals (main actors). It is a list of the scenes that one character is in (e.g., Ali: Sc. 02, Sc. 04, Sc. 06, and Sc. 08) along with a description that entails the character's emotional state. It is a marvelous way to become familiar with the story and assess the intertwining journeys of each character.
>
> I also do a *lift breakdown*. This is a list of scenes with the estimated timings that I think are candidates for the editing room floor. It is good practice to estimate timings and then compare them to the final cut. These skills will serve you well in the future. The rule of thumb is 1 minute per page.
>
> —ljc

2.13 Order the Supplies

By now, you have spent at least six hours working for free. You will find that this investment of your time will save you countless hours of stressful confusion after you start working. It will also be so appreciated by the editor and coproducer that they will be inclined to hire you again!

It is important to know where the editor would like his editing system to be placed in the room. This might necessitate a visit to the cutting rooms before your first day on the job to evaluate your space. Some editors have a vested interest in how they set up their rooms. For example, some editors dislike having their backs to the door and will specify which wall the Avid or FCP setup should be placed against.

The last chore to accomplish before your first day on the job is to make a list of supplies and furniture needed for the cutting rooms (see Table 2.3). This list should be faxed to the post supervisor, who will decide which items need to be ordered and which need to be permanently borrowed from the production office. If you are setting up a film room, these lists still apply, except the editing machines will include Moviolas or flatbeds and some additional paper supplies. Keep this master list and add to it from job to job.

Table 2.3 *Supply list for a digital or film room*

Sharpies (red and black)	1 box
Pens (black, blue, red)	3 boxes
Pencils	1 box
Pencil sharpeners	1 for each of you
Highlighters	1 box yellow, 1 box blue
Scissors	1 for each of you
Stapler	1 for each of you
Staples	1 box
Staple remover	1
Tape	1 box
Tape dispenser	1 for each of you
Envelopes	1 box
Rulers	1 for each of you
White out	1 for each of you
Paper clips	1 box for each of you
Pen and pencil holders	1 for each of you
Push pins (multicolored)	1 large container
Push pins (clear)	1 large container
Index cards (multicolored)	1 pack
Index cards (white)	1 pack
Three-hole punch	1 for each of you
Two-hole punch	1 for the assistant
Clipboard for paperwork	1 for each of you
Legal pad (8 1/2×11 inch) (three hole punched)	3 for each of you
Steno pad	2 for each of you
Post-its (2×2 and 1×1 inch) (multicolored)	Large pack of each size
Three-ring notebooks:	
(3-inch D-ring)	1 for each of you (to start with)
(2 inch)	4 for each assistant (to start with)
Tab dividers (minimum of eight)	10 sets
White paper (three-hole punched and plain)	2 packs each
Bulletin board (8×10 feet)	1 for each of you
Bulletin board (4×6 feet)	1 for each of you
Printer–fax connected to editing machines	
Printer ink	
DVDs and jackets	1 box

There are few films edited on film these days, but for those of you who might have the opportunity to work in that environment, Table 2.4 is a basic list of supplies you will need to order.

Table 2.4 *Supply list for film room (in addition to the digital room supplies)*

Trim boxes	6 dozen (to start with)
Trim racks	5
White masking rape (1 inch)	6 rolls
White masking tape (1/2 inch)	3 rolls
Trim tags	2 boxes
Rubber bands	2 boxes
Splicing tape (white)	6 rolls (each person)
Splicing tape (clear)	6 rolls (each person)
Butt splicer	1 each
Butt splicer blades	1 box
Synchronizer with sound heads (6 gang or 4 gang)	1 each
Flanges (keyed and nonkeyed)	1 each
Split reel	1 for each assistant
Cores	1 dozen
Spring clamps	1 each
Sound reader	1 each
Editing bench (American or English)	1 each
Moviola/flatbed	1 each
Moviola bulbs	1 dozen
Light bulbs for Moviola tray	1 dozen
White gloves (large and small)	1 dozen each
Grease pencils	2 dozen
Velvet	1 each
Webril wipes	2 rolls
Acetone	1 bottle
Yard stick	1
Reels (1000 feet)	3 dozen
Yellow leader	3 rolls
Fill leader	3 rolls
Academy leader	1 roll
Sound pops	10 feet
Trim bins (large and small)	3 each
Oversized trim bags	3 each
Electric rewind	1
Coding machine	1
Dolly	1

Table 2.5 is a list of furniture you will need to order for the editing suite.

Table 2.5 *Furniture list for a digital or film room*

Couch	1 for each room
Editing chair/editing stool	1 for each of you (best you can get)
Guest chair	1 for each of you
Standing lamp	1 for each of you
Desk lamp	1 for each of you
Book shelf	1 for each of you
End table	1 for each of you
Coffee table	1 for each of you

The post producer chooses the rental company for the editing equipment. It is good to know about the equipment, however, so that you can request upgrades (e.g., an oversized screen for viewing cuts).

Along with the script, it is also imperative that you request all the paperwork that the production office generates. Ask them to email these lists to you or to send a hard copy with your script. They should include the cast and crew list, one-liner, production schedule, and shooting schedule. Put these in your newly created three-ring notebook.

Yay! Your advance paperwork is now complete. It's exhausting, and you haven't started the film yet (or been paid). But these advance preparations will pay off. Now you are ready to start your first day.

Chapter 3

Your First Day

The editor and assistant begin work on the first day of principal photography. Very exciting. Create the project windows in the editing systems. Bring some media with you to test all the equipment, and make sure the supplies and furniture have arrived. Prepare the three-ring notebooks for the editor and yourself. They will be filled with telecine reports, camera reports, sound reports, the script supervisor's log, and lined script pages. Make additional tabs for ADR, MX, SFX, VFX, titles, stock, network formats, and spec sheets for the music and sound department. Look at the templates as a guide, and you will be on your way.

Today is the day you get to meet and greet the script supervisor, camera department, and sound crew. Tomorrow you will receive your first day of dailies.

3.1 Setting Up the Project Window

Editing systems are constantly evolving, dictated by the need to keep pace with technological advancements and improvements. Film has been replaced with tapeless media in the cutting room. However, the work flow remains essentially the same. The assistant needs to import, download, ingest, digitize, etc. He needs to organize and rename things and prepare the film for the editor to cut.

Regardless of which film or editing system you use, the first task is to test the equipment, digitize and generate an output, calibrate the soundboards (you *must* call the tech in for this), test the microphone and recording ability, and adjust the monitors.

When you have completed testing the equipment, your next task is to start prepping for the following day's dailies by creating the *project window* for your editor. Because you will most likely be on Unity or SAN, the editor will have access to his colleagues' episodes in his editing room.

> **DEFINITION**
>
> Unity (for Avid) and SAN (for FCP) are the systems used to connect editing computers. They allow each editor to have access to media at the same time.

DOI: 10.1016/B978-0-240-81398-1.00003-1

In the project window, you should create the project with the episode number and several standard bins (see Figure 3.1); for example, A. Workpix (or current cut), Act, ADR, Banners, Gag, Scenes (individual scenes), Z1 Assembly, Z2 EC1 (editor's cut 1), Z3 DC1 (director's cut 1), Z4 PC1 (producer's cut 1), Z5 SC1 (studio cut 1) through NC1 (network cut 1), to name a few. You will create folders for Act bins, Scenes, SFX, SMX, Stock, and VFX.

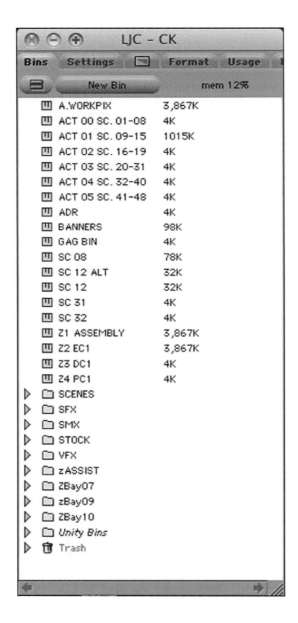

Figure 3.1 *Project bin*

There is usually a bin in which the editor keeps his current cut. Each editor has his own preference on how to name it; for example, Current Cut, Cuts, or Editor's Cuts. After all the dailies have been completely cut, the editor will work out of this bin.

TIP

In our projects, we call the current cut A. Workpix so that it will default to the top of the project window.

Next you can create an Act bin (see Figure 3.2). It is labeled with the act number and the scenes it contains. When the scene is cut, it is placed in its appropriate bin. This is one of the many ways to organize scenes and acts.

○ ○ ○	ACT 01 SC. 09–15	
Brief **Text** Frame Script		
Name	**Duration**	
ACT 01 SC. 09 - 15	8:56:02	
SC. 10	50:15	
SC. 11	7:12:02	
SC. 12	1:24:17	
SC. 13	5:19:23	
SC. 14- 15	3:14:05	
Duration		

Figure 3.2 *Act bin*

Add a bin for ADR into which you will place the temp ADR that is recorded in the editing room. Also create a Banners bin for the miscellaneous banners (see Figure 3.3).

○ ○ ○	BANNERS	
Brief **Text** Frame Script		
Name	**Duration**	
DIGITIZED BLACK	1;00;02	
DIGITIZED WHITE	2:00:00	
END CREDITS	2:00:00	
END LOGOS	8:00	
MAIN TITLE	18:04	
MISSING SCENE	1:59:26	
MISSING INSERT	2:00:00	
MISSING STOCK	2:00:00	
VFX	2:00:00	
Duration		

Figure 3.3 *Banners bin*

In it you will place the following:

1. Digitized black
2. Digitized white
3. End credits (or slug for end credits denoting length, such as "End credits—30 secs") (sweetened with EC MX)
4. End logos
5. Main title (or slug for main title denoting length, such as "Main title—20 secs") (sweetened with MT MX)
6. Missing scene
7. Missing insert
8. Missing stock
9. VFX

> **DEFINITION**
>
> Banners are space holders for future media drop-ins that can be created by the assistant in title tools.

These are items that the editor will need to cut in, and he will appreciate that you have anticipated his needs.

Create a Gag bin so that your editor can place the materials that can be used for the gag reel at the end of the show. A Scene bin will be created for each new scene you receive during dailies.

Editors have different systems of keeping their various iterations of cuts. We like to keep our versions in separate Z bins.

> **TIP**
>
> We place a Z in front of each title so that they will sort to the bottom of the project window. Z1 represents the first assembly (see Figure 3.4). After we have completed cutting all the dailies, assembled our scenes into acts, and joined these acts together, we now have an assembly of the entire show.
>
>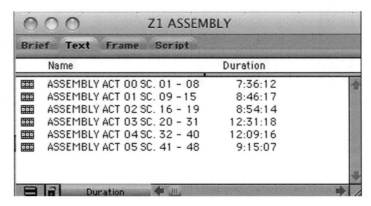

Figure 3.4 *Z1 assembly*

This bin remains untouched now because it is the only copy of the entire show—without lifts or missing dialog—and is an exact replica of the script. This bin is then copied to the A.Workpix bin, in which the next set of changes is done (see Figure 3.5).

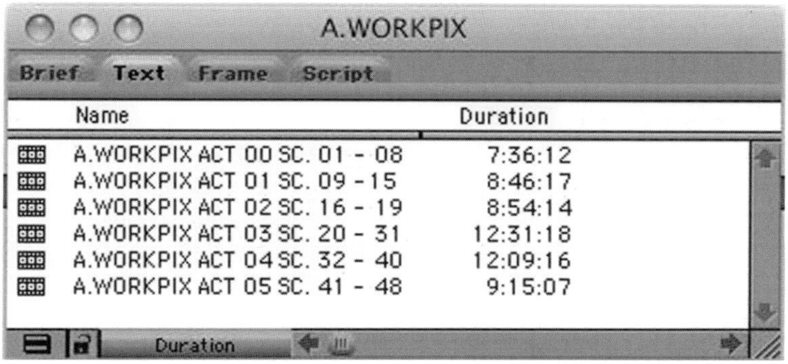

Figure 3.5 *A.Workpix*

Note that even though this is a copy of the assembly, we change the title and rename it A.Workpix for each act. This is essential for making sure the editor is always working in the most current cut. It is a huge waste of time when the changes are made in the wrong version of the show.

When the next set of changes is complete, a copy of the A.Workpix is dragged into the next bin, Z2 EC1, and the title is changed to EC1 (see Figure 3.6).

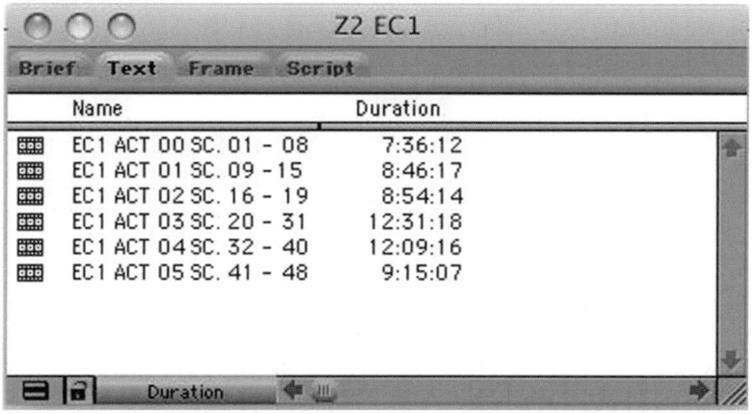

Figure 3.6 *Z2 EC1*

When you create these bins in the project window, be aware that there is sometimes more than one version of each phase of the cut. Editors might have time for EC2, and the director's cut might go to DC3 or DC4, and so on. You must change the Z number accordingly. Pay careful attention to saving the various versions because the editor is often asked to go back to an old cut. One of the best notes we receive is, "Put it back the way you had it in the editor's cut."

Now you create various folders. One folder is for the scenes that the editor has completed cutting that will eventually contain every scene in the movie. Two critical folders to create are for sound effects (SFX) and music (SMX).

> **TIP**
>
> Because the project window sorts alphabetically, we place an S in front of FX and MX because we like these bins to follow each other.

Next, the stock folder contains two bins. The Stock Production bin contains the establishing shots that have been provided by production and can be used without cost by postproduction. The Stock Purchased bin contains the stock that you have ordered from an outside stock house that costs money. Separating these two bins makes it easier for the editor to choose from the available free footage first. If the right shot is not available, then the editor will select from the purchased stock. It will also be easier for the assistant to identify what stock needs to be ordered before the online occurs.

3.2 Settings

It is now time to create the settings for your editor's project. Make sure the audio is set to drop frame, nondrop frame, or 24 or 30 frame project; create the user settings; and select 16:9 or letterbox or 4:3. Discuss these settings with your post supervisor and editor.

> **TIP**
>
> If your editor has special visual effects or transitions he uses frequently, you can set up a Favorites bin (this is primarily important on FCP). If you have a snapshot of his settings and know how he remaps his keyboard, you can prepare these in advance of his first day of cutting.

We suggest that you re-create your settings instead of importing them from your last film because it can corrupt your new project. You can save settings in the Unity or SAN after you re-create them.

The Unity (or SAN) should be maintained at least once a month by your techs. Sometimes this task falls to the assistant editor. You are in charge of making sure the drives are not too full and that not too many files are on any one partition. Double check that media is placed on the correct drives (i.e., music is on the music drive, etc.).

3.3 Import FX and MX

Begin importing the sound effects and music. Contact the supervising sound editor and MX editor and ask them for help in gathering together a suitable library for your current show. Their contact information will be on the cast and crew list. Remember to request this list before your first day so that you can contact them in advance. This way you will hopefully receive the requested media by your first day on the job.

The composer's music editor will have an eclectic collection of his scores from previous films. These can be used as temp score. In television, after you receive the score from the first few shows, you will have more appropriate thematic music to use for your current episode. On features, if the composer has been hired when you start dailies, the same rules apply. It is more common on theatrical releases for the editor to find a temp score from various composers. Oftentimes the director and editor have discussed the vibe of the MX and will suggest film scores that would be good to have in the editing system for temp use.

While the media is digitizing, multitask and begin organizing your notebooks.

3.4 Binders and Paperwork

Hopefully you have received some of the paperwork generated by the production office. Check that you have the latest schedules and any outstanding lists—cast and crew, production schedule, shooting schedule, weekly prep schedule, one-liners, day-of-days, and the most current draft of the script. Remember to visit the production accountant to collect your startup paperwork. It is *very* important to get on the production email list to get copied on the paperwork that is generated by their office. Otherwise, you will not know what is going on!

Prepare the binders—the editor's notebook as well as your own, with cover sheets, spine sheet, and tab dividers. The contents and tab dividers will be different for the editor and assistant. Place all the paperwork in the notebook under the specified headings.

You will know the scene numbers contained in each act from your script breakdown. Use a tab divider for each act. Label them with the act number as well as the scene numbers contained in that act. For example, the first label will say TEASER Sc. 01–06, then ACT 01 Sc. 07–15, etc. The assistant will place the most current script into each of these divided sections.

Create labeled tabs for the following categories:

Tab labels	Contents
Continuity	Act and scene breakdown
Breakdown	Script breakdown
Locater lists	Color-coded markers
Editor's cut	Notes for changes
Director's cut	Notes for changes
Producer's cut	Notes for changes
Studio cut	Notes for changes
Network cut	Notes for changes
ADR	Notes on added or changed lines of dialog
SFX	Notes on SFX needed for film
MX	Notes on MX needed for film
VFX	Notes on VFX to be created
Reprise	Notes for suggested content and changes
Titles	List of opening credits and end credits
Format	Network specs/format sheet
Shooting schedule	List of scenes that will be shot each day
Cast and crew lists	Contact information
Day-of-days	Which actors work on which days
One-liner	AD breakdown of shooting script

DEFINITION

The script supervisor lines the script to show which dialog was covered in which shot and who was speaking on camera, with detailed descriptions and technical details written on a facing page.

Many editors have their own set of preferences about their notebooks and user settings. The assistant editor must ask the editor about this. Do not assume anything. Tailor your work to suit his needs. Some editors have only the lined script in front of him and pay little attention to the rest of the paperwork.

One of the nice things about working with the same editor is that most questions about preferences have been answered before, and a natural rhythm and work flow has evolved.

Prepare the two assistant editor's notebooks. The first notebook contains the paperwork for an individual episode. This includes the camera reports, sound reports, telecine reports, negative discrepancy reports, editor's logs, copies of the lined script, and copies of memos and emails. In features, you will only need one notebook because there is only one episode. The second notebook has the information that is germane to the entire show. There are additional categories for this second notebook, which include the specs from the sound effects department, music department, and the network. The network will have spec sheets for delivery requirements as well as a format sheet. The second notebook also contains contact sheets for the cast and crew, telecine house, ADR stage, and dub stage. Make sure you stay abreast of the paperwork each day.

Here are the contents of the first notebook for the individual episode:

Labels	Contents
Continuity	Act and scene breakdown
ADR	Notes on added or changed lines of dialog
SFX	Notes on SFX needed for film
MX	Notes on suggested drops or needed MX
VFX	Notes on VFX to be created
Reprise	Notes for suggested content and editing changes
Titles	List of opening credits and end credits
Shooting schedule	List of scenes that will be shot each day
Cast and crew lists	Contact information
Day-of-days	Which actors work on which days
One-liner	AD breakdown of shooting script
Editor's log	Takes, shot timings, list of incomplete scenes from the script supervisor
Lined script	Script pages lined with takes and coverage
Telecine reports	Post facility report of transferred dailies
Camera reports	List of all shots and circled (chosen) takes
Sound reports	List of all shots and circled (chosen) takes
Audio EDLs	Printout of sound cuts and dissolves in finished film
Picture EDLs	Printout of PIX cuts and dissolves in finished film

Figure 3.7 is an example of the cast and crew contact information you will receive from the production office.

MUSIC

Music Supervisor	Wendy.... wendy...@gmail.com	(c)	310-555-0100
Composer	Mike....	(o) (c)	310-555-0101 310-555-0102
Music Editor	Elliott.... gold....@ornette.com	(o) (h)	323-555-0103 323-555-0104

POST PRODUCTION

Associate Producer	Tom.... Ziggy....@yahoo.com	(o) (c)	661-555-0105 661-555-0106
Editor	Nathan.... n8....@earthlink.net	(o) (c) (h)	661-555-0107 310-555-0108 310-555-0109
Editor	LoriJane.... lcol....@sbcglobal.net	(o) (h)	661-555-0110 818-555-0111
Editor	David.... david....@verizon.net	(o) (c) (h)	661-555-0112 323-555-0113 310-555-0114
Asst. Editor	John.... jvor....@aol.com	(o) (c)	661-555-0115 310-555-0116
Asst. Editor	Carsten.... carsten....@gmail.com	(o) (c)	661-555-0117 661-555-0118
Post Coordinator	Michael.... roland....@gmail.com	(o) (c)	661-555-0119 661-555-0120
Post P.A.	Ryan.... ryan....@gmail.com	(o) (c)	661-555-0121 661-555-0122

Figure 3.7 *Cast and crew template*

This information will change often, so be sure to replace old paperwork with the newest copy in the notebooks. Make copies for each notebook and one copy for each bulletin board in each editing room. These lists are where you will find the names and contact information necessary to do your job. The postproduction department will generate their own list pertaining to the people and facilities involved in post only. Place the updated versions in your editor's notebook and on his bulletin board.

The day-of-days list is for determining which actors will be working on which days (see Figure 3.8). Though it is not often referred to during the shoot, it will be useful when ADR is needed from a given actor. On occasion, the production soundman will be able to get a *wild line* that you can place in your editor's cut before delivery to the director or the producer.

ACTORS DAY OUT OF DAYS		Date	
Production Company	Production Title	Script Date	
Producer	Director	Prod. Manager/Asst. Director	

Rehearsal -R	Hold - H	Day Number..	M T W T F S S M T W T F S S M T W T F S S M T W T F S S
Started -S	Travel - T	Date	
Worked - W	Finish - F	Day of the Week..................................	
On Call - C			

No.	Character	Cast Member	
1			
2			
3			
4			
5			
6			
7			
8			
9			
10			
11			
12			
13			
14			
15			
16			
17			
18			
19			
20			

Figure 3.8 *Day-of-days template*

DEFINITION

A wild line is a line of dialog recorded without rolling the camera. An editor will ask production for a wild line to replace dialog that is either recorded off microphone (*off mic*), garbled, or to add a line of dialog that will help clarify a story point.

A one-liner is generated by the 1st AD and contains a description of the scene, the scene numbers, the location of the shoot, the number of pages, and which cast members are involved (see Figure 3.9). It is presented on a first to last day shooting order. The 1st AD's work is a great cheat sheet in preparing your continuity, but remember to still take the time to edit his work. You might have to take out the humorous asides or include more specific information.

Note that this piece of paper is sometimes called a *one-line schedule*. Sometimes it has no title at all, but you will be able to recognize it now!

CONTINUITY SYNOPSIS/ONE LINE					
TITLE: _____			PROD. PER. _____		
DIRECTOR: _____			DATE: _____		
SCENE NOS.	SET	DESCRIPTION	D/N	PAGES	CHARACTERS

Figure 3.9 *One-liner template*

As shown in Figure 3.10, the production office also generates the *prep schedule* (preparation schedule). It is a calendar of daily meetings, their times, meeting places, and invitees. It reflects the day's work in the director's schedule as he prepares to shoot. It also contains scheduling information about the concept meeting (what the show should look like and more) and tone meeting (where the writers and executive producers share their vision of the show with the director). The tone meeting often takes place the day before the first day of the shoot, and the time of this meeting often shifts. It is always a good idea for the editor to be included

TITLE: _____	**PREP SCHEDULE**
Ep. _____ "_____"	Updated November, 30, 2010 @ 6:00pm

TUESDAY	Dec. 1, 2010 PREP DAY 2 – EP. 116
2nd ½ of Crew lunch	LOCATION SCOUT (EXT/INT Police Station)
All Day	EPK Interviews with Cast on Stage 2
WEDNESDAY	Dec. 2, 2010 PREP DAY 3 – EP. 116
10:00 AM	TABLE READ on Stage 8
THURSDAY	Dec. 3, 2010 PREP DAY 4 – EP. 116
9:30-10:30 AM	PRODUCER'S CASTING SESSION
FRIDAY	Dec. 4, 2010 PREP DAY 5 – EP. 116
2:00 PM	TONE MEETING

Figure 3.10 *Prep schedule template*

in the tone meeting, so the assistant has to make sure that his editor is informed about the changes in the prep schedule.

An important piece of paperwork is the script supervisor's daily production report, also known as the *editor's log* (see Figure 3.11). When it is filled in correctly, it is the assistant editor's lifeline to the set. At the end of each day's shoot, the script supervisor will fax the editor's log to production. It contains the numbers of scenes shot; which ones are complete, partial, or incomplete; and the number of pages attributed to each scene and their timings. Usually the post PA will pick it up in the morning and bring it to the editing rooms. If this does not happen in a timely fashion, the assistant editor should go and pick it up himself.

The assistant editor must be able to determine from this paperwork whether a scene is complete or incomplete. A mistake in this area will result in wasted time and stress for the editor because partially completed scenes are often not edited until the entire scene has arrived in the cutting room. It is the assistant's job to develop a clear and concise way to have this information communicated to him by the script supervisor. If the script supervisor overlooks this information or if his notes are unclear, the assistant must take the time to get to the bottom of the problem and fix it quickly.

Script Supervisor's Daily Production Report

EPISODE: Day   of Photography   Date

Slate Numbers Shot: (Set-Ups)

Scene Numbers COVERED:

TOTALS: Today		Previous	To Date		Total in Script	To Be Taken
	# of SET UPS					
	# of SCENES COVERED					
	# of PAGES COMPLETED					
	Rough ESTIMATED TIME					

CALL TIME   LUNCH   CAMERA WRAP

FIRST SHOT   FIRST SHOT   SS/CC OUT TIME

AM SET UPS   COMPANY MOVES

Camera Rolls: Sound Rolls:

REMARKS:

Figure 3.11 *Editor's log template*

It is also the script supervisor's job to fax the *lined script* (see Figure 3.12) and its facing page to the production office at the end of each day. If this proves to be inconsistent, it is the assistant editor's job to make sure that the process is ironed out. Without the paperwork, it is very hard to get the dailies prepared in a timely fashion for the editor. You can ask for the associate producer's help in streamlining this process.

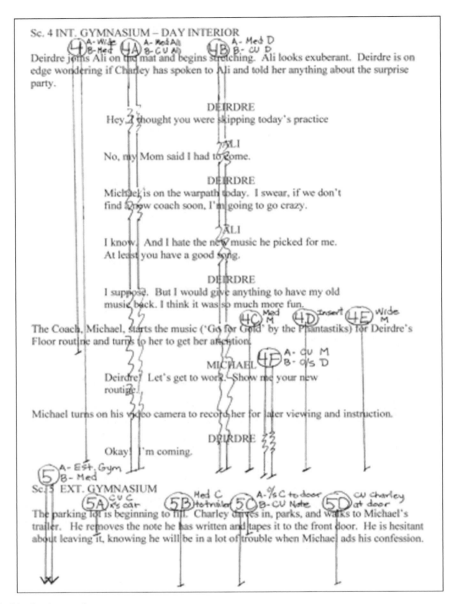

Figure 3.12 *Lined script template*

The lined script is a copy of the script page with lines drawn from top to bottom denoting which lines of dialog are on or off camera. Note that each line has a scene number and take, which indicates which shots cover that part of the script and where the coverage begins and ends. Hopefully each line has a brief description (e.g., A Cam: c.u. Ali; B Cam: 2/shot Michael & Deirdre). This information is valuable during cutting because you can tell by the straight line on the page that that bit of dialog is *on* camera, and the squiggly lines mean it is *off* camera. Knowing where the pickup (p.u.) of a scene starts is helpful.

The *facing page* is filled with essential information about what has been shot (see Figure 3.13). It is called the facing page because it is placed opposite the lined script page it describes.

TITLE: "THE SURPRISE PARTY" SCRIPT PAGE # 5

DIR: AMANDA ZAR   SCRIPT SUPERVISOR MARIA L.

SLATE	TK	TIME	COMMENTS	SHOT DESCRIPTION	LENS	CR	SR	DATE/COMMENTS
4	①	:40	Comp. ok	Master INT GYM DAY	35	A20	4	10/28 Track Deirdre
	②	:42	Comp. good	Dancers, Cam. pans to include ALI				
4	①	:50	Comp.	Same CLOSER	zoom lens	B21	4	10/28 TK1 - Need to zoom out faster
	②	:52	Comp. good					
4A	①	:45	comp. ok	MED. ALI	zoom lens	A20	4	10/28
4A	①	:45	comp. ok	CU ALI	zoom go	B21	4	10/28
4B	1	:20	inc. NG Dial.	MED DEIRDRE	35	A20	4	10/28 TK1 - saw boom at top
	②	:50	Comp. good					
4B	②	:10	FS	CU DEIRDRE	75	B21	5	10/28 TK2-NG snd.
		:51	Comp. good					
4C	①	:15	Comp. ok	MED MICHAEL	50	A20	5	10/28
4D	①	:45	Comp. good	INSERT BOOM BOX VARIOUS SIZES	50	A21	5	10/28
4E	1	:15	Comp. NG	WIDE MICHAEL	50	A21	5	10/28
	②	:20	Comp. good					
4F	①	:22	Comp. gd.	CU MICHAEL	35	A21	5	10/28 *use for Line # 6
4F	①	:22	Comp gd.	9/s D to MICHAEL	70	B22	5	10/28
5	①	:55	Comp. gd.	Estab. GYM DAY Charley drives in	100	A30	9	11/04
5	①	:55	Comp. gd.	MED CHARLEY drives in	250	B28	9	11/04
5A	1	:10	F.S.	CU CHARLEY X's car.	40	A30	9	11/04
	②	:15	Comp. ok					
5B	①	:30	Comp. gd.	MED CHARLEY WALKS TO TRAILER	35	A30	9	11/04
5C	①	:30	Comp. good	O/s CHARLEY to DOOR/TRAILER	35	A30	9	11/04
5C	①	:15	Comp. gd.	C.U. NOTE various sizes	40	B28	9	11/04
5D	①	:15	Comp. ok	CU. CHARLEY at door. X's cam L.	35	A30	10	11/04 Tk 1-end * Tk 2-start *
	②	:18	Comp. gd. *					

Figure 3.13 *Facing page template*

Denoted on the facing page is the slate and take number, timing of each take, whether it was complete or incomplete, a shot description, the lens that was used, the camera roll, the sound roll, the date shot, and comments. If you are working with Red or P2, there will be a numbering system like card 1 to card 2. During the course of the shoot, there are multiple takes filmed of each setup, and only a few are selected for print. For example, the c.u. was shot eight times, but only takes 2 and 3 are selected by the director. These are the circled takes that will be telecined (film to tape), transferred (tape to tape or hard drive), or printed (film negative prepped for development at the lab) for the editor to cut.

If you are shooting on film, the dailies first go to the lab, where they are either prepped for telecine (digital) or for developing (film). If you are shooting high def, it goes directly to telecine, where the telecine editor transfers the dailies onto a hard drive or tape. He follows the paperwork directives received from camera, sound, and script about which takes were selected to print. The takes that are not circled become the B negative. This hard drive or tape is picked up in the morning by the postproduction assistant (post PA) and delivered to the assistant editor along with the paperwork from the production office.

The second assistant cameraman (2nd AC) keeps a log of all takes shot on the set (e.g., Sc. 33–1, –2, –3), their timings, whether the takes are complete or incomplete, notes regarding possible focus issues, runouts (when the camera has run out of film during the shooting of a take), lens flares, etc. The timings of these shots become important to determine whether the take is complete. A copy of the *camera report* is sent to telecine and to the production office (see Figure 3.14).

Sometimes the B negative is ordered to find a different performance, search for better camera moves, or find a take without negative damage. The 2nd AC fills out the camera report, which reflects the date shot, the camera roll number, and denotes whether it is the A or B camera. He circles the chosen printed takes, and when the scene is complete or at the end of the day, he will confer with the script supervisor to make sure the correct takes have been circled.

The production sound mixer (soundman) or his assistant keeps a log of all takes shot on the set, their timings, and notes regarding NG (not good) sound, BG (background) noise, and preferred takes for sound. He also records wild tracks and wild lines. These wild tracks will be denoted on his sound report and hopefully cross-referenced on the facing page of the lined script (see Figure 3.15).

DEFINITION

Wild tracks are sound recordings without picture to be used for BG presence.

When the scene is finished, the soundman will confer with the script supervisor to confirm the chosen takes. Note that he has circled the chosen takes to be printed.

On most films, the script supervisor is responsible for making sure that camera, sound, and script notes are in accord. The paperwork from these three departments are sent to the telecine editor at the end of the day's shoot, and copies are sent to the editing room via the production office. The post producer chooses the post facility where the film gets transferred, onlined, and finished. This is also the facility where the VFX are created for the final version of the film and where the online is color corrected (timed) to become the final air master (color-timed master, or CTM).

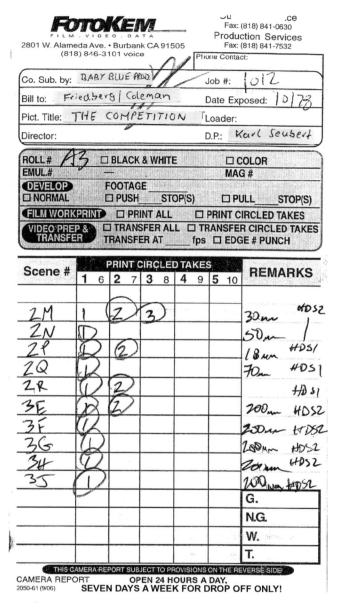

Figure 3.14 *Camera report template*

Unfortunately, mistakes happen on the set. For example, Sc. 33–1 and 33–2 are circled by sound, and takes 2 and 3 are circled by camera, and the script supervisor has circled all three takes. The mistake is missed on the set, and it is up to the telecine editor to defer to the paperwork provided by the script supervisor, thereby printing all three takes. When in doubt, it is a good idea to transfer all the takes in question. For example, if

SOUND REPORT

ROLL No. 2

PRODUCTION COMPANY	PRODUCTION TITLE	PROD. No.	DATE
BABY BLUE PROD.	THE COMPETITION	1012	10/28/09

DVD Roll #	HD#	Folder#	Mixer:	CAMERA FORMAT
1	1	102	SIMON HERBERT	(35mm) 16mm VIDEO

PILOT Hz	NR TONE	TONE REFERENCE LEVEL	RECORDING FORMAT	CAMERA SPEED FPS
50 6	■■■	-20 db		(24) 25 30 PA NTSC

DIGITAL SAMPLE RATE	USER BITS	USER BIT COMMENTS	AUDIO TIME CODE PPS
44. 48	: : :		24 25 30 (29.97)

TRANSFER TO:	Location:
35mm 16mm R-DAT OTHER	Int. Gym

SCENE	TAKE	SEG	Notes	CH 1	CH 2	CH 3	CH 4
-20db	(1)	01					
2	(1)	02		Mix	Boom	N.C.S Wire	
	2	03					
	(3)	04					
2A	(1)	05					
2B	(1)	06					
3	1	07					
	(2)	08					
	3	09					
	(4)	10					
3A	(1)	11					
3B	1	12					
.	(2)	13					
3C	(1)	14				✓	
3D	(1)	15					
C3	1	16					
	2	17					
	(3)	18					
	(4)	19					
	5	20					
	6	**21**					
	(7)	22					
	(8)	23					
	(9)	24					
C3A	(1)	25					
C3B	(1)	26		✓	✓		
	(2)	27					

Figure 3.15 *Sound report template*

sound circles take 1 but no one else does, make sure it gets transferred anyway. The script supervisor is usually correct, but better safe than sorry. The assistant editor must determine the takes that should have been printed and order them as a B negative after digitizing the dailies.

The telecine editor or his assistant generate paperwork for the dailies they transfer. This report includes comments about flares, negative dirt or scratches, hairs in the gate, and focus issues (see Figure 3.16). They will include a negative discrepancy report when there is serious damage.

KEYLOG Tracker HD Video Dailies Summary Report by VT Roll

Facility: **KEEP ME POSTED**
Project: **eps_1012**
Assistant Editor:

Downconverted Video Std: NTSC
Total Time: 00:59:09:20
Date of Transfer: October 29, 2009

VT Roll: **101202**

Event #	Scene	Take	Downconverted Video Timecode In	Out	Duration	Snd Rl#	Original Audio Timecode In
1	2G	1	02:00:01:04	03:45:16	03:44:12	1	16:41:13:08
Cam Rl#	A2						
2	2H	2	02:03:45:16	05:58:C0	02:12:08	1	16:54:57:00
Cam Rl#	A2						
3	2J	1	02:05:58:00	08:26:04	02:28:04	1	17:21:24:22
Cam Rl#	A2						
4	2J	2	02:08:26:04	11:03:12	02:37:08	1	17:24:23:27
Cam Rl#	A2						
5	2K	4	02:11:03:12	12:27:00	01:23:12	1	17:33:16:21
Cam Rl#	A2						
6	2L	1	02:12:27:00	14:05:20	01:38:20	1	17:38:01:14
Cam Rl#	A2						
7	2M	2	02:14:C5:20	17:56:08	03:50:12	1	18:21:08:12
Cam Rl#	A3						
8	2M	3	02:17:56:08	20:24:16	02:28:08	1	18:25:54:15
Cam Rl#	A3						
9	2N	1	02:20:24:16	22:00:20	01:36:04	1	18:29:52:13
Cam Rl#	A3						
10	2P	1	02:22:00:20	23:44:00	01:43:04	1	18:49:01:07
Cam Rl#	A3						
11	2P	2	02:23:44:00	25:21:16	01:37:16	1	18:52:05:05
Cam Rl#	A3						
12	2Q	1	02:25:21:16	26:29:20	01:08:04	1	18:55:16:22
Cam Rl#	A3						
13	2R	1	02:26:29:20	31:47:16	05:17:20	1	19:13:06:12
Cam Rl#	A3						
14	2R	2	02:31:47:16	33:14:20	01:27:04	1	19:18:39:27
Cam Rl#	A3						
15	3E	1	02:33:14:20	35:35:16	02:20:20	1	19:55:41:29
Cam Rl#	A3						
16	3E	2	02:35:35:16	40:19:08	04:43:16	1	19:59:51:07
Cam Rl#	A3						
17	3F	1	02:40:19:08	41:27:12	01:08:04	1	20:09:12:07
Cam Rl#	A3						
18	3G	1	02:41:27:12	43:16:20	01:49:08	1	20:21:58:24
Cam Rl#	A3						
19	3H	1	02:43:16:20	46:45:04	03:28:08	1	20:24:57:21
Cam Rl#	A3						

Printed October 29, 2009   T3.2.003   cr8.5.00   Page 1 of 2

Figure 3.16 *Telecine report template*

When the negative discrepancy report indicates damage, it is a red flag for you and must be acted on immediately. Production will want to know if the editor can cut around the damage. The assistant editor must digitize the scene in question as soon as possible, inform the editor that there is negative damage, and prepare the dailies so the editor can cut the scene as soon as he can. The editor will cut around the damage and show the scene to the director and producer. It will then be determined whether the scene needs to be reshot. The answer is time sensitive. The production might lose the actor that day, or the set might be scheduled to be torn down.

The cause of the negative damage needs to be identified quickly. If it is a camera problem, then that camera will need to be replaced. If it is a lab or telecine issue, then different adjustments will be made. Remember, all problems and solutions come down to time and money, and production is hoping for *no reshoots and no extra costs*.

3.5 Spec and Format Sheets

The second notebook that you create will contain the paperwork that affects every episode, including the delivery requirements. If you are on a television show, ask your post producer for *spec sheets* (specifications of delivery requirements). These spec sheets from SFX and MX will let the assistant know exactly what should be delivered to them after the show is locked (see Figure 3.17). The network specs will have delivery

```
Green Post Sound Turnover Specs. We require:

A Quicktime Movie with a Visual Time Code Burn in.  DV Codec 720x480
                    or
    1 DVCAM videocassette with Visual Time Code Burn in and 48K Audio
                    or
    DVD Video can be substituted as long as they have a Visual Time
Code Burn In

Production audio and Temp ADR on CH 1

FX ( no music ) on CH 2

SMPTE time Code on CH 3 a.k.a Address Track

VITC on lines 12-14

Time Code Window Burn in the Upper Right

EDLs:

The EDL should be in CMX 3600 format and put on a CD-R as well as e-
mailed to edls@smartpostsound.com.

The EDL needs to be for Audio only, include scene/take, and with sound roll number and sound roll
Time Code. The sound roll number should reflect the production rolls of the dailies, i.e.
have the same name.We also ask for a second EDL with Address Track Time Code for trouble shooting.

OMF:

The OMF needs to be OMF 2.0, Consolidated and Embedded with at least 300 frame handles,
AIFC Audio format. Please try to keep the OMF file and Media files folder together in one folder.
If you reach the "2 GB FIle Size Limit" break up the OMF by Act, or break the Act up into sections.

Documentation:

We ask for a copy of the Lined script as well as a copy of all sound reports and telecine logs.

Call (818) 555-0100 with any questions.
```

Figure 3.17 *Spec sheet templates (SFX and MX)*

requirements for air—the amount of black between acts, the amount and length of bumpers, the main title lengths and position, the end credit lengths, and many more specific requirements.

When you have gathered all of the necessary information about your total program time, the assistant editor is responsible for determining what the target time is. Each editor will have his own preference regarding what to include in this target time. The assistant editor creates a cheat sheet that reflects the measurement necessary to be on footage. This can be a confusing process but must be done with great accuracy. Table 3.1 is an example of a cheat sheet for a TV show with a target time of 43:45:00.

Table 3.1 *Target footage*

Content	Target footage
Story only	42:00:00
Story with main title (:20 sec)	42:20:00
Story with main title, logos (:10 sec)	42:30:00
Story with main title, logos, EC bed (:30 sec)	43:00:00
Story with main title, logos, EC bed, recap (:30 sec)	43:30:00
Story with main title, logos, EC bed, recap, blacks (:15 sec)	43:45:00

> On one of my shows, I was given the wrong format footage, and the producer's cut that we delivered to the network was off by 2 minutes. This could have been an egregious mistake. Fortunately, it was caught before we locked the show. If we had onlined at 2 minutes under, it would have become an expensive mistake, literally and figuratively. It might have cost the assistant editor his job, and we would have had to recut and reonline the episode.
>
> —ljc

The *format sheet* is different on every show. The durations of black, total program time, target delivery time, and whether you deliver in drop frame (DF) or nondrop frame (NDF) changes all the time. The length of the show should be clearly denoted as to whether it is in drop or nondrop frame. DF and NDF are both ways of labeling or addressing video frames for NTSC video. Television in the United States does not run at 30 fps; it runs at 29.97 fps. NDF counts at exactly 30 fps. (The trick to recognizing NDF is that it is denoted with a colon. For example, the total running time is 42:30:08, which is read as 42 minutes, 30 seconds, 8 frames.) It boggles the mind, but these are vital details you need to understand. You must ensure that you have the correct settings for your project.

The post producer receives the delivery requirements from the network and gives the information to the assistant editor, who then prepares the format sheet template on the first day (see Figure 3.18). The length of the main title is determined by the network.

TIP

The benefit to nondrop frame timecode is that all frame numbers are sequential. Drop frame (denoted with a semicolon, such as total running time 42;30;08) compensates for this by dropping numbers. The benefit to DF is that the timecode duration matches the running time. NDF assigns a sequential number for each frame. DF skips some numbers (not the actual frame, just the number assigned to it) so that the final sequence reflects the true running time on air. To make matters worse, some HD formats are DF and some are NDF.

DEFINITION

MOS denotes the term *mit out sound*—a German term adopted in America that means recorded without sound.

The blacks are inserted for a commercial break or a bumper (title card with the name of the show). The bumper card usually has a voice-over recorded by one of the actors stating "[the name of the show] will return in a moment." Sometimes the bumper card is MOS.

On the last day, as the assistant prepares for the online, the start and duration columns are filled in with master timecodes and delivered to the post producer.

Show Title/Season

Production #_____   Title_____   Date_____

ELEMENT	START	DURATION
SEGMENT 1 (10 to 16 minutes) **Includes:**		
RECAP	01:00:00;00	
TEASER	01:	
MAIN TITLE	01:	
ACT1 (w/ opening credits)	01:	
BREAK 1 (1 second of BLACK)	01:	1;00
SEGMENT 2 (5 to 9 minutes)		
ACT 2	01:	
BREAK 2 (1 second of BLACK)	01:	1;00
SEGMENT 3 (5 to 9 minutes)		
ACT 3	01:	
BREAK 3 (1 second of BLACK)	01:	1;00
SEGMENT 4 (5 to 9 minutes)		
ACT 4	01:	
BREAK 4 (1 second of BLACK)	01:	1;00
SEGMENT 5 (8 to 12 minutes)		
ACT 5 (Includes 3 sec Executive Producer Card)	01:	

Figure 3.18 *Format sheet template*

BREAK 5 (1 second of BLACK)	01:	1;00
SEGMENT 6 (MUSIC ONLY over entire segment)		
FULL FRAME LOGOS	01:	4;00
(Includes Prod. Logo AND Network Logo)		
END CREDITS	01:	30;00
(Cards left 1/3 w/show logo at top & Video Montage right 2/3)		
MUSIC AD CARDS	01:	15;00
(1 card = 10 sec, 2 cards = 15 sec, 3 cards = 20 sec)		
TOTAL RUNNING TIME		44:15;00
TOTAL BLACK		5;00
TOTAL PROGRAM TIME		44:10;00
TARGET DELIVERY TIME		44:10;00
	OVER/UNDER	
BLACK (One minute between end of program and textless)		1:00;00
TEXTLESS MATERIAL – M.O.S.	01:	

Notes:

- Program time includes Recap, Teaser, Main Title, Program Segments, End Credits, Logos, and Music Ad Cards
- Program time excludes Breaks/Blacks.
- Any deviation from stated Segment lengths need to be run by your Post Production Executive.
- Segment times should be computed from the first frame of audio or video to the last frame of audio or video.
- Show length and timings are NTSC DROP FRAME.
- The first 30 seconds of a program must not have supers or matte material extending into the upper left corner or upper right corner, title safe areas of the television picture so that program rating and closed caption icons can be inserted in these areas.
- Programs must not have supers or matte material extending into the lower 1/3, title safe area of the television picture so that graphics can be inserted into this area. When exceptions are necessary, contact your Post Production Executive.
- Program bumpers are not allowed in any programming.

Figure 3.18 (*Continued*)

Call the various departments to confirm the specs and introduce yourself. Specs change, and you want to make sure you have the current versions so you don't have to redo work later! On one show, the SFX spec sheets given to us by our A.P. were outdated, and my assistant had to output the show multiple times.

Yay! Your project is set up, your binders are organized, and now it is time to meet some people on the set.

3.6 Meet the Crew

After you have finished the work described in this chapter is a good time to introduce yourself to the crew members. It is essential to begin a dialog with the script supervisor, camera assistants, and the sound crew. If they are on location, make a point to get a ride out there, time permitting. Start your relationship on a friendly and cheerful note, and discuss paperwork, communication methods, and preferences. Your first day is your last free day without dailies to digitize, so make good use of your time. Introduce yourself to the people in the production office, postproduction office, on the set, and the MX and SFX editors. You might not be able to accomplish all of this on your first day, but give it a go. Whatever is left on your list will have to be revisited at a later date.

We realize the tasks that need to be accomplished on your first day are enormous. Successful completion of these tasks is largely determined by how well-prepared you are.

Congratulations! You have finished your first day on the job. This was the relatively easy day. Now comes the first true test of your skills—dailies!

> **TIP**
>
> *Anticipation* and *preparation* are key ingredients for maintaining a smooth-running editing room, and they are the cornerstones of a successful career as an assistant editor.

Chapter 4

Your Second Day

It's your second day on the job, and dailies have arrived. Showtime. Your dailies will come to you on tape, hard drives, or film. Whichever form you get, they need to be organized into Scene bins for the editor to start cutting.

There are three major responsibilities during the assistant editor's tenure on a film that can result in his being fired. These areas of concern are *dailies*, *measurements*, and *online*. It is of utmost importance to pay close attention to the timecode, key numbers, tape numbers, and circled takes. Being meticulous is the best way to keep your job.

4.1 Importing Dailies

You will receive an ALE that will contain the information about your dailies (see Figure 4.1).

This information, especially the information about the audio timecode from the set, needs to be carefully checked by the assistant editor to prevent duplicate numbers or typos. The telecine report, negative discrepancy report, and flex file (or ALE) is sent along with the transferred dailies. The ALE is also emailed directly to the assistant editor so that preparation work for digitizing or importing the dailies can be started in advance of receiving the tape or hard drive. Remember that there are different formats for disks, and these specs for inputting the dailies on your editing system have been discussed and predetermined by your associate producer.

First, check your email to download the flex file or ALE before digitizing or importing.

Second, you must check the default settings on the machine; make sure the audio is set correctly to 48 kHz (*not* 44 kHz). If you miss this, you will have to redo your dailies. In Avid, this is under audio settings in your project window. If you are digitizing in analog audio, check the tone levels of your dailies using your mixing board. If you are digitizing in digital audio, check that the audio levels are coming into the system correctly using the audio tool. If you are digitizing digital audio via FireWire, FCP does not provide any audio setting control. If you receive tapeless media, FCP will set audio settings automatically.

DOI: 10.1016/B978-0-240-81398-1.00004-3

Heading

FIELD_DELIM	TABS	TRACKER_VERSION	3.2.003	Sort Order: [Video TC In]
VIDEO_FORMAT	1080			
FILM_FORMAT	35mm, 4perf			
AUDIO_FORMAT	48kHz			
TAPE	101201			
FPS	23.976			

Column

Data

Name	Tracks	Tape	FPS	Start	End	Duration	Labroll	Camroll	Dailyroll	Shoot Date	Sound TC	Soundroll	Scene	Take	Slate	Descript	Comments	KN Start	KN End	Pullin	Ink Number	TC 24	ASC_SOP	ASC_SAT
2-1	VA1	101201	24	01:00:01:20	01:01:27:12	00:01:25:16	8650176	A1		10/28/2009	09:08:56:23	1	2	1			short preroll no stix			AA			( )( )( )	
2-3	VA1	101201	24	01:01:27:12	01:02:51:20	00:01:24:08	8650176	A1		10/28/2009	09:17:24:01	1	2	3						AA			( )( )( )	
2A-1	VA1	101201	24	01:02:51:20	01:04:17:00	00:01:25:04	8650176	A1		10/28/2009	09:22:35:14	1	2A	1						AA			( )( )( )	
2B-1	VA1	101201	24	01:04:17:00	01:05:53:16	00:01:36:16	8650176	A1		10/28/2009	09:26:34:11	1	2B	1						AA			( )( )( )	
3-1	VA1	101201	24	01:05:53:16	01:06:56:20	00:01:03:04	8650176	A1		10/28/2009	09:40:55:01	1	3	1						AA			( )( )( )	
3-2	VA1	101201	24	01:06:56:20	01:08:42:04	00:01:45:08	8650176	A1		10/28/2009	09:42:14:06	1	3	2						AA			( )( )( )	
3-4	VA1	101201	24	01:08:42:04	01:10:21:12	00:01:39:08	8650176	A1		10/28/2009	09:48:26:18	1	3	4			short preroll no stix			AA			( )( )( )	
3A-1	VA1	101201	24	01:10:21:12	01:12:11:00	00:01:49:12	8650176	A1		10/28/2009	09:51:44:04	1	3A	1						AA			( )( )( )	
3B-1	VA1	101201	24	01:12:11:00	01:13:48:08	00:01:37:08	8650176	A1		10/28/2009	09:54:55:09	1	3B	1						AA			( )( )( )	
3B-2	VA1	101201	24	01:13:48:08	01:15:42:20	00:01:54:12	8650176	A1		10/28/2009	09:58:01:11	1	3B	2						AA			( )( )( )	
3C-1	VA1	101201	24	01:15:42:20	01:19:14:12	00:03:31:16	8650176	A1		10/28/2009	10:07:59:23	1	3C	1			short preroll no stix			AA			( )( )( )	

Figure 4.1 *Flex file template*

3D-1	VA1	101201	24	01:19:14:12	01:22:30:16	00:03:16:04	8650176	A1	10/28/2009	10:41:00:13	1	3D	1	AA	( )( )( )
C3-3	VA1	101201	24	01:22:30:16	01:23:41:16	00:01:11:00	8650176	A1	10/28/2009	11:47:09:15	1	C3	3	AA	( )( )( )
C3-4	VA1	101201	24	01:23:41:16	01:24:47:20	00:01:06:04	8650176	A1	10/28/2009	11:49:49:20	1	C3	4	AA	( )( )( )
C3-6	VA1	101201	24	01:24:47:20	01:25:53:08	00:01:05:12	8650176	A1	10/28/2009	11:54:13:10	1	C3	6	AA	( )( )( )
C3-7	VA1	101201	24	01:25:53:08	01:28:13:08	00:02:20:00	8650176	A1	10/28/2009	11:56:45:07	1	C3	7	AA	( )( )( )
C3-8	VA1	101201	24	01:28:13:08	01:29:28:00	00:01:14:16	8650176	A1	10/28/2009	11:59:47:10	1	C3	8	AA	( )( )( )
C3-9	VA1	101201	24	01:29:28:00	01:31:43:08	00:02:15:08	8650176	A1	10/28/2009	12:02:31:03	1	C3	9	AA	( )( )( )
C3A-1	VA1	101201	24	01:31:43:08	01:35:49:20	00:04:06:12	8650176	A1	10/28/2009	12:17:48:29	1	C3A	1	AA	( )( )( )
C3B-1	VA1	101201	24	01:35:49:20	01:36:46:16	00:00:56:20	8650176	A1	10/28/2009	12:29:41:05	1	C3B	1	AA	( )( )( )
C3B-2	VA1	101201	24	01:36:46:16	01:38:19:16	00:01:33:00	8650176	A1	10/28/2009	12:31:23:02	1	C3B	2	AA	( )( )( )
C3C-2	VA1	101201	24	01:38:19:16	01:39:38:16	00:01:19:00	8650176	A1	10/28/2009	12:47:23:18	1	C3C	2	AA	( )( )( )
2C-4	VA1	101201	24	01:39:38:16	01:41:55:04	00:02:16:12	8650175	A2	10/28/2009	13:54:03:13	1	2C	4	AA	( )( )( )
2D-1	VA1	101201	24	01:41:55:04	01:42:17:12	00:00:22:08	8650175	A2	10/28/2009	13:58:54:01	1	2D	1	AA	( )( )( )
2D-2	VA1	101201	24	01:42:17:12	01:43:13:16	00:00:56:04	8650175	A2	10/28/2009	13:59:35:26	1	2D	2	AA	( )( )( )
2E-1	VA1	101201	24	01:43:13:16	01:47:12:12	00:03:58:20	8650175	A2	10/28/2009	16:00:43:24	1	2E	1	AA	( )( )( )
2E-2	VA1	101201	24	01:47:12:12	01:54:11:00	00:06:58:12	8650175	A2	10/28/2009	16:07:09:29	1	2E	2	AA	( )( )( )
2F-1	VA1	101201	24	01:54:11:00	01:55:53:08	00:01:42:08	8650175	A2	10/28/2009	16:18:26:17	1	2F	1	AA	( )( )( )
2F-2	VA1	101201	24	01:55:53:08	01:59:58:00	00:04:04:16	8650175	A2	10/28/2009	16:22:45:14	1	2F	2	AA	( )( )( )

Figure 4.1 (*Continued*)

Third, you have to determine that the key codes, audio timecode, and names assigned to your tape are correct. Check that each tape has a unique name (e.g., 201R03) that matches the name on the flex file or ALE. There must be no duplicated tape names. Dailies have a visual burn-in with the running key codes and audio codes. Check to make sure that these numbers match the flex or ALE files and your other paperwork. You might want to ask your editor if he prefers not having key code run throughout the take. On FCP, you need to use Cinema Tools to create the database that will track flex file data automatically when the clips are captured. Cinema Tools is integrated into FCP in the tools menu.

Fourth, start digitizing your dailies. Discuss with your editor which scenes he prefers to have digitized first. Some editors like to have the largest, hardest scenes in the morning while they are fresh. Some want to warm up to that and are happy with a couple of smaller, less challenging scenes. As long as you have at least one bin fully prepared for your editor to work on when he walks into the cutting room, you are in good shape.

Sometimes it cannot be the editor's prerogative because telecine has not sent you the B camera for some of the scenes, or telecine has not finished transferring a complete scene, or there were no complete scenes that made it to telecine from the set. All sorts of factors enter into the decision-making process when you attack the morning's deluge of film. Just remember, you are always aiming to keep your editor cutting, with little or no downtime between scenes. So throw the first tapes in to start the process before you have prioritized the order in which you should digitize. This way, the machine is working while you figure out your paperwork. No time is wasted getting the dailies into the system. If you have begun to import a scene that is incomplete or not the right one, you can stop (it will all be saved) and switch over to the scene your editor prefers to cut first.

4.2 Interpreting Paperwork

Fifth, start to organize the paperwork and decide which scene should be first up for your editor. You have to determine that all the film that should have arrived according to the paperwork is indeed in your possession. The film you receive should reflect the circled takes. These selections, as we have said, are determined by the director on the set. The assistant must compare the editor's log to the facing pages of the lined script, the sound reports, and the camera reports. This purpose of this process is to make sure that all of the circled takes were included; then you check the telecine report to make sure that the post facility has transferred all the circled takes.

Many assistant editors use colored highlighters to mark their cross-referenced takes while they organize their dailies. For example, when you find 32G-4 on the telecine report and then confirm that you have it on your flex file or ALE, you can highlight the telecine report in one color until all of the takes on the reports match up. When there is one take left that is not highlighted, you will know it has to be researched further and possibly ordered up as B negative. If telecine has missed one of the circled takes, then you must make sure it gets ordered and is telecined for the next day's shipment of dailies. During the editing process, circled takes might have performance or technical issues, so a B negative is ordered by either the editor, director, or producer. Some associate producers like to be consulted before a B negative is ordered.

4.3 Watch the Dailies

If you digitize dailies, it is important that you take time to keep a watchful eye on them. You are the second frontier for noticing any flares, scratches, negative damage, or excess dirt, as well as color, focus, and exposure issues (telecine is the first to send a negative discrepancy report to the AP). You will be able to flag these problems for your editor. It is also an opportunity to watch the film with editing in mind so that you can discuss with your editor the coverage, performance, and technical issues you have observed. This is invaluable to your editor so that he can address these issues immediately.

4.4 Continue to Digitize or Begin to Organize

So you have a scene digitized into the machine. Then what? Should you continue to digitize or should you organize the bin for the scene you've just completed? The answer to this varies daily. Some of the factors to consider are the amount of film, the editor's preferences, and if he already has enough scenes in his project. If the editor has not received any film to cut yet, then you must set a bin and get him working! As you know, the goal is to always keep your editor busy with dailies. Try to estimate how long it will take before you need to provide another scene. This will help you determine what you should digitize next. Let's proceed with setting the bin for this first scene.

4.5 Setting the Bin

Each scene has its own bin (see Figure 4.2). It contains all the materials pertaining to that scene—each take, all wild lines, all wild tracks, all playback, selected needle drops, etc.

Figure 4.2 *Scene bin*

The bin now needs to be organized according to your editor's specs. Some editors prefer their A and B camera joined in a multicam group clip. Sometimes an editor will request that the dailies be strung together into one long sequence called a *kem roll*. As you can see in Figure 4.3, the preference is to have the group clips at the top of the bin, with the individual camera takes organized at the bottom. The single camera coverage is normally hidden at the bottom of the bin out of view. Note the preference for the takes for each setup to be touching. Some

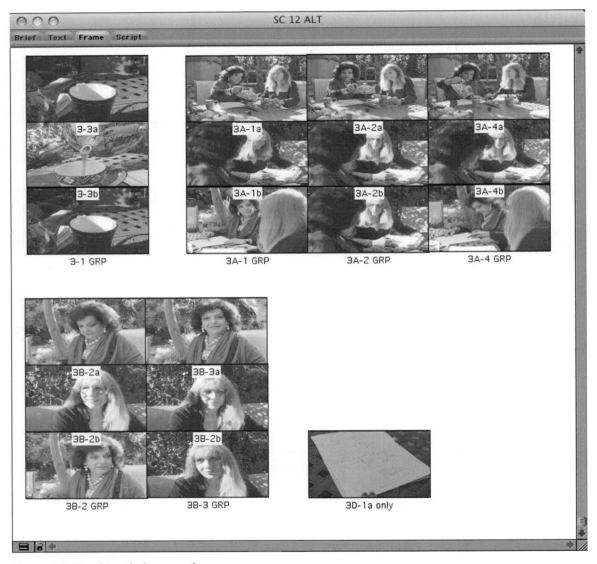

Figure 4.3 *Scene bin with alternate preferences*

editors prefer their group clips at the bottom of the bin, and some like A cam and B cam takes to be attached to their group clip.

The size of the icons in the bins is adjustable. Make sure to include the wild lines, playback material, and presence (room tone recorded on set) for the scene. In the AVID you can remove any stray periods and unnecessary information in the description of the take when you create a group clip (see Figure 4.4).

3A-4GRP.Grp.01

Figure 4.4 *Group clip that needs to be tidied*

When working on an Avid, this group clip designation should be tidied and should look like Figure 4.5.

Now that the Scene bin is set, do one last check against both the script supervisor's report *and* the lined script to make sure that all of the shots are in the bin. For example, if the lined script or its facing page says that Sc. 33–4 was circled and it is not in the bin, you have to go back to your paperwork and determine why this has happened and if you need to order a B negative. Later, when the director asks your editor why the close-up of the phone was not used in the cut, it should not be because the assistant editor neglected to put it in the bin.

3A-4GRP

Figure 4.5 *Group clip that has been tidied*

Now scroll through each clip to make sure the dailies are in sync and digitized correctly. In film and 24 fps projects, the machine sometimes captures the wrong frame, which causes a stuttering effect on the film.

> I call it the *RoboCop* look, which makes my assistants smile at my ignorance. It is called an A frame issue because the take was captured on a frame other than the A frame. It is easily fixed by redigitizing the clip.
>
> —ljc

If you are working with high def, the cameras on the set need to be periodically resynced to make sure they are generating the same timecode. When the camera crew does not perform this task, your A and B cameras can be two to six frames out of sync and need to be adjusted manually.

Check all the takes in each scene. Organize the takes into bins. If you have done your homework in advance of receiving the film, you will also provide the SFX that your editor will use to cut the scene. For example, phone rings, cell phones, office computers, fax machines, police backgrounds (BGs), crime scenes, sirens, traffic, country birds, crickets, car interiors, and car, truck, and train horns all should be available *before* the editor cuts the scene. This is a great opportunity for you to offer to cut the FX in when the editor is done with the scene!

4.6 Communicating

When a scene is ready to cut, the assistant editor can place a Post-it on the edge of the editor's lined script with the scene number and any other pertinent information—whether the scene is complete or incomplete or what is missing and why (e.g., "Sc. 32G–4: Circled but not received. Ordered for tomorrow" or "Sc. 32G–4: Negative damage on right side of frame").

The Post-its can be color coded to reflect the day the scene was received. For example, dailies input on Monday are posted with blue, and dailies from Tuesday are amber, etc. This way the editor knows how much of that day's work is completed and what bits are still outstanding. This method is one more safety net to assure that all dailies have been edited and the scene is in the editor's cut.

> This system was created based on an embarrassing day when I was working on *Picket Fences*, and I ran my editor's cut with a scene missing. Luckily, the director had a sense of humor and said, "Hmmm, interesting. It works better without that scene. However, let's take a look at it."
>
> —ljc

Upon completing a scene, the Post-it is removed, and the measurement for that scene is written onto the wall chart continuity in the column for the editor's cut. These two safety nets will avoid the possibility of inadvertently turning over a cut with a scene missing. The Post-it method is just one channel of communication between the assistant and the editor, and it minimizes the amount of verbal interruptions during the editing process.

4.7 Archiving as You Go

From the very first day of dailies, you should set up a bin into which you can place the *production stock*. This is any establishing shot of the exteriors of the locations used in your show—the library, family home, police precinct, etc. The production stock will be used by the editor every time an establishing shot is necessary for the beginning of a scene. At the end of your season, the studio will ask for this bin to be sent to their stock library and archived for future rental. Keep a watchful eye out during dailies for shots that can be used as establishing shots.

Another bin that should be created for each project is the *Gag bin*. This is where you archive all those lovely foul-ups, comedic moments, actors missing their lines, laughing during a take, and sometimes cursing. These are the outtakes. Make sure you create a bin for yourself as well as the editor. While you are watching dailies, make notes so that you can add bits to your bin. Ask the editor to place whatever he can into his Gag bin. This will save you precious time when you are in a great hurry to collect all the funny material before the wrap party.

SHINE NOTE

Take the opportunity to shine as an editor, and cut a memorable gag reel. The producers will take note of your work and are more likely to consider moving you up to editor if a position becomes available.

Everyone wants to see the gag reel, and it usually falls to the assistant editors to cut it for the wrap party. Editing the gag reel often entails hours of overtime (paid and unpaid). Try to include everyone from the cast, as many crew members as possible, and all your colleagues in postproduction. You can find great music to tie it all together and create a wonderful tribute that will be admired and remembered.

At the end of the season, some networks require that all the *lifted scenes* be archived and shipped to them. This bin needs to be set up for each episode and addressed when you have locked the show.

4.8 MX and Needle Drop Bins

Name	Duration	Comments
1001 1m14 Kaylee and Boyfriend	1:03:29	KAYLIE AND CARTER THEME
1001 1m16 Lauren Schemes 2	34:10	
1001 1m18 Source Replace	2:05:14	
1001 1m19 Right Decision	37:12	
1001 1m20 Wake Up ALT	31:29	
1001 1m21 The Big Day 02	35:21	
1001 1m25 Lauren Falls 01	45:04	
1001 1m26 Emily Beam ALT	2:02:09	
1001 1m27a Emily Vault	1:48:10	
1001 1m27a Lauren's Vault 01	1:15:16	
1001 1m29 Emily's Big Shot 04	7:29:29	
1001 1m31 Nailed It 01	2:32:22	
1001 1m31 Nailed It 04	2:03:17	
1001 1m33 Not the End ALT	2:10:16	
1001 1m34 The Rock is sunk 01	2:59:26	
1002 0m2 Opening FIX	42:04	
1002 0m4 Payson Falls FIX	24:09	SAD TENSE
1002 1m6 Talk to Marty FIX	2:02:02	
1002 1m8 Gonna Be Fine	28:05	SAD RESOLVEY
1002 1m10 Beautiful Face	57:01	KAYLIE CARTER THEME
1002 1m11 Wiggle Replace	21:02	
1002 1m12 Lauren Walks In	42:11	SAD SOMETHING'S WRONG
1002 1m13 Laundry Frolic	1:10:19	KAYLIE AND CARTER THEME
1002 1m14 Crunch Time FIX	37:20	ROCK N ROLL
1002 1m17 Go To Denver FIX	19:09	TENSION
1002 1m19 Marty 1	26:16	
1002 1m23ab On the DL FIX	2:05:26	SAD BAD NEWS
1002 1m25 26 What About Friendship FIX	3:15:07	
1002 1m29 Pretty Princesses	1:07:27	
1002 1m30 HomeLateEDIT	2:48:10	
1002 1m31 Adulterers	1:42:02	
1002 1m33 Little Game is Over FIX	46:12	
1003 0m2,3A,3B Tanner & Sasha	2:13:25	
1003 1m1 We Need You Here	1:13:15	
1003 1m2 Sasha Speech	1:31:25	
1003 1m3 Spruce Juice Bumper	14:22	
1003 1m4 Rock Stars Logic	32:25	
1003 2m1 Totally Screwed	14:16	
1003 2m3 Paysons Gonna Party	38:09	

Figure 4.6 *Score bin*

The way you set up your MX bin for both the score and needle drop is critical. In the Score bin, the assistant should organize the music by the episode number and the number of the cue in the body of the film (see Figure 4.6). For example, *1001 1m14* means that this cue is in the first episode (1001) and is in the first act (1 m) and is the 14th cue (14). The composer usually gives the cue a name (in this case, Kaylee and

Name	Artist	Duration	Cost	Folder2	Comments
This Is Our Life	Maziarz	3:56:21	$	SSW	PROM
Til Then	Maziarz	3:21:01	$	SSW	
Two Satellites 1	Maziarz	3:27:19	$	SSW	
Breathless	Miranda Lee Richards	5:15:22	$	SSW	USED 1004 FINAL;
Wait For You Here *****	Molly Jenson	4:48:22	$	SSW	PROM
OK OK	Ringer	3:10:10	$	INDIEPOP	
2-16 Gots' To Be The S	RJ Sureshot	2:46:07	$	Electronic	
Who We Are	Ryan Calhoun	3:28:00	$	SSW	USED 1002 FINAL;
City of Dreams	Samantha Farrell	4:20:04	$	SSW	
Where Do We Go	Sandrine	2:48:15	$	SSW	
Atomic Strike	Session 5	3:56:20	$	From Wendy	USED 1004 FINAL;
Sound The Alarm	Shapes of Race Cars	2:42:10	$	INDIEPOP	
New Solution	Shirock	3:43:07	$	SSW	
Vulnerable ****	Stephanie Lang	3:23:27	$	SSW	Lori Fave; PROM
Save Your Best	Steve Reynolds	4:24:14	$	SSW	
Count To Three	Story One	3:15:02	$	Rock	Unverified Clearable
Dark Black	Sumo	4:11:21	$	House	USED 1013 PC
Burn	Taryn Manning	3:26:06	$	INDIEPOP	
I Saw Lightning	Telekinesis!	2:12:05	$	SSW	Lori Fave
Rust	Telekinesis!	2:06:06	$	SSW	Diana Fave
I Thought About You	The Beautiful Girls	3:21:07	$	INDIEPOP	
Girls With Attitude	The Fame	2:55:14	$	Pop	
NOT COMING DOWN	The Fame	3:23:26	$	Pop	
Show You The Door 1	The Fame	3:12:14	$	Pop	
Show You The Door 2	The Fame	3:13:05	$	Pop	
Supersonic	The Fame	2:58:29	$	Pop	
Supersonic_Instr	The Fame	2:58:29	$	Pop	
Boom, Snap, Clap	The Flame	3:37:04	$	Pop	USED 1002 FINAL;
The End	The Windupdeads	3:55:25	$	INDIEPOP	
READY#37	Toby Lightman	3:19:24	$	INDIEPOP	
I've Got A Secret	WHIZBANG	3:57:07	$	From Wendy	
Keep Breathing	Ingrid Michaelson	3:25:17	$$	Indie	PROM
I'll Be In The Sky	BOB	4:08:05	$$	Rock	
I Like It_WHIZBANG	Chris Brush	3:54:06	$$	Rock	
Practice Makes Perfect	Cute is What	3:46:02	$$	Rock	
Catch Me If You Can	Gym Class Heros	5:09:26	$$	RAP	
Let's Go	Hipjoint	2:59:21	$$	Rock	USED 1005 FINAL;
Here With Me ***	Jennifer O'Connor	4:02:19	$$	Indie	
Watch ME Walk	Keri Noble	3:44:15	$$	SSW	PROM
Senses	La Rocca	5:04:09	$$	SSW	
Don't Upset The Rythm	Let It Rock	3:51:01	$$	Rock	
Give It Up	ParaFlux	2:47:21	$$	From Wendy	
Rock Your World (sq#SBD3	Ryan Lovel	6:06:27	$$	Rock	

Figure 4.7 *Needle Drop bin*

Boyfriend), and there should be a column for the duration of the cue as well as a comments column in which the editor can make notes.

The assistant editor will create a separate bin for the needle drops and create columns for the name of the artist, name of the song, duration, cost, genre, and comments (see Figure 4.7).

The setup for the Needle Drop bin should be done so that each column can be sorted (keyboard combination Command+E) according to the way the editor needs to view information. Some editors prefer to find a song by the artist's name, and some prefer to sort by the name of the song. Sometimes the editor is looking for a certain genre—hip-hop, rock, or emo. Sometimes a tune is selected based solely on what will please the producer, and his favorites can be found in a column of his comments. When the song is locked for the show, that information should be denoted in this bin so that it is not mistakenly temped into another episode.

For a needle drop show, the assistant editor has extra tasks to keep the music organized efficiently. The MX supervisor will send countless drops via CD or website. These tunes need to be imported into the Unity or SAN, burned to CD, and copied for your producers. Their comments need to be gathered and incorporated into your Needle Drop bin. Then the drops need to be distributed to all of the editors.

				"SHOW TITLE" EP. # "EPISODE TITLE"			
ACT	**SC**	**MASTER TC**	**DUR**	**TITLE**	**ARTIST**	**COST**	**COMMENTS**
						TOTAL	
						BUDGET	

Figure 4.8 *Needle drop template*

The template in Figure 4.8 was created to help organize each episode's music during the editing process.

It is essential to stay on top of all music that is sent to you. Import and distribute it to your editors immediately!

All music that editors track with (other than playback) is only temporary. It will be replaced with music written and scored by the composer or needle drops that will be licensed at a future date. Many times an editor cuts in a song that remains in the show because it is well-loved or eminently affordable.

It is the assistant's responsibility to keep all incoming media organized in such a way that any editor working on the show will be able to easily find what he needs. It is also important to make sure that each editor knows when new material has arrived and if there have been comments or selections made by the producers or director.

Put a Post-it in the editor's script when a song arrives that has been specifically chosen for a certain scene. If a new CD has been imported into the Needle Drop bin, it is a good habit to leave a Post-it note on the editor's bench so that he is informed about all the new music.

4.9 When Dailies Are Completed

Congratulations! You have finished setting all the bins for your editor and ordered the B negative, if necessary. It is time to check your list from the day before to see if there are any unfinished chores. It is a good time to check on the supplies that have not yet arrived and expedite that process.

TIP

Communicating with Post-its is useful on several levels. It informs your editor of all new media (stock, B negative, SFX, and MX). It preempts unnecessary interruptions while your editor is cutting. It covers your ass (CYA). There will be times when your editor insists that he was never informed about new materials, and all you have to do is point to the Post-it. It is wise to leave a written trail for *many* of your communications—with the A.P., the MX supervisor, the producers—email is a great way to confirm conversations and protect you during difficult situations.

By now it's time for lunch. Ask your editor when he would like to break. If he is staying in, ask when it would be okay for you to leave. It is always nice to offer to bring back food in case he is not going out.

Check the call sheet to see when the crew is breaking for lunch. If your show is not on location that day, the caterer will provide food, and it's always nice to have a free lunch! If you haven't met the script supervisor, soundman, or second assistant cameraman, coordinate your lunch hour with their break time to seek their company and chat.

After lunch you will have time to continue organizing SFX, MX, and banners. You can also prepare for the next day's dailies by looking on the call sheet or one-liner to see what will be shot the next day. This way you can prepare your Post-it notes with the scene numbers in advance and check to see if the next day's shoot includes visual or MX playback. If picture playback is called for, the assistant will need to remind the editor and prepare the cut playback footage for the A.P. and the set. If the scenes need more specific sound effects, now is the time to make sure the SFX editor sends them to you, or you should download them.

If you have not had the chance to complete all your continuity and wall charts, now is the time to catch up. *Everything* should be completed by the end of this day.

You will repeat the dailies routine in episodic television for the next 6 or 7 days. Trust us, it gets easier!

Your duties as an assistant are now well underway, and you will establish a well-oiled routine that will keep your editor working and happy. The next step in the postproduction process is for your editor to complete his first cut, view it, and make some final changes before the assistant outputs it for the director.

Chapter 5

Edit and Distribute the Cut

After all the dailies have been shot, the editor has a certain amount of time to complete his first cut of the edited scenes and make the necessary changes to complete his editor's cut. The film will be viewed, and there will be certain changes that need to be made and moments that need to be enhanced. He will add stock shots, alter transitions, recut scenes, and decide where music and sound effects should be added, deleted, or volumes adjusted. When the editor's cut is complete, it is sent to the director first. The assistant is responsible for taking notes, recording temp ADR, downloading music, preparing QuickTimes for the dub stage or music department, ordering the B negative, preserving copies of each version, updating the continuity with scene timings, denoting lifted scenes, adding act timings together to arrive at the total measurement, and cutting a recap from first cut to a locked cut.

5.1 Editor's Cut

Viewing the editor's cut is a very important screening for the editor. It is the time for him to view the film as a fresh audience—letting the scenes wash over him as if he were viewing the movie for the first time. On another level, he must at the same time identify the problem areas. He must decide where to add or delete music, where to start scenes with stock shots, how to transition between scenes better, where to add dissolves, where to jump cut, what to trim or expand, and a multitude of other fixes that occur to him during this virgin viewing.

5.2 Taking Notes

The assistant should be ready with paper, pen, and the continuity to take notes. With the continuity in hand, the assistant will be able to designate the correct scene number to the given note. There is an art to taking good notes. If your handwriting is challenging to read, type your notes afterwards, or bring your laptop to the screening. Remember to get permission for this because the editor might be distracted by the noise of clicking keys and long fingernails. You will learn the shorthand necessary for good note-taking through time and experience.

DOI: 10.1016/B978-0-240-81398-1.00005-5

> **TIP**
>
> Here are some useful abbreviations for taking notes:
>
> head trim (ht)
> tail trim (tt)
> exterior (ext)
> interior (int)
> close-up (cu)
> medium shot (med)
> two-shot (2/s)
> over shoulder (o/s)
> wide shot or master (ws or mast)
> jump cut (jc)

Because there will be scenes to adjust, SFX and MX to be added or deleted, stock shots to be ordered, and levels of dialog to be fixed, it is a good time to jump in and offer to help cut the SFX and **shine**.

5.3 Recording Temp ADR

The assistant will record the temp ADR in the cutting room for the editor to place in the cut. Be prepared to set the audio levels, lower the master volume buttons, and configure the machine and microphone for recording added dialog. It sounds easy, but you cannot imagine the horrible, high-pitched feedback the machine emits when the wrong buttons are pushed. It can be quite embarrassing in front of company. Have a checklist prepared, and do a test recording *before* the first day you are asked to perform this task.

5.4 Preserving Copies

Before you start the next version of the show, the assistant editor must make a copy of the editor's cut in the project.

> **TIP**
>
> We like to keep copies of previous versions of the show at the *bottom* of the project window and the current cut at the top. This is accomplished by placing a Z before the preserved cut. We call our current cut A.Workpix so that it goes to the *top* of our project window.

When you copy the current cut down to Z1 EC1 (editor's cut 1), make sure you change the name of each act from A.Workpix to EC1. As discussed earlier, this is important because you do not want to make editorial changes in the wrong sequence! Management of the various cuts is essential during the editing process. The assistant editor must be aware of whatever system the editor would like to use and stay on top of it. In general, whenever there is an output of a cut, it is natural to make a copy of that version and file it away. Sometimes there is no output of a version, but you will still need to make a copy of it in case you need to refer to it later. Consult with your editor about this daily.

> **TIP**
>
> We prefer to leave the scene on the continuity list in its original position and gray out the background color. It is good to leave the duration filled in so everyone knows how much time was deleted when the scene was removed.

5.5 Lifts

If the editor removes a scene (this scene is now called a *lift*), the assistant needs to denote that on the continuity. Every show has a preference on how lifts are reflected on the continuity (see Figure 5.1).

Some producers and networks like to have the lifts added to the end of the continuity. This is something you will need to discuss with your A.P. in *advance* of the day that you distribute the cut.

"THE COMPETITION"
EP. 103 – "The Surprise Party"

SC #	D/N		
		RECAP	31:05
SC #	D/N	TEASER	6:09:29
01	D1	**EXT. ESSEX, ENGLAND:** A mini drives past a sign: Buckhurst Hill, 12 KM	10:16
		lifted	
		DX SCHOOL (STOCK, IN HOUSE)	4:04
02	D1	**INT. THE SCHOOL – GYM FLOOR** Deirdre enters, sees Ali finishing her routine.	55:17
04	D1	**INT. THE SCHOOL – GYM FLOOR** Deirdre and Ali – Coach plays MX for Deirdre's routine. *MX: 'Go for the Gold' THE PHANTASTIKS*	31:24
05	D1	**EXT. STONE HOUSE – ENGLAND** David drives up to his house	16:28
06	D1	**INT. THE SCHOOL – GYM FLOOR** Deirdre finishes routine. Coach is not happy.	58:01
07	D1	**EXT. STONE HOUSE – ENGLAND** David enters his house, finds it in disarray. Calls the police.	2:11:26
08	D1	**INT. THE SCHOOL – GYM FLOOR** Deirdre and Ali discuss the new music for both routines. Ali realizes that Deirdre doesn't know about her surprise party.	1:16:25
SC #	D/N	ACT 1	8:59:01
		DX SCHOOL (STOCK, IN HOUSE)	4:23
09	D1	**INT. THE SCHOOL – COACHES OFFICES** *(Reader – enter description of all the following scenes from your script here)*.	52:02
10	D1	**INT. THE SCHOOL – GYM FLOOR – CONTINUOUS**	38:01
11	D1	**EXT. THE SCHOOL – CONTINUOUS**	57:04
12	D1	**INT. THE SCHOOL – PARENT'S VIEWING AREA – LATER**	21:16
13	D1	**INT. THE SCHOOL – GYM FLOOR – CONTINUOUS**	1:55:18
13A	D1	**INT. THE SCHOOL – BAG PILE – MOMENTS LATER**	41:19
		DX MALL – (STOCK, IN HOUSE)	2:17
14	D1	**EXT CAFE – LATER**	3:24:13

Figure 5.1 *Continuity with the lifts highlighted*

SC #	D/N	ACT 2	10:03:24
		DX NEIGHBORHOOD – (STOCK, IN-HOUSE)	3:15
15	D1	**INT. SMITH APT. – LATER**	1:22:22
		DX JONES HOUSE – (STOCK, IN HOUSE)	1:26
16	D1	**INT. JONES HOUSE – KITCHEN**	1:20:29
17	N1	**INT. JACKSON MANSION – DEIRDRE'S ROOM**	1:58:00
		NX SMITH APT. (STOCK, IN HOUSE)	2:06
18	N1	**INT. SMITH APT. – SAME TIME**	56:10
		NX SMITH APT (STOCK, IN HOUSE)	2:24
19	N1	**INT. SMITH APT. – LATER**	1:57:17
21A	N1	**EXT. PARTY – CONTINUOUS**	50:14
		NX RESTAURANT – (STOCK, IN HOUSE)	2:15
22	N1	**INT. RESTAURANT**	1:35:14
SC #	D/N	ACT 3	5:25:16
23A		**EXT. PARTY – SAME TIME** *MX: "Rock On" – 1-69*	3:39:11
24	N1	**INT. RESTAURANT**	1:46:02
SC #	D/N	ACT 4	7:49:06
25	N1	**EXT. PARTY** *MX: 'Last Night' – THE BACKWARDS*	2:17:08
25A	N1	**EXT. PARTY** *MX: 'It Takes Two' – SPEECHES*	1:29:01
27	N1	**EXT. PARTY – LATER**	1:21:10
		NX ROAD – (STOCK, IN HOUSE)	1:26
27A	N1	**INT. DAVID'S CAR – SAME TIME** ****VFX TO COME: STABILIZATION**** *MX: '5 Men' – THE BACKWARDS*	42:10
28	N1	**EXT. PARTY/CABIN – A LITTLE LATER**	1:58:15

Figure 5.1 *(Continued)*

SC #	D/N	ACT 5	5:03:19
29	N1	**INT. DAVID'S CAR**	53:16
		NX SMITH APT. – (STOCK, IN HOUSE)	2:14
29A	N1	**EXT. SMITH APT. – FRONT DOOR**	1:17:21
		NX JACKSON MANSION – (STOCK, IN-HOUSE)	2:16
30	N1	**INT. JACKSON MANSION – DEIRDRE'S ROOM– LATER THAT NIGHT** *MX: 'Follow Your Dreams' – BRAD NEXTOWN (thru scene 31)*	1:11:01
31	N1	**INT. CABIN – SAME TIME**	1:42:22
		*TOTAL RUNNING TIME	**45:00:06**
		OVER/UNDER (+/-)	**+47:26**
		LIFTED SCENES	
01	D1	**EXT. ESSEX, ENGLAND:** A mini drives past a sign: Buckhurst Hill, 12KM	10:16

Figure 5.1 (*Continued*)

5.6 Scene Timings and Total Measurements

As mentioned earlier, the topic of measurements is serious. If the assistant miscalculates the running time of the show, it is grounds for being fired. The old axiom "measure twice, cut once" applies in your cutting room and helps avoid the embarrassment and ill will that is caused by a miscalculation. As the film progresses toward lock, it becomes that much more essential to have an exact measurement. A mistake in measurement becomes more expensive as you travel up this ladder from editor's cut to network cut.

A continuity is included with each output. It is necessary to measure each scene and fill in the column with that information. These columns need to be updated for each output.

As each scene measurement changes, so does the act timing. These need to be carefully changed on the paperwork. You need to give a total measurement of all the acts and compare that footage to the *target footage* for air. Also denote the amount of time you are over or under footage. This information is contained on the continuity as well as the cover sheet for the continuity. These measurements need to be archived for the editor on the footage chart you have printed out and placed on his bulletin board (see Figure 5.2).

Keeping track of the changes in the duration of each act and each version will be helpful during the post process. It gives an enormous amount of information at a quick glance. One can see which acts have remained the same and which acts need to be rebalanced if they are longer or shorter than the network target footages.

	Assembly	EC1	EC2	DC1	DC2	PC1	PC2	PC3	NC1
"THE COMPETITION"									
EP. 103– "The Surprise Party"									
Date: _____									
Day: _____									
TEASER	6:20:01	6:09:29							
ACT 1	9:22:24	8:59:01							
ACT 2	10:05:03	10:03:24							
ACT 3	6:30:11	5:25:16							
ACT 4	7:59:21	7:49:06							
ACT 5	5:04:04	5:03:19							
TOTALS:	45:22:04	43:31:07							
FORMAT:	**42:15:00**	**42:15:00**							
+/−	**+3:07:04**	**+1:16:07**							

Figure 5.2 *Filled-in footage chart template*

Networks are concerned with where the act breaks fall and when they are going to commercial break. They do not want to have a commercial break on the half hour because they do not want to lose their audience to another show. These target times change constantly as audience viewing habits change, so it is very important to have the latest published target times. The assistant can get this information from the post supervisor. Make sure to post these times clearly for your editor.

5.7 Building a Cut

When the editor's cut is completed in television, it is time for the assistant editor to build the show (put all the acts together into one time line sequence). Remember to ask your editor how much black he wants between the acts. Prepare a title card in the title tool for the beginning of the show. It should contain the name of the show, episode number, version (e.g., editor's cut), total running time, how much time you are over or under the format footage, and the date. Fade in and fade out on this card and place a second or two of black before the body of the film.

In features, the show can be divided into 2000-foot reels, and these are then built to allow for a maximum of 3-hour time lines. If your film is longer than 3 hours, you might consider dividing it into two 2-hour time lines.

Ask the editor and your associate producer if they would like to include the main title, the end credits, and the end logos for each of the cuts that are sent out. This media exists in your Banner bin, which you created on your first day. The main title and the logos are often updated throughout the season. The end credits have not been generated yet, but a space holder—a 20- to 30-second banner that says *End Credits*—can be attached to the end of the film. The composer's MT and EC music should be attached to these banners. This enables the editor to cut them in as one piece of media.

Be careful when you add the main title, recap, and logos to your edited show because they change the footage measurement, and this is where mistakes are often made. This is when your cheat sheet that you created with your format sheet at the beginning of the show will come in handy. It includes the various measurements with and without these elements.

Remember to add a few seconds of black to the end of the sequence before you output. The Avid or FCP might mistakenly stop on the last frame of film if there is no digitized black added to the last frame of film even though the soundtrack continues.

> This happened to us once on a pilot. Near the end of the output of the producer's cut, which we were about to send to the network, the machine stopped recording. On the last frame of picture, we had cut to black and extended the music for another 10 seconds. However, the Avid did not continue recording past the picture, cutting off the emotional music for the end of the movie. The output was ruined, and our time window for getting the cut out had passed. It was almost two o'clock in the morning, and the pilot needed to be duplicated and delivered by seven o'clock that morning. We were unable to do an insert edit on the DVCAM because the machine had not been set up correctly or tested in advance. The associate producer would not allow us to redo the output from scratch, and it went to the network with the abrupt ending. The show was not picked up, and the executive producer felt it was partially due to this editorial error. The associate producer was in the doghouse for a long time. The executive producer never hired me again.
>
> —ljc

5.8 Cutting the Recap

During editor's cut there is enough time for the assistant editor to start thinking about and assembling the reprise for the episode. It is not always the assistant's job to create the recap, but when possible, volunteer to do it.

The recap usually runs between 30 and 60 seconds, or sometimes longer. It precedes the show and informs the audience of the events that led to the episode they are about to watch. The writers sometimes provide the salient story points that need to be touched upon. Many times these decisions are left to you, so it is necessary

SHINE NOTE

Cutting a recap is a wonderful opportunity for the assistant editor to **shine**. The segment you put together will provide a great opportunity for quality time with the editor and producer. Your effort, attitude, and storytelling style will be duly noted and appreciated.

The reprise is usually attached to the show during the producer's cut so that it is included for the network to view. There are often notes from many people with different ideas, so buckle your seat belt and smile. Cutting trailers, teasers, and reprises is a special art. They include tremendous amounts of information edited at a frightfully fast pace. Learning to edit the recap is a skill that is fun to hone and important to add to your fast-growing list of abilities.

to have an intimate knowledge of previous episodes. You must show your audience the important moments that are germane to the show that is about to be aired.

5.9 Shipping

Create the output of the film by recording it onto a DVD. Because your equipment has been checked and you have done a mini output test *prior* to the day you need to ship the film to the director, you know that recording is not a problem. You have ordered DVDs in advance, so you have the materials necessary to create this output. The post PA duplicates the assistant's DVD output of the show and archives one DVD for the post department. The output and duplication process continues throughout the editing process, from the first output of the editor's cut to the network cut and all the way to the locked cut. You will create labels for the DVD unless you have arranged for the post PA to do this. You have created the cover sheet for the continuity, which has been updated with new scene timings and act timings.

One very important task is that you must know the director's home address and if he wants his DVD to be sent there or somewhere else. You must find out if he wants it left at the guard gate or front door; if the post PA should ring the bell, knock, or phone in advance; and if there is an hour at which it is too late to deliver. You must always include the continuity with the output. You must know if the DVD is being sent by courier to the director and what the cutoff time is for the courier. This way you can determine at what time the editor needs to stop cutting and when the output must start. You must find out the tracking number and the estimated time of arrival (ETA) so that when the director calls in the morning and complains that the DVD has not arrived, you will be able to troubleshoot. You must know the director's phone numbers and email address. It is a good idea to email the director as soon as the output has left the studio, what the ETA is on the following day, and the courier's tracking number. Ask the editor if he would like to include a note with the DVD. These questions need to be answered *before* the day of the output. Figure 5.3 is a cover sheet for the continuity.

After the editor's cut has been sent to the director, it is a good idea to confirm with the editor when he and the director will start work in the morning. It is always pleasant to have special edible goodies available in the cutting room to make your guest happy. This also applies to the next round of visitors (the producers). The editing room should be an inviting and creative environment—a place in which the directors and producers are comfortable.

"THE COMPETITION"

Episode # 103

"The Surprise Party"

August ___, 2010

EDITOR'S CUT

TRT: :48:04

FORMAT TIME: :46:00

Over/Under: +02:04

Figure 5.3 *An example of a cover sheet for the continuity*

5.10 Director's Cut

The director's cut is my favorite phase (though I love dailies too!) of the post schedule. I get to discuss the film—its virtues and challenges—*honestly* and hear the inside stories of how scenes evolved on the set. The director's sensibilities, vision, and interpretation of the script are often-times surprising and enlightening. When the director is especially tuned in to editing, the communication is inspiring and can be the most uplifting part of the process. The chances for happy accidents for the style of the show increase exponentially with a gifted director.

—ljc

During the director's cut, the chores for the assistant remain substantially the same. You will be responsible for changing the continuity sheet to reflect the newly ordered sequences (scenes may be transposed or moved to different acts). There will be new measurements for many scenes that also affect the overall footage of each act, and therefore the duration of the entire movie. B negative might need to be ordered to find that perfect performance the director is absolutely certain was captured on film and not yet printed. After getting approval from the associate producer (there is sometimes an extra cost involved in ordering a B negative), the assistant will order it, digitize it, and place another Post-it in the editor's lined script so that he will know that new material has arrived. When using Final Cut Pro, our assistants color code the B negative in the Scene bin so that it is easy to find. On the Avid, the assistant will label it *B neg*. New music or stock is also frequently ordered, digitized, and similarly denoted for the editor to cut in.

> **SHINE NOTE**
>
> You can **shine** by duplicating the sequence, placing it in a newly created Alt MX bin, and cutting the new music alts to picture. This will help your editor tremendously. When a new alt is selected, you can cut it into the current cut.

When you ask the MX supervisor to help select alt needle drops, he will need to take a look at the sequence. The assistant will create a QuickTime (QT) and post it on the MX supervisor's server. The MX supervisor will send his choices via Internet and/or a compilation on a CD that needs to be transported to your cutting rooms. This process changes according to geographic hurdles and the urgency of the request. The assistant will alert the MX supervisor that there is an imminent arrival of a QT and a request for alts. In your informational email, include the name and episode number of the show, the length of the scene, the notes or commentary from the director and the editor, and a short story update about what immediately precedes and follows this scene. Sometimes it is good to send the pages from the script that precede or follow the scene as well.

When there are sound effects that need to be ordered to supplement your library, be very specific when emailing or describing your request to the supervising sound editor. It is also helpful to compile a list of needed sounds throughout the day. Add to the list for a couple of days before disturbing the sound department unless there is an urgent request. Most of the time the SFX editor will upload several choices via the Internet.

It is never too early to search for great stock shots. It is a time-consuming task that initially may take more than a day or two. Ultimately the assistant editor will provide stock choices for the editor to cut in, but the post supervisor can often be a big help in this area.

During the director's cut, the needed VFX will be discussed at length. Try to include your associate producer and his staff in this process as early as possible. Show them the work you have temped. The assistant editor should create a QuickTime of the shots (with a handle of a few shots on either side of the VFX shot) to be sent to the VFX editor for a cost breakdown. Write down the number of frames, total duration of the shot, timecodes, camera roll number, master tape number, and date shot. Save a copy of this information in your assistant's notebook, and copy your post supervisor and the VFX editor. Your telecine house needs this information so they can pull the original master tape of this shot for the VFX editor to start work.

The director's cut lasts for a certain amount of days depending upon the format. According to the Directors Guild of America (DGA) contract, there are 4 days minimum on episodic TV; 20 days for a 2-hour film for TV; 30 days for a two-part, 4-hour miniseries; and 10 weeks for a feature with a budget greater than $3,605,000. These numbers are legal guidelines and are sometimes negotiable.

There should be a distribution list generated by the post producer with the names of people who will receive the director's cut. Remember to change the labels to say it's the director's cut! The post PA receives the assistant editor's output of the director's cut and duplicates it for distribution. He should also label each DVD with the appropriate name, date, and footage information provided to him by the assistant editor. Remember to provide a continuity for the post PA to duplicate and attach to each DVD.

The director's cut goes to the producers, who will make their changes during their allotted time. The assistant will output the producer's cut and send it to the studio and then the network. Sometimes the producer's cut goes to the studio and the network at the same time, and both sets of changes are performed simultaneously. Sometimes there is no studio cut, so you send the producer's cut straight to the network. For all the different versions that follow the director's cut, all the same steps are repeated. The assistant must ask for the distribution list, know what the cutoff time is for a timely output, know where the DVD will be sent, update and include the continuity, quality check (QC) the master DVD for sound and picture before sending it to duplication, and measure the show accurately. As you deliver the film higher up the ladder, these measurements become more critical. You are reaching a lock on your film and need to be frame accurate. There are assistant editors who have lost their job due to an incorrect measurement. Check, double check, and *triple check*!

In features, the process is ultimately the same, except there is no network delivery. The total running time (TRT) of the movie is not restricted by format footage timings or a target time. The length of the movie is determined by the overall viewing experience, though the studio will often ask for the film to be cut down from 3 or more hours to 2 or less hours. The process of updating the current timings of all scenes is universal. Categorizing lifts, stock, music, and gags is desirable throughout the industry, regardless of the venue.

At this point of the film, only the editor, the assistant editor, and the director have viewed the film. It is forbidden by the DGA rules to show anyone in production any edited footage without the director's permission. However, there is a trend in television for producers to ask to see cut scenes during dailies or the editor's cut. This is a tough position, and as an assistant editor, you must defer to your editor's decision on how to handle the situation *before* screening or giving out DVDs. The assistant has access to lots of creative content that only authorized eyes are supposed to see. Part of your job is keeping that content restricted to the editing room.

5.11 Privacy in the Editing Room

A sensitive issue in the cutting room is to understand that it can be a very private and revealing place for a producer or director. In some cases, these executives have been working for many months on their shows, especially in the case of features. This first cut represents years of their creative talents exposed, the battles they have had to fight, the indignities they have had to endure, and the disappointments on the set. This screening in the editing room is the first time they see their movie in its entirety.

When the director sees the editor's cut, he sees all the directorial mistakes and the bad things that happened along the way—the actors who didn't show up on time so he couldn't get the shots he wanted; the weather that did not cooperate and all the production details that hindered the shooting; the blocking of scenes that might seem awkward; the focus that might be soft; or the actors who never got the lines right. That is what a director usually responds to in the first cut of a show, and his emotional reaction can be intense. His disappointments, histrionics, and all your conversations must stay private.

What happens in editing, stays in editing.

5.12 Producer's Cut

Next comes the producer's cut. Because the executive producers are inundated with questions and problems that arise in casting, writing, and production, editorial is often put on a back burner during the day. Waiting for their notes is often the hardest part for the editors and their assistants. Maintain a good attitude so that

Table 5.1 *Network requirements*

Act 00 (teaser)–01	10–16 minutes
Act 02	08–10 minutes
Act 03	08–10 minutes
Act 04	06–09 minutes
Act 05	10–12 minutes

when the producers do arrive, the atmosphere is inviting and energetic. It is always a good idea for the assistant editor to determine the producers' preferences for food or drinks and make sure the editing rooms are well-stocked. This will help facilitate a smooth transition from director's cut to producer's cut.

Because the producers are busy with all the other details of making a film, their brief time in the cutting room is spent with a special eye on the clock. Whenever you have a moment of their attention, you must make the best use of it! Be organized and prepare lists of questions that need to be addressed (such as the recap, music alts, and added lines of dialog). The assistant will output the show quite often during this phase, and it is important to diligently update the continuity with new scene timings.

Make sure your acts are within the timing requirements of the network format. Even though your continuity has reflected the act timings during each output, the post producer must be made aware of the aberrant act lengths. He will then contact the network and ask for a variance (special permission from the network that allows an act to be longer or shorter than the prescribed format). If the network denies the variance, then scenes have to be moved out of the long acts or into the short acts, and the producers need to be aware of these problems. This is when accurate scene footages reflected on the continuity will be extremely helpful.

Place the network act footage information on the bulletin board next to your continuity and footages chart (see Table 5.1). These lengths vary with different networks.

If one of the acts is under or over these timings, a red flag should be raised. Even though the continuity reflects the act timings, the post producer should be informed. Hopefully these timing issues will be addressed before the picture is locked. The film will have to be restructured by moving scenes into different acts and/or changing the lengths of scenes.

DEFINITION

Standards and Practices is a division of the network that monitors the use of language, levels of violence, and modesty.

After your producers have completed their cut, an output of the show is made for the studio and network, who will then email or phone in their final notes. Editorial will also hear from Standards and Practices.

Sometimes other represented affiliates attached to your show will be given an advance copy of the film for their notes as well.

On my third episode of *Make It or Break It* we had actors playing ESPN broadcasters narrating gymnastics for the nationals competition. ESPN was given a DVD of the network cut, and they asked for changes to be made to the dialog. These notes were addressed before we locked the show.

—ljc

After the network notes have been addressed and approved by everyone, the assistant editor does a final check of the total length of the show. Be very accurate. The editor will be asked to get it on format footage or close to it, and every frame is important.

Sometimes locking a show goes like clockwork. Schedules are met; format footages have been satisfied; stock is selected, ordered, and cut in; VFX are approved; and needle drops are all agreed upon, affordable, and licensable. However, there are times when an element is still pending at lock (e.g., a stock shot, insert, or a scene is missing) and will have to be dealt with afterwards. The assistant must keep a vigilant eye on the incomplete tasks. Keeping lists is very important. Making sure all of the details are finalized is ultimately the post producer's job, but the sign of a *great* assistant editor is one who follows the film to its completion.

In television, when the lock takes longer than the schedule allows, the assistant editor must multitask and start preparation for his next show. This overlap occurs frequently. Sometimes the assistant will have *three* shows on his plate, all in different states of completion. This is when your meticulous notes will keep your work life sane.

5.13 The Locked Show

Please be aware that after you have locked the show, done all the preparations for online, and calculated a final measurement, there can be last-minute changes that need to be incorporated. Perhaps one network executive had not seen the show when network notes were delivered, or an executive producer has changed his mind about a scene and wants it shorter or longer. Sometimes an ADR line must take the place of the original dialog, and the scene must be recut to allow for that new line. Sometimes a composer wants to add a second of black to the end of every act for ringout. The assistant must take these changes in stride.

> This is why I refer to locking as *latching* instead. Maintain your sense of humor and make the changes—it is only time (yours) and money (theirs).
>
> —ljc

Now you have completed the cycle of changes that will constitute a locked show. Yay! Get ready for your third and most challenging task as an assistant editor—the online.

Chapter 6

Get Ready to Online

Now that the picture is locked, the process referred to as *online* (in the digital world) or *negative cutting* (in film) takes place. It is *showtime*. The online is where the original master tapes are assembled and matched frame for frame (by timecode) to the final locked picture. This is done because the quality of the original media is the best resolution, whereas the editor has been working with compressed media. Dailies are digitized into your editing system at a lower resolution to save hard drive space. For television, the resolution needs to revert to the original video–digital masters to meet broadcast standards. This final tape version is called the *master, final master,* or *color-timed master (CTM)*. After it has been dubbed (the process of mixing the dialog, SFX, and MX on a dub stage), it is called the *final sweetened master* or *sweetened CTM*. On film, when the negative has been cut, a *digital intermediary (DI)* is created so that color correction, titling, and VFX can be done in the digital world before a print is struck.

Television shows currently online the video only. After the film has been onlined, the post facility stripes the picture as a guide for the sound department with a mixed-down version (dialog, SFX, and MX) of the film editor's work. An audio EDL that represents all of the film editor's sound work is sent to the sound effects department so they can match the originally recorded production dialog back to this locked cut. The original sound is recorded on DAT or hard drive; it varies according to the equipment used by the production mixers.

It is very important that the online goes smoothly because an error at this point is costly—financially *and* careerwise. If you have done all of your work correctly during dailies (audio and video timecodes are correct, tape numbers have not been duplicated, and source material from outside the production has arrived at the post facility), there should be no problems.

Here is a checklist of tasks that should be completed to prepare for online:

1. Create a Locked Sequence bin
2. Remove add edits or match frame edits
3. Do a cut-to-cut check for jump cuts
4. Format the locked sequence
5. Complete the format sheet
6. Create the locked continuity and locked needle drop sheet
7. Prepare the ADR list
8. Prepare the VFX list

DOI: 10.1016/B978-0-240-81398-1.00006-7

9. Reassign tracks
10. Create the chase cassette (DVD)
11. Create the audio EDL, picture EDL, and OMFs
12. Prepare for SFX and MX spotting
13. Duplicate the script and sound reports per the spec sheets for SFX

6.1 Create a Locked Sequence Bin

When you have been given the green light to start the online, your first task will be to create a new bin into which you will place a copy of the locked cut. A good precaution to take at this point is to lock all the tracks so that no further changes are inadvertently made in this version. When you have formatted the cut, it will be the final copy of the show. The *master timecode (MTC)* will start at 01;00;00;00 (if you are in drop frame) on the first frame of picture. This MTC information will be used uniformly for sound, music, online, VFX, and the dub stage.

6.2 Remove Add Edits and Check for Jump Cuts

It is good to remove all unnecessary add edits or match frame edits if you are on an Avid. (Avoid this step on FCP because it will remove the VFX on the media.) Highlight the entire sequence and then go to Edit (in Avid). Click on the Remove Matchframe edit button. This will delete all the false edits in your list. The assistant should then do a cut-to-cut check of the show. This means that the assistant must check the video for inadvertent jump cuts by going through the movie and making sure each video splice begins and ends on a different image. Sometimes during the course of changes, work is done so rapidly that mistakes happen. A frame or two can be missing from a shot, and it will need to be reconstituted properly. The assistant can do this by turning on the video track only and hitting the button that takes you to the next cut. If the picture that appears on your source side is the same as the picture that appears on your record side, there is a jump cut.

SHINE NOTE

If you find a jump cut, let your editor know *immediately* and ask him if it is intended. If not intended, have him decide what the fix will be. This will save time and money at the online as well as keep your picture and track in sync. Life is so much better when you catch jump cuts *before* the online, and it is a good opportunity to **shine**!

6.3 Format the Locked Sequence

After you have removed the add edits and checked for jump cuts, you will format the show. Add the main title (not to be confused with the opening credits), the format blacks, the end credits, and the various logos. This will be the final sequence assembled from the first frame of formatted black footage to the final identifying network logo. Duplicate this locked sequence and copy it down into the Z bins to preserve your work. Create a new bin called Spotting Sequence and lock all the tracks. This is the sequence that you will screen during your separate FX and MX spotting sessions the day after you lock the show.

6.4 Complete the Format Sheet

The format sheet is now filled in with the master time code for each act (see Figure 6.1).

TIP

Creating and formatting the locked sequence is the most important part of the online. This sequence *must* be formatted correctly, or everything you create from it (PIX and audio EDLs, the chase cassette, DVDs for FX and MX, etc.) will be incorrect. Check your sequence. Check it again. Check it a third time for kicks. It is easy to make a mistake here, but it is also easy to catch and fix it *before* anyone spends a great deal of time and money working on an incorrectly formatted show!

"THE COMPETITION" Season 1		
Production # 103 Title: "The Surprise Party" Date: January 05, 2010		
ELEMENT	START	DURATION
SEGMENT1 (10 to 16 minutes) **Includes:** **RECAP**	01;00;00;00	32;00
TEASER	01;00;32;00	6;08;27
MAIN TITLE	01;06;40;27	18;04
ACT1 (w/opening credits)	01;06;59;01	7;37;16
BREAK 1 (1 second of BLACK)	01;14;36;17	1;00
SEGMENT 2 (5 to 9 minutes) **ACT 2**	01;14;37;17	8;17;15
BREAK2 (1 second of BLACK)	01;22;55;00	1;00
SEGMENT 3 (5 to 9 minutes) **ACT 3**	01;22;56;00	7;47;25
BREAK 3 (1 second of BLACK)	01;30;43;25	1;00
SEGMENT 4 (5 to 9 minutes) **ACT 4**	01;30;44;25	6;39;17
BREAK 4 (1 second of BLACK)	01;37;24;14	1;00
SEGMENT 5 (8 to 12 minutes) **ACT 5** (Includes 3 sec Executive Producer Card)	01;37;25;14	6;42;07
BREAK 5 (1 second of BLACK)	01;44;07;21	1;00
SEGMENT 6 (MUSIC ONLY over entire segment) **FULL FRAME LOGOS** (Includes Prod. Logo AND Network Logo)	01;44;08;21	4;00
END CREDITS (Cards left 1/3 w/show logo at top & Video Montage right 2/3)	01;44;12;21	30;00
MUSIC AD CARDS (1 card = 10 sec, 2 cards = 15 sec, 3 cards = 20 sec)	01;44;42;21	15;00
TOTAL RUNNING TIME		44;52;21
TOTAL BLACK		5;00
TOTAL PROGRAM TIME		44;47;21
TARGET DELIVERY TIME		44;10;00
	OVER/UNDER	+37;21
BLACK (One minute between end of program and textless)		1:00;00
TEXTLESS MATERIAL – M.O.S.	01;45;42;21	

Figure 6.1 *Filled-in format sheet template*

Note that the duration of each act is also filled in. We know from the original format sheets we have received from the network what timings exceed or comply with their requests.

The format sheet, though daunting at first blush, is really quite simple when all of the questions about blacks, main title length, the number of logos and their allotted time, and the recap timing has been sorted out. Fill in the paperwork carefully—check it twice!

6.5 Create the Locked Continuity and MX Sheet

Remember to create the final locked continuity with all the updated footages for each scene and act. Include the timings for the scenes that were lifted as well. Make sure the final time of the locked show is denoted. Date all paperwork and remember to create a final locked music sheet if you are on a needle drop show.

6.6 Prepare the ADR List

The *automated dialog replacement (ADR)* or looping sheet is a list of dialog lines that need to be recorded. These lines will replace, change, or be in addition to the production dialog (see Figure 6.2).

"The Surprise Party"					
SPOTTING SESSION: ADR / LOOP NOTES					
DATE:	As of: 02/02/2010				
TO:	Email addresses of Post/Snd/Editors				
EPISODE # 103		EPISODE TITLE:	"The Surprise Party"	Form completed by: L. Smith	
Act 1	10	01;19;40;15	Doctor	More determined	"Please, I'm her doctor." Loop for performance. Per Producer
Act 1	12	01;20;03;02	Coach	ADD	"Come on Ali, you're not going anywhere." Per Director
Act 1	12	01;20;06;12	Coach	ADD	"Keep pushing." Per Producer
Act 1	12	01;20;33;01	Coach	ADD	"We need to work harder!" Per Producer

Figure 6.2 *ADR template*

Act 2	13	01;21;59;11	Agent	More upset	"In Deirdre's gym bag we found…" Per Producer
Act 2	13	01;22;24;23	Mandy	Change name	**"Hathord"** instead of "Hatfield. "
Act 2	13	01;23;22;15	David	ADD	"and they got it on video." Per Producer
Act 2	15	01;26;51;08	Reporter	ADD	"Excuse me sir." Per A.P.
Act 2	16	01;27;18;13	Coach	ADD	"Okay Dave, so what do you have for me tonight?" Per Network
Act 2	16	01;27;42;29	Reporter	ADD	"It's Emma Jones". Per Network
Act 3	17	01;29;27;27	Ali	ADD	Can I give it a try **"Coach."** Per Exec. Producer
Act 3	17	01;29;28;20	Ali	ADD	"I've wanted this for ten years." Per Exec. Producer
Act 3	20	01;31;15;15	Deirdre	ADD	"Uh huh. Let me see." Per Editor
Act 3	20	01;31;31;15	Coach	ADD	**"Everybody here is"** free to come and go. Per Director
Act 4	24	01;36;24;26	Coach	Replace dialog	This added DOD **"Could"** put you in first place (Replace "would") Per Network
Act 4	26	01;39;22;08	Ali	angrier	**"I miss him so much"** for performance. Per Studio
Act 4	28	01;41;04;25	Coach	Change dialog	**"The best doctor is"** wanted ????
Act 4	28	01;41;11;00	Coach	Noise	"We believe she is the **only** one who can help." Per Writer

Figure 6.2 (*Continued*)

It is important to include in your list which person suggested the ADR note. The executive producer might disagree with a directive, and the origin of a note is of great subsequent importance. Note that the timecode of the ADR line is the *new* master timecode. These numbers are filled in after you have created the locked sequence.

6.7 Prepare the VFX Notes

Make sure you remind the associate producer about the shots affected by VFX. He will need the master time-code of each event, their durations, and possibly a QuickTime of the shots if the VFX are done somewhere other than the original post facility that is in charge of your dailies. Depending upon the machine used at online, there are some effects that might need to be addressed in a separate bay at the post facility. The post coordinator will then create the VFX after the online.

> I update my color-coded locator list every time I cut in a VFX. It contains pertinent information for the post coordinator (e.g., VFX Sc. 10 < 45 frames > – Burn-in video game on television monitor). The assistant should update the list then print and distribute it to streamline the post process before and after the lock. This locator list is in *addition* to the comments typed into the EDL, which is generated by the assistant editor.
>
> —ljc

6.8 Reassign Tracks

On an Avid, the editor tries to cut using only eight tracks because that is the playback capacity without doing a mixdown. Currently, the latest version of Avid will play back sixteen tracks. When cutting a scene that requires more than the amount of tracks that can be played back simultaneously, the editor will assign dialog to a track that is traditionally reserved for SFX and cut SFX into tracks normally used for MX. There are quadruple amounts of playback tracks on FCP, but reassigning tracks still needs to be done when dialog, FX, and MX tracks intermingle.

The assistant will reassign the audio tracks in preparation for the online in such a way that all dialog, SFX, and MX do not overlap each other. For example, if dialog needs four tracks, move sound effects down to track 5. If SFX requires six dedicated tracks, move music down to start on track 11.

If you have color coded your sound effects and your music, it will be easy to see in the time line just where these overlaps have occurred. For example, in the following editor's time line, dialog is on the first three tracks, SFX is on four tracks (intermingled with dialog on track 3), and music is on six tracks (intermingled with both dialog and FX) (see Figure 6.3).

When preparing these tracks for online, the assistant must move the music down to occupy tracks 7 and 8, 9 and 10, and 11 and 12. Note that he was able to consolidate sound effects from four tracks down to three tracks after the music was moved down, and SFX now lives on tracks 4, 5, and 6 (see Figure 6.4).

The end effect is that there are dedicated tracks for dialog, SFX, and MX. They must *never* share the same track in the time line for the online. An output of the locked show will go to the dialog editor, who needs to hear it clean (no SFX or MX) to better determine whether the lines have to be looped. When the composer scores the film, he needs to have the ability to toggle the temp MX on and off. Being able to listen to the temp score is helpful if he has been asked by the producers to emulate it or reproduce its vibe.

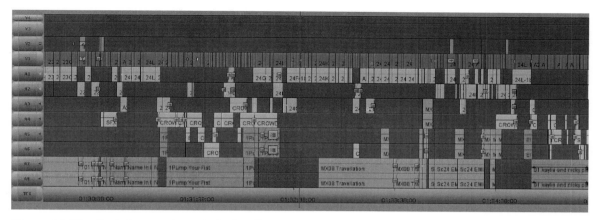

Figure 6.3 *Time line before separating tracks for the online*

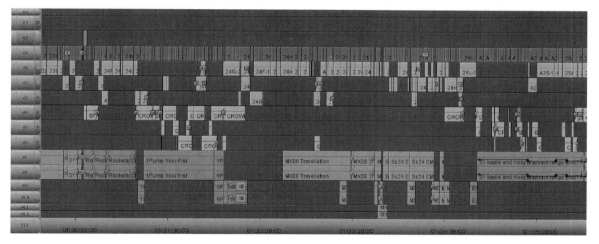

Figure 6.4 *Time line after separating tracks for the online*

When the assistant outputs the show for the sound department and the music editor, he will be responsible for reassigning the audio tracks—dialog, SFX, and MX—to their proper channels based on the specs previously received from each department. For example, dialog tracks are assigned to channel 1, temp ADR to channel 2, FX to channel 3, and MX to channel 4.

6.9 Create the Chase Cassette (DVD)

The assistant editor will make a chase cassette, which is an output of the locked show. This output is a visual reference

> **TIP**
>
> It is wise to color code temp ADR when you record and place it in the Temp ADR bin. This way, it can easily be seen in the time line. Assign all temp ADR lines to the same dialog track so they will sort sequentially on your locator list. Mark it with a colored locator chosen specifically for ADR. This organization will help you complete the ADR list for the spotting session.

played simultaneously with the video assembled master (VAM) by the online editor to ensure that his online matches the output exactly. There are four split tracks: A1 is production dialog, A2 is temp ADR, A3 is SFX, and A4 is music. The online editor then lays back the editor's four audio tracks that have been sent to him by the assistant. The VAM will be used to create dubs for the FX and MX departments according to their individual specs. You will create picture and audio EDLs (edit decision lists) that will go to online and the sound department.

6.10 Create the PIX and Audio Edit Decision Lists (EDLs) and the OMFs

The edit decision list (EDL) is a list of the beginning and ending timecodes for every event (cut)—dissolve, transition, title, or picture and track. The system used for online (e.g., Grass Valley, Nitris) affects the formatting of the EDL. It is a good idea to speak directly with the online editor to confirm on which form they expect their bins or EDLs to arrive. Make a habit of sending over a test bin before the online to make sure your systems communicate properly.

When your show contains more than one video track (i.e., VFX on track V2), it is imperative to create a separate EDL for each video layer (see Figure 6.5).

The audio EDL is for your sound department. They use the EDL to match back to the original tracks recorded on the set. These original tracks replace your work tracks because they are better quality (see Figure 6.6).

You have now completed most of the preparation for the online. Well done. The EDLs and/or Avid bin are emailed in advance or sent to the post facility. This Avid bin contains the formatted show and permits the online editor to get started with the process even as the assistant continues to make outputs for various departments.

6.11 Prepare for SFX and MX Spotting

The next task is to prepare for the SFX and MX spottings. You already have the ADR lists filled in for the dialog editor. You need to fill in the needle drop list if you are on a show with licensed music so the composer and the music editor know which spots call for a score to be written and which needle drops need to be replaced with a score. Estimate the number of people who will be at the spotting session in advance of their arrival and prepare the editing room with enough chairs to seat your guests.

Make copies of the paperwork (continuity, ADR, and needle drop list) to distribute. Remember to make a copy for the editor's notebook as well as yours.

The assistant should arrive at the cutting room in advance of everyone so that he can be a good host—start the coffee, distribute the paperwork, and arrange the chairs. Remember, these people are your guests. Make them as comfortable as possible when they visit your editing suite.

If you are on a feature that is doing a film finish instead of a digital finish, some of the steps are different. On a film finish, you create a negative cut list for your negative cutter. A Digital Intermediate (DI) is created, which is a scan of the original negative. This allows the color correction, VFX, titling, and finishing of the film to be done digitally before striking a print of the movie for release in theaters. Many of the online steps are exactly the same for a DI as a film finish.

```
TITLE:   ACT.00  1016  SC. 01-04
FCM: NON-DROP FRAME
001     BL    V    C        00:00:00:00 00:00:00:00 01:00:00:00 01:00:00:00
001  10       V    D    024 03:17:41:09 03:17:50:14 01:00:00:00 01:00:09:06
* TO CLIP NAME:   1-3
002  10       V    C        03:20:14:10 03:20:15:06 01:00:09:06 01:00:10:01
* FROM CLIP NAME:   1A-4
003  10       V    C        03:17:50:23 03:17:57:06 01:00:10:01 01:00:16:10
* FROM CLIP NAME:   1-3
004  10       V    C        03:22:43:01 03:22:44:15 01:00:16:10 01:00:17:28
* FROM CLIP NAME:   18-2
005  10       V    C        03:18:00:23 03:18:04:10 01:00:17:28 01:00:21:11
* FROM CLIP NAME:   1-3
006  10       V    C        03:22:48:20 03:22:49:18 01:00:21:11 01:00:22:09
* FROM CLIP NAME:   18-2
007  10       V    C        03:20:25:01 03:20:28:06 01:00:22:09 01:00:25:15
* FROM CLIP NAME:   1A-4
008  10       V    C        03:22:52:18 03:22:55:15 01:00:25:15 01:00:28:11
* FROM CLIP NAME:   18-2
009  10       V    C        03:20:31:03 03:20:33:03 01:00:28:11 01:00:30:11
* FROM CLIP NAME:   1A-4
010  10       V    C        03:24:26:16 03:24:31:19 01:00:30:11 01:00:35:15
* FROM CLIP NAME:   1C-1
011  10       V    C        03:20:39:15 03:20:47:09 01:00:35:15 01:00:43:08
* FROM CLIP NAME:   1A-4
012  10       V    C        03:24:39:07 03:24:42:12 01:00:43:08 01:00:46:14
* FROM CLIP NAME:   1C-1
013  10       V    C        03:20:50:07 03:20:55:02 01:00:46:14 01:00:51:08
* FROM CLIP NAME:   1A-4
014  10       V    C        03:24:46:11 03:24:48:08 01:00:51:08 01:00:53:04
* FROM CLIP NAME:   1C-1
015  10       V    C        03:20:56:23 03:21:00:07 01:00:53:04 01:00:56:14
* FROM CLIP NAME:   1A-4
016  10       V    C        03:23:25:08 03:23:30:14 01:00:56:14 01:01:01:21
* FROM CLIP NAME:   18-2
017  9        V    C        02:46:40:04 02:46:47:18 01:01:01:21 01:01:09:09
* FROM CLIP NAME:   2-7
018  10       V    C        03:14:50:01 03:14:51:04 01:01:09:09 01:01:10:13
* FROM CLIP NAME:   2C-2
019  10       V    C        03:10:02:07 03:10:06:03 01:01:10:13 01:01:14:08
* FROM CLIP NAME:   28-5
020  9        V    C        02:46:51:22 02:46:53:04 01:01:14:08 01:01:15:15
* FROM CLIP NAME:   2-7
021  10       V    C        03:10:07:10 03:10:08:17 01:01:15:15 01:01:16:24
* FROM CLIP NAME:   28-5
022  10       V    C        03:06:02:15 03:06:03:23 01:01:16:24 01:01:18:04
* FROM CLIP NAME:   2A-1
023  10       V    C        03:14:06:13 03:14:11:04 01:01:18:04 01:01:22:23
* FROM CLIP NAME:   2C-2
024  10       V    C        03:06:10:18 03:06:13:08 01:01:22:23 01:01:25:10
* FROM CLIP NAME:   2A-1
025  10       V    C        03:12:30:06 03:12:33:05 01:01:25:10 01:01:28:09
* FROM CLIP NAME:   2C-1
026  9        V    C        02:47:07:22 02:47:15:04 01:01:28:09 01:01:35:16
* FROM CLIP NAME:   2-7
```

Figure 6.5 *PIX EDL template*

```
TITLE:   ACT.00  1016  SC. 01-04
FCM: NON-DROP FRAME
001  10      A      C          20:45:31:01 20:45:32:29 01:00:01:00 01:00:02:28
* FROM CLIP NAME:  1-3
002  10      A      C          20:45:33:24 20:45:36:19 01:00:03:23 01:00:06:18
* FROM CLIP NAME:  1-3
003  10      A2     C          20:54:46:19 20:54:52:15 01:00:06:18 01:00:12:14
* FROM CLIP NAME:  1A-4
004      AX   NONE  C          00:00:00:07 00:00:00:11 01:00:08:04 01:00:08:09
AUD   3
* FROM CLIP NAME:  SFX PHONE; FLIP PHONE, FUNCTION BEEP 2
005  10      A      C          20:45:39:19 20:45:45:27 01:00:10:01 01:00:16:10
* FROM CLIP NAME:  1-3
006  10      A      C          20:45:48:01 20:45:52:22 01:00:16:10 01:00:21:01
* FROM CLIP NAME:  1-3
007  10      A2     C          20:45:47:15 20:45:48:02 01:00:16:15 01:00:17:03
* FROM CLIP NAME:  1-3
008  10      A      C          21:12:12:16 21:12:13:22 01:00:21:01 01:00:22:08
* FROM CLIP NAME:  1B-2
009  10      A      C          20:54:59:25 20:55:07:29 01:00:22:08 01:00:30:11
* FROM CLIP NAME:  1A-4
010  10      A      C          21:14:52:13 21:14:57:04 01:00:30:11 01:00:35:03
* FROM CLIP NAME:  1C-1
011  10      A      C          21:14:57:04 21:14:57:04 01:00:35:03 01:00:35:03
011  10B     A      D      008 20:55:14:01 20:55:22:12 01:00:35:03 01:00:43:14
* BLEND_AUDIO_DISSOLVE
* FROM CLIP NAME:  1C-1
* TO CLIP NAME:  1A-4
012  10      A      C          21:15:05:08 21:15:08:08 01:00:43:14 01:00:46:14
* FROM CLIP NAME:  1C-1
013  10      A      C          20:55:25:04 20:55:35:04 01:00:46:14 01:00:56:14
* FROM CLIP NAME:  1A-4
014  10      A      C          21:12:49:11 21:12:54:06 01:00:56:14 01:01:01:09
* FROM CLIP NAME:  1B-2
015  9       A      C          18:56:43:02 18:56:51:10 01:01:01:09 01:01:09:18
* FROM CLIP NAME:  2-7
016  10      A      C          19:58:04:27 19:58:06:02 01:01:09:18 01:01:10:23
* FROM CLIP NAME:  2C-2
017  10      A      C          19:45:06:05 19:45:09:20 01:01:10:23 01:01:14:08
* FROM CLIP NAME:  2B-5
018  9       A      C          18:56:55:07 18:56:56:14 01:01:14:08 01:01:15:15
* FROM CLIP NAME:  2-7
019  10      A      C          19:45:10:29 19:45:11:21 01:01:15:15 01:01:16:08
* FROM CLIP NAME:  2B-5
020  10      A      C          19:05:17:05 19:05:17:21 01:01:16:08 01:01:16:24
* FROM CLIP NAME:  2A-1
021  10      A      C          19:05:17:25 19:05:18:27 01:01:16:24 01:01:17:26
* FROM CLIP NAME:  2A-1
022  10      A      C          19:57:20:26 19:57:25:22 01:01:17:26 01:01:22:23
* FROM CLIP NAME:  2C-2
023  10      A      C          19:05:25:29 19:05:27:25 01:01:22:23 01:01:24:19
* FROM CLIP NAME:  2A-1
```

Figure 6.6 *Audio EDL template*

6.12 Duplicate the Script and Sound Reports

The sound editing department is composed of a dialog editor, an ADR editor, an FX editor, and a Foley editor. Sometimes these jobs overlap. Each person will need a copy of the script and the sound reports. Make sure this paperwork is done and available by the time the spotting session takes place.

Congratulations! You have completed your first show from soup to nuts.

In episodic television, the department will finish the rest of the show—VFX, titling, dirt fix, color correction, ADR, group ADR, dubbing, layback, and delivery. In features, pilots, movies of the week and documentaries, the editor is often present for these sessions as well. The world of documentaries and reality (nonscripted television) differs greatly from network and cable television. However, there are some commonalities that prevail regardless of venue. The assistant is still responsible for the dailies, outputs, and online; he needs to anticipate the needs of the editor, pay close attention to detail, and remain energetic and focused.

Chapter 7

Assisting Protocols for Documentaries

With the advent of cable television in the 1980s and 1990s, the world of documentaries and reality shows exploded in popularity. Today they are still boasting an ever-increasing market share in the world of television viewing. They have become the hot new genres.

To work as an assistant on either a documentary or a reality show, you will need the same basic skills and knowledge of the editing room required by other venues. What will differ, however, is *what* you digitize or import, the *organization* of the B roll, and *how you organize your material and set bins* to suit the needs of your editor.

Documentaries and reality shows shoot great amounts of footage and require exceptional organizational skills as you bring order to what seems like chaos. There are different production techniques and shooting styles employed by both of these genres. Documentary coverage usually reflects a controlled shooting style on a single camera where every shot is planned and carefully composed. Reality is shot in real time, capturing events as they happen, and there are often multiple cameras shooting the action from different angles, usually handheld and generally much more proactive in coverage. Working in these different styles will affect your work flow as an assistant.

7.1 Elements of a Documentary

Within the genre of documentary there are various approaches to capturing the subject matter. One of the standard methods of making a documentary is to settle on the subject or theme. A research team will find the following:

- The best locations
- Relevant interviews and interviewees
- Stock footage (to be licensed from a stock house)
- Stills (obtained from the subject of the show or licensed from a stills library)
- Music that might be used for the show or that might form part of the story

> **DEFINITION**
>
> B roll is footage that is used to illustrate the story and will be used as cutaways for an interview.

DOI: 10.1016/B978-0-240-81398-1.00007-9

DEFINITION

Re-creation is a dramatic reenactment of a situation (historic or contemporary) that portrays an event or action that highlights or dramatizes a story point in the show.

A producer, cameraman, sound mixer, and small production crew will then go on location to record the interviews, shoot the B roll, and capture any sound or music that is relevant to the story.

Another popular and important device used to tell the documentary story is the re-creation. These dramatizations can sometimes be major production events utilizing actors, extras, sets, and complicated lighting setups. They can be quite costly. Sometimes these re-creations can be shot rather simply and will rely on postproduction techniques to heighten their drama.

Re-creations are, for me, the most exciting part of editing and creating a documentary. This is where the dramatic world of theatrical production meets the nonfiction world of harsh reality. I have edited many nonfiction works that have relied heavily on re-creations to dramatize events. These re-creations form an integral part of the mood and the visual look of the show. A simple cart being pushed slowly along a road by a man against a stunning sunset became the key symbolic element in a story called "Black Death" for the series *History's Mysteries*. African men walking past the camera with bare feet in front of a slave fort in Ghana symbolized the slaves being herded onto the dreaded ships for the New World in "World on a String."

Many times these re-creations need to be treated in some way to take them beyond the immediate reality and to create another time and place. Many popular methods include speeding up the shot (ramping) or doing a slow motion effect (slow-mo) to create more tension or make the scene more surreal. Editors are always looking for fresh and effective ways of treating shots when they are used as re-creations or flashbacks in a story. This becomes a perfect moment for an assistant to suggest new concepts using the latest available programs or technology that might be available for the editing programs. Offer up suggestions and contribute whenever the opportunity arises.

—df

When the shoot is complete (there are always pickups of some sort needed to help flesh out a story), all the material (on whatever format it was shot on) is brought back to postproduction and prepped for inputting or ingesting. Again, every production house has its own specific setup, and you will familiarize yourself with all the technology particular to that editing system. All the interviews will need to be transferred by the assistant onto a tape format (specified by the transcriber) with visible time code (Viz TC) and sent to be transcribed. These transcriptions will have a shooting timecode (TC) denoted in the margins on every paragraph for visual reference for the writer. The writer–producer will select relevant statements made in the interview (bites) and will write a script based on these selected bites. He will denote the TC on his script for the assistant. This enables the assistant to scroll through the interviews and use both the timecodes and the corresponding typed transcripts to find the selected material required for digitizing. The writer–producer will write a guide narration in and out of each bite, which will become the story outline for the show. Many creative writers–producers will also suggest visuals and B roll material that could be used over the narration and interviews (the cutaways). This is a paper cut of the film and is the first script the editor has to work with.

There are many different documentary formats and styles, and most people will approach their subject matter in a method that is best suited to that subject matter. Many shows are not scripted at all. Some documentaries could be compilation films, using clips from old movies, for example. These films might incorporate an onscreen host to start and end the show. The onscreen presenter is the actor who will be shot on a stage or on location and will be setting up the narrative and talking directly to the camera. Often he is the voice-over (VO) narrator for the entire film. Often the editor has to craft the show with the on-screen host already shot. Sometimes this narration will be written only after the show is cut. The host will be tagged to the head and tail of the show, and his off-screen narration will be written after the show has a final cut.

Sometimes a producer–cameraman will go on location and shoot as much material as he can with a story in mind. The footage will be brought back, and the final film will be created in the cutting room from mounds of footage. There is no script, and guidelines for the story outline will be in rough note form from the director. Often the amount of coverage is enormous, and finding shots can become a nightmare unless there is meticulous organization of the material. Discuss a method of breaking down the material with your editor, and take careful note of how he wants the footage digitized and bins set up for fast and easy reference. Endless styles of shooting will dictate the work flow and organization of dailies and B roll. Your contribution in managing the material will be essential for the success of the show.

7.2 Sort the Footage

The assistant has the job of breaking down all the tapes (media) shot on location, which includes the B roll and interviews. Usually the interviews will be interspersed with the B roll on the same tape. You will log and digitize or import all the material into the editing system.

To begin trying to organize all the material, it is a good idea to make a brief log of what is on each tape you receive. Often there will be no time for slates or any real kind of identification of the material shot. Go through all the tapes and make a log for each one. Make sure that all tapes and/or tapeless folders have unique names to be referenced during digitizing. Break down the material into B roll and interviews, and note the date shot. Add timecodes where possible for easy reference when searching for bites, special shots, or scenes on the tape. Put all these sheets with the lists of information in the editor's binder so he has a tangible record of all the material that was shot. This process is the same whether you are working with tape or material from a tapeless media—P2 or EX (media on tapeless formats is stored in a folder).

Here is an example of a breakdown of the contents of a tape. Note the italicized commentary that the assistant has added.

> **SHINE NOTE**
>
> When sorting material, if you see some really pertinent or great beauty shots, make comments on the logs. This is a great way to **shine** and help your editor go to the great moments quickly.

Tape 1

12/16/09

1. Interior B roll–Village Green restaurant
2. Street scenes–Jerusalem (*3rd shot is most active!*)

3. B roll–Alleys, etc. near falafel shop (quiet)
4. Ext. Vegetarian Society
5. Signs–"Event"
6. Interview Mr. Jack Cohen (chief electrician)–T/C: 00:05:17

Tape 2

12/17/09

1. Interview Joseph Jacobs–T/C: 0:00:00
2. B roll–Joseph in his office (talks to someone, goes to the computer, etc.)
3. Interview Barry Jones, owner Village Green rest–T/C: 00:17:57
4. Jerusalem from top of Tower Building (late afternoon) (various)
5. Sunset over Jerusalem from top of Tower Building (*great–4th shot has best focus!*)
6. Interview Dr. John Black (dentist)–T/C 00:26:48
7. B roll–Dr. John Black and patient

Tape 3

12/18/09

1. Interview Eran Ben Shack (Green Course. Instructor seen in B roll)–TC: 00:00:17
2. B roll–Driving shots. Traffic, congested roads (Tel Aviv), many high-rises and tall, modern buildings can be seen. Freeways. (All shot through the windscreen.)
3. 0:10:04–Freeway. Buses, train zooms past, busy. (*nice and colorful!*)
4. Freeway to Jerusalem (through windscreen) (0:19:50 new bridge construction)
5. 0:21:47–Entering Jerusalem (through windscreen)
6. 0:22:20–Old City, Dome of the Rock. Shot from vantage point. Various. Zooms etc. (Modern settlements in B/G.) Dome shines brightly. Pans. Reveals.
7. Old City Shouk
8. 0:40:20–Nice shot of Dome of the Rock
9. 0:45:50–Lutheran church bells
10. Jerusalem street scenes and pedestrians (*great car-bys and kids!*)
11. 0:56:00–High angle, Old City from vantage point

After you have made a rough list of all the material on the tapes, start logging material on each tape. Give them appropriate labels and arrange them in a B roll bin. Make sure that you label them in a way that will enable your editor to find shots quickly. It is not necessary to log a shot at every camera stop where there is continuous timecode.

If you are using tapeless media, which separates each individual shot before ingesting it, use your judgment on how you want to organize the material. Group the shots together in a logical order. It is best to log a segment of material shot in one location; for example, the farmyard and the animals as one clip instead of separating the chicken, duck, and horse shots. It is easier for the editor to scroll through all the farmyard material (if the clip is a reasonable length; maximum of 8–10 minutes) and make his own selects or subclips in a separate bin. Use your discretion when logging all the material, and come up with a simple way to name and identify shots in the bins. The editor usually has a wide choice of shots to work with, and you need to set up an efficient and organized system that helps make the work flow seamless. This is key to your assisting skills. If you have any queries, discuss them in detail with your editor and get his feedback on what works best for him and, again, his preferences for organization.

In documentaries, the cameraman will be tempted to capture many things that oftentimes might not be integral to the story. However, it is wise to digitize all the B roll material for the editor so he has the best possible selection. It is often that unscripted sunset that the cameraman captured while everyone was on coffee break that could be the perfect transition shot that the editor needed to bridge day and night. Digitize all B roll and only scripted bites for the interviews.

Set up your project and make bins for Re-creations, Stock, Stills, Music, Sound Effects, B roll, Banners, Lower Thirds, and Interviews. Then create your Cuts bins and label them as you would for narrative programming.

Prepare binders and keep all paperwork you receive (e.g., camera report sheets) and all the logs you have created neatly filed and labeled. Place the current working script into the editor's binder and label it in much the same way as you would for a television show. When you receive the typed transcriptions of the interviews, place them all in a huge binder and put tabs on the side with each interviewee's name so you can find the interviews easily. This binder is gold and will often be consulted by the director–editor during editing when he looks for some other relevant bite he would like to add to the cut to help the story. Keep all the paperwork that you receive from the stock houses or still libraries in the assistant's binder, as well as copies of scripts as they are worked on. Scripts in documentaries are rewritten many times and will change with each cut as narration is refined and polished. Keep your editor's binder up to date with each and every rewrite.

7.3 Create a Radio Cut

If your show is being created for a network, the first script written will generally be sent to network producers for approval. The assistant will use this first script (paper cut) as a guide to start pulling the interview sound bites to create a spine for the show.

Create a bin in the project labeled Interviews. Go through all the interview material that was shot, find the scripted bites on the tapes or hard drive (using timecode and transcriptions as a guide), and digitize or import them into the project and into the Interviews bin. Then label them with the interviewee's name, and for ease of reference write the first and last three words of the interview bite next to the clip that corresponds to the script (e.g., Stern, Max: "I wish he had … and then he left"). Go through the whole script and digitize all the bites. It is a good idea to keep all the interview bites of one person together and keep all your characters listed alphabetically in the bin for easy reference.

Often the assistant will do a rough read of the narration in the script and record it into the computer to be used as a guide track or temp narration track. The pace needs to be steady and not too fast. If you are unable to deliver a reasonable read, we suggest you find someone else in post who will be happy to read for you.

Record his voice as the temp track. The final narration, with the designated professional voice, will generally be recorded when the show is locked. Create a VO bin (or Temp Narration bin), and digitize the reading into the bin.

Create a Cuts bin and make a new sequence called the radio cut. By following the script, you will assemble the radio cut, intercutting the guide narration (on track 3) with the interview bites (production sound on tracks 1 and 2), usually leaving 1 second of black between the bite and the narration. The radio cut is the first cut that the editor will receive in his Cuts bin, and he will begin working on the show with this spine or assembly. As in episodic television, the assistant will be responsible for formatting the acts with commercial breaks, cutting in main titles, end credit cards, and following many of the standard procedures that were previously described for television programming. Make sure you create all the banners for shot missing, re-creation to come, end titles, etc. and place them in the Banners bin for your editor.

Here is an example of a first draft script that the assistant will follow to pull the bites, record the guide narration, and create a radio cut. Note that sometimes the writer will pull a long bite but will only use parts of the statement and will denote that there have been cuts by using the markings //0//.

Act Two

TC	Video	Audio
	Clear water. Sparkling. Sunlight reflecting off a lake, creek, or river. Something beautiful.	NARRATOR: ONE OF THE MOST PRECIOUS AND THREATENED COMMODITIES AT STAKE IN THIS ARID REGION IS WATER.
	Rain slashing against windows. Rack focus to buildings in Tel Aviv in the background. • Tape 14	NARRATOR: IN A LAND WHERE RAIN IS SPARSE AND WATER RESOURCES FEW, CONSERVATION OF THIS PRECIOUS COMMODITY IS CRUCIAL.
	Interview Jack Frost	Interview Jack Frost Tape 27 (T/C: 00:37:11–00:38:06) The problems of river pollution as well as ground pollution are serious in Israel. We have many, many wells which have been polluted, so the problem of water pollution in Israel is certainly widespread.
	Start CU on bird strutting next to water. All looks well and peaceful. Zoom out. This is the heavily-polluted Yarkon River that flows through Tel Aviv. On either side of the concrete channel, traffic and trains run by. • Tape 35	*Hear at first the call of a gull. Mainly silence and nature sounds. As the camera zooms back, the sounds of traffic and city noise override the natural sound and rise in intensity. (It must shock the senses to discover where we really are … a big city, not the countryside.)*

(Continued)

TC	Video	Audio
		NARRATOR: THIS IS THE YARKON RIVER THAT FLOWS THROUGH THE HEART OF ISRAEL'S BIGGEST CITY, TEL AVIV.
		NARRATOR: NORTH OF THE CITY THE YARKON IS SO POLLUTED THAT MERELY TO SWIM IN ITS TOXIC SLIME WOULD BE LIFE THREATENING. MANY BLAME GOVERNMENT AND PUBLIC SHORTSIGHTEDNESS AND A LACK OF AN ENVIRONMENTAL AGENDA FOR DISASTERS LIKE THIS.
	Interview Sam Waterman	Interview Sam Waterman Tape 12 (T/C: 00:37:18–00:38:34) The rivers of Israel are just open sewage canals. //0// The environmental crisis of Israel is quite serious.

Here is an example of a final script of a locked show ready for recording the final narration:

Raising Baby Jenny
Domestic Version–Final draft
June 19, 2010

Cold open

TC	Video	Audio
	Newborn Jenny	NARRATOR: THIS IS AN AFRICAN LION CUB NAMED JENNY.
	Jenny nurses	NARRATOR: REJECTED BY HER MOTHER AT BIRTH, SHE WAS SAVED BY ZOOKEEPERS AND IS NOW BEING RAISED BY HAND.
	Jenny peeks around corner	NARRATOR: FROM THE START, JENNY IS FEARLESS.
		JACKIE GREEN: She knows no boundaries, she has no limits yet. We haven't found anything she won't do yet.
	Jenny at 2 months	NARRATOR: BECAUSE OF HER EASY-GOING TEMPERAMENT, HER CAREGIVERS REALIZE THAT SHE'S AN IDEAL CANDIDATE FOR A VERY IMPORTANT TASK— ALLOWING PEOPLE TO SEE HER UP CLOSE AND LEARN ABOUT WILDLIFE CONSERVATION.

(Continued)

TC	Video	Audio
	Jackie Green	JACKIE GREEN: We would like her to be able to go to events where she can be an example of why animals are so important in our life.
	Jenny with Amanda	NARRATOR: JENNY WILL BE PREPARED FOR THE ROLE OF WHAT IS KNOWN AS AN ANIMAL AMBASSADOR. BUT AN AFRICAN LION HAS A REPUTATION FOR BEING A DIFFICULT ANIMAL TO DEAL WITH.
		DAVID NIELS: There are so many things that you have to consider. They're incredibly strong and can potentially be very dangerous.
	Jenny flees TV studio Alt: Jenny backstage at African Safari. Jenny growls.	NARRATOR: BUT WITH THE PERSEVERANCE AND DEDICATION OF HER KEEPERS, JENNY EXCEEDS ALL EXPECTATIONS AND SUCCESSFULLY ACCOMPLISHES THE GOALS SET FOR HER …
		NARRATOR: … ON *RAISING JENNY*.
	SHOW TITLES	MUSIC THEME UP FULL

End cold open

7.4 Stock Footage

Stock footage is often an integral part of a documentary. It could be historic footage of World War II, or it could be home footage shot by the family about whom the film is being made. Whatever the origin, it needs to be carefully logged and sources noted. The post supervisor or the producer–writer will usually do the research and view tapes they have ordered from various stock houses. When they have deemed what might be of potential use to the editor in telling the story, they will give you the viewing tapes from the source library to digitize into the project. Keep all the paperwork from the different libraries carefully filed in the binder. The lists contain their library tape numbers, timecodes, and shot descriptions of all the footage they have sent for viewing and selection. Ultimately, you will have to reference back to these logs when the final cut is made, and you have to order the final clean versions of the viewing material to be inserted into the final show.

Digitize the selected library shots into a bin named Stock Footage for your editor. Label each segment you receive with the library source name on it and with a brief description. In this way, it is easy to identify the source by just looking at the time line or clicking back from the time line into the bin.

This footage is only a working copy and will have visible timecode on every frame. When the final cut is locked, you will order up the shots from the library and give exact timecodes, including exact frame counts at the head and at the tail of the timecode numbers. This footage is usually very expensive to purchase, and it is priced by the second, so it is vital that you be infinitely precise when ordering up the final stock.

I edited part of the documentary series *Ancient Mysteries*, hosted by Leonard Nimoy, for the A&E channel. One of the shows, "The Neanderthals," was written and produced by my husband, Lionel Friedberg. The film told the story of the lifestyle of a Neanderthal man who lived more than 100,000 years ago. What footage do you use to illustrate this tale and cover the fascinating narration and interview bites? Exactly, there is no footage! Hence, stock became my greatest friend.

The assistant had done a great job digitizing endless stock footage that had been collected from stock houses around the world, such as museum exhibitions and robotic Neanderthal figures, archaeological digs in France, worldwide locations where Neanderthals had roamed, etc. In the end, the show looked great, but the cost of all the footage was prohibitive. Each supplier puts their own value on their footage and sets up their own pricing per second or per shot. I approached our production office about shooting some suggestive re-creations, but they were loath to spend money on shooting any footage. Eventually, the assistant editor went through tapes of other stock, finding cheaper footage to match what I had used. His resourceful persistence helped me cut the stock cost by a third. The compromise between cost and aesthetic choices is an eternal battle fought in the documentarian's editing room. The show was extremely well-received. The lessons to be learned here are when given the opportunity, **shine** as a creative partner for your editor, contribute creative suggestions when called upon, and strive for aesthetic excellence. If you can assist your editor in this way, it will help promote you to the cherished seat with lightning speed.

—df

When the show is locked and the final replacement footage from the library is received, you must match and replace the working print that is in the cut with the new, clean version from the stock house. The new shots must match up perfectly—to the frame—to the working copy. Because the editor has probably gone to great pains to select exactly the right shots and has more than likely added SFX and MX to sync with the footage, you must cut in the footage correctly. If there is a problem and the new footage you receive does not match the editor's cut, you have to inform him immediately. Cut in the replacement footage on the track above the old footage, and double-check that it is accurate and matches perfectly frame by frame. Triple-check your work by running the new footage with the soundtrack. You do not want to begin the online with a mismatch of stock footage!

7.5 Stills

Another very important element often used in creating a documentary story is the use of stills and old photographs. These are often bought from various libraries that specialize in licensing images. Today, many of these are emailed as JPEGs, TIFs, or PNGs and can be imported directly into the project. Often the editor will create moves on these stills using his program tools. These can be used as final images, but on higher-budget shows, the post producer will probably order hard copies of the stills and shoot various moves on a rostrum camera for more accuracy and polish. This is a motion control camera that is positioned over a tabletop that enables the operator to perfectly control his camera moves over images that are placed on this tabletop. The motion control enables smooth and carefully paced pans, tilts, zooms, and even multiple moves over the smallest of pictures. This offers the editor a greater choice of how to play his still image for the best emotional or storytelling effect.

Often the temp stills that the editor has used for cutting and viewing purposes will have to be replaced with the newly shot stills of better quality created with the rostrum camera. Match the new camera moves exactly to replace the temp shots. If there is a problem, always inform your editor.

While editing a documentary series, *A History of Sex*, produced for the History Channel, stills became a major element in the visual illustration of historic stories. I had to be resourceful in manipulating these photographs so that R-rated activity was never shown in the film; it was only suggested.

How to make painted sex imagery on a Grecian urn appear tasteful was a challenge! Finally, when all these barriers were overcome and great shows were locked, the producers bemoaned the fact that we were over budget. We were instructed to minimize the number of stills used. Nothing can be more frustrating for an editor than having to start the reverse engineering process of your finely honed work due to budgetary constraints. The assistant jumped into the reconstructing process, and with paper and pencil in hand, together we reviewed the film. We planned where we could lose shots and how we could use images more than once in a different configuration. There is usually no cost if you use the same image more than once in the same show. We devised new moves on previously used stills, and my assistant sent the lists to the rostrum operator for further shooting. We were able to disguise the fact that these images were already in the show, and with layering of B roll, I was able to give a whole new feel to the same image. Thanks to the help of the assistant, we were able to remedy the budgetary problems and still keep the inherent integrity of the visuals. This series has been one of the most successful offerings on the History Channel, with many spin-offs following since its initial airing in the late 1990s.

—df

Stills, like stock footage, come with fairly high prices if they are obtained from outside libraries. Keep all the paperwork with reference to the used stills and their source for the postproduction supervisor. All of this information is vital for licensing the material.

7.6 Titling

One feature that is important in documentaries is the use of titles or lower thirds. These are the names and titles of the interviewees. When the show is locked, an important job is to make sure that there is a complete list of all the people in the show who require lower-third identifications. Check with your post producer to be sure you have the correct spellings of their names and the final identification that is to be used. Using the timecode of the formatted show, create a list of all the lower thirds and the precise minute, second, and frame count where they should fade up and fade down as denoted on the cut. This list will be used if the titles are to be re-created in a postproduction titling facility. Time is money, and anything you can do to help speed up the process and time spent in the titling facility will make you **shine**.

7.7 Use of SFX and MX

In the documentary world, the use of SFX and MX is utilized in much the same way as with all other genres. However, because of the normally lower budgets of documentaries, producers will often negotiate great licensing deals with music libraries and will rely more on needle drops for the dramatic underscoring of their show. Sometimes needle drops are used only as a guide for the composer, who will come aboard and spot and score the film when it is locked.

If a library is to be used for either permanent scoring or temping, you must set up different bins and group the music into categories; for example, dramatic, tension, classical, stings, lyrical, ethnic or world, etc. This facilitates the search for the editor when he is hunting for a specific style or mood of music to enhance the scene.

A good SFX library is also necessary. Create bins in the project and organize the sound effects alphabetically so the editor can scroll through the lists and find what he needs quickly. Offer to help lay in SFX when needed.

7.8 Finishing the Documentary

The routine of assembling the film, formatting, outputting, and finishing the show follows many of the same rules as dramatic shows. The final narration will be recorded to time to make sure the narration readings are as close as possible to the temp VO. The new narration is laid in to replace the temp exactly to the frame. Sometimes, because of variants in reads, slight visual adjustments will have to be made by the editor to accommodate the new narrator. Often on documentaries, the sound is mixed on ProTools or a similar system. One of the assistant's jobs, besides preparing for the online, is to convert all the final cleaned soundtracks to OMF files to give to the sound mixer. As in other genres, a QuickTime on a DVD or a chase cassette of the locked show is generated, which will be used for visual reference during the online.

The documentary world is very often the low-budget end of the editing venues, but on a personal level, it can certainly offer rewarding experiences. The subject matter embraces the world as your canvas—from history to science, culture to religion, and natural history to space exploration. Documentaries enrich your personal perspective and understanding of life on this planet and beyond.

Chapter 8

Assisting Protocols for Reality Shows

As there are different formats and methods for making documentaries, each reality show also has its own personality and style. Every production house will create its own procedures for shooting and posting its shows. Reality television relies on capturing events as they happen with multiple cameras rolling simultaneously. What all productions have in common is usually hours of footage providing great coverage and multiple choices for the editor. Again, meticulous organization of material and group clipping of multicam setups becomes essential. Most production companies use some shared editing system so that all the editors and assistants have access to the same media whether they are posting on Avid or FCP. Similarly, each house finishes a project differently. Some have in-house online systems, and some use outside post houses to online and title and color correct. But once again, there is a commonality in the work flow and in taking a show from dailies to online.

One of the great advantages of getting a job as an assistant on a reality show is that they usually staff with nonunion personnel. It is a good place for assistants to secure entry-level jobs and learn the business. Many shows have multiple—sometimes seven or more—editors and several assistants prepping the work for editing. You will most likely share the workload with other assistants and could well land the night or graveyard shift. Be prepared!

The assistants all prepare the footage, group the multicam shots, organize the B roll, create the GFX, and organize SFX and MX; they format the shows and then prepare and do the outputs when the show is locked. The assistant could also be the online assistant if the online is done in-house. On a large show, you will work long hours with probably no overtime. But remember, when you start a task, you must finish it before going home. Do not leave an output or work half done.

> **TIP**
>
> Work past your shift when you need to. This is one of the ways to impress your producers and **shine**.

Some work flow suggestions for assisting on reality shows, using the Avid DX Nitris, follow.

DOI: 10.1016/B978-0-240-81398-1.00008-0

8.1 Dailies

One of the first tasks for the assistant is to load all the dailies into the system. Most shows manage the media on an Avid Unity (or SAN; XSAN if you are on FCP). The assistants partition the drive space for projects, renders, media, VO, music, and OMF. It's best to keep each unity partition at 400 GB or less. When digitizing, if you reach 400 GB on one drive partition, you should make a new media partition, e.g., MEDIA_01, MEDIA_02, etc. Avid does not like dashes, symbols, or spaces, so it's best to use underscores or no spaces at all.

8.2 Basic Management

To keep the Unity functioning at its best, on Avid there is a defragmenting operation called Optimization. The unity drives organize the media to be continuous and occupy the fastest part of the disks. Always optimize after digitizing large amounts of film or purging media. This is done in the Avid Unity Administration Tool. The assistant does not need to perform this function on FCP because it optimizes automatically.

8.3 Work Space Synchronization

Unity allows users to protect drives, or what Avid calls mirroring. When enabling or disabling protection if a work space already contains data, assistants synchronize to make sure all files truly have a mirrored copy. In the Avid Unity Administration Tool, two small pieces of paper appear near the work space icon, which indicates synchronization is needed. This usually happens after changing work space protection. Adding protection to a work space will require double the disk space (i.e., a 250 GB work space requires 500 GB of disk space). Disabling protection and then synchronizing a 250 GB work space will free up 250 GB.

8.4 Offline and Online Management

Media drives for offline and online should be kept separate so that the media formats are not mixed. When editing a show in SD 30i NTSC, 10:1 m, but finishing in HD 1080i/59.94, DNxHD 220, have separate media drives and project drives on the Unity.

To save drive space, 10:1 m is the (low) resolution recommended for offline editing. Full resolution is 1:1, so 10:1 is 1/10 the resolution of the full-quality picture, which means you can digitize 10 times the amount of footage at 10:1 m than at 1:1, and it would use equal drive space. It is useful to offline edit at a lower resolution because you can fit a lot more footage on the Unity drives. The *m* in 10:1 m refers to multicam, and in older versions of Avid you needed to digitize with an m resolution to make grouping possible. With the newer versions of Avid, grouping is no longer restricted to the m resolutions.

It's best to not even give the offline editors Unity login access to the online drives, so they don't have to worry about rendering to the wrong drive. On the same note, creating a separate login to the Unity for the online editor and only giving him access to the online media, project, and renders ensures he won't render HD media to the SD drives.

8.5 Digitizing and Organizing Dailies

To digitize a large amount of footage for offline editing, using 10:1 m or 15:1 s will take up less space than higher resolutions. The designation 15:1 s means the media is 1/15 the resolution of the original media, and *s* stands for single field. Both of these resolutions can be group clipped on the Avid DX Nitris. Older versions of Avid, such as Meridian, needed the media to be m, or multicam, to be groupable. This is not an issue with the newer versions of Avid. Digitize footage from the deck being used (e.g., XDCAM deck), targeting one of the media drives on the unity. Some shows digitize in one video track, four audio tracks, and the timecode from the tape. Media is coming in at 10:1 m. The bin, file name, and tape name in Avid should all be the same as the tape name that production gave to the tape so that there is no confusion when looking for or sorting footage. Under Settings in the Project window, and then under Capture Settings, always make sure Capture Through Timecode Breaks is selected so that Avid knows to continue capturing even if there happens to be timecode breaks on the tape. Do a custom preroll of 1 second so that the Avid does not default to 4 seconds. If the editing machine prerolls for 4 seconds, you could end up losing a few seconds of a scene on the top of each clip.

Some reality shows have each episode in its own separate Avid project, all located on the Projects_Users partition on the unity. There is a separate AssistProject that contains all footage and everything that the other projects contain so that the assistant editor can easily switch between episodes if necessary. When there is enough footage to begin organizing, sync the dailies if necessary (sometimes the audio is recorded right onto the tape and not to a separate audio recording device), and then group the footage that can be grouped.

Grouping can go pretty fast if the production jam-synched the cameras on set frequently and the timecodes of each camera angle match up perfectly. Sometimes production jam-syncs the cameras only once before starting to shoot, and by the afternoon they have drifted several frames out of sync. The assistant will need to check each group clip now for sync. It is still groupable, it just takes the assistant a little more time to adjust the sync for the group clip.

...Step 1: Stacking

Combine all footage into one long sequence, or create a *sync map*, as some people call it. In other venues it is called a *kem roll*. Usually do one sequence for each shooting day. The master timecode of the sequence corresponds to the timecode of the cameras. You can do this by changing the start timecode of the sequence in the Avid to match the first clip's start timecode. Also, make sure your sequence timecode is set to match whatever the cameras were shooting—drop frame or nondrop frame. The start timecode of the sequence can be changed in the bin by typing the correct timecode into the Start column in the bin or by clicking on the record monitor and then select Get Sequence Info from the File menu and type the correct timecode into the window that pops up. The best way to build the sequence is to lay in the first and last clips of the day. Then add filler between the two until the sequence is long enough to go from the timecode of the first clip to the timecode of the last clip. After this is done, just type the timecode of the next clip into the record monitor, the cursor will jump to the correct place, and then put the clips in the sequence. If the bin is sorted by timecode, then by tape name, it seems to go faster because they are in the correct order. Keep each camera on a separate video track (V1 for cam A, V2 for cam B, etc.). When you have laid in all of the clips from that day into the sequence, you will have one long sequence that, if played in realtime from the beginning, will exactly re-create the shooting day.

...Step 2: Overlapping Clips

When all the footage is in a sequence, it's easy to see what you need to group. Any time there are overlapping clips, more than one camera was shooting at the same time. That is what will need to be grouped together.

...Step 3: Check for Timecode Drift

Pick a few points throughout the sequence and play the audio from one camera with the video from another to see if they match up. If audio was only recorded on one camera, check for sync on the video side and look for a distinctive frame of video that will be easy to tell if it is the same on each camera (e.g., a blink, hand clap, or something to that effect).

...Step 4: Synching Each Camera to the Base Camera on V1

There might be some timecode drift, and if there is, the footage needs to be adjusted and put in sync. When adjusting, it's important to not move any video that's on V1 because that is the base camera. Slip what needs to be slipped, putting things into sync. Audio waveforms are sometimes a useful tool to slip things back into sync.

...Step 5: Set Auxiliary TC for the Base Camera

Under the Bin menu, under Headings, the assistant editor should click AUX TC to display that column in the bin. For the base camera on V1, copy the Start Timecode into the AUX TC column. This is because you did not shift the base camera around, so its AUX TC and Start TC will be the same.

...Step 6: Adjust the Aux TC for the Rest of the Cameras

Starting with track V2, because V1 is the base camera, step through the edits of the sequence using the fast-forward button. Enter the sequence master timecode of the first frame of each clip into the corresponding Auxiliary TC column for that clip. The TC will differ from the Start TC of the clip only if it is one of the clips that you had to slip for sync reasons.

...Step 7: Add Edits at Every Place on the Sequence Where a Clip Starts or Stops

Make sure all of the tracks in the sequence are highlighted, and put the cursor on the first frame of any camera that drops out or comes in. Do an Add Edit at each point throughout the entire part of the sequence that needs to be grouped. The edit should go through all of the tracks. This will divide all of your clips into smaller pieces, and each of the smaller pieces is the same duration so they can be grouped together.

...Step 8: Creating the Subclips from the Sequence

After all the add edits are done, these smaller pieces need to be *subclipped* back out to group. The easiest way to do this is by setting keyboard shortcuts for commands 1 through 7 on the keyboard (e.g., they could be F1 through F7 at the top of the keyboard). When all the subclips are created, you will have a bin of hundreds of subclips. The correct auxiliary timecode for each subclip should have transferred from its original master clip.

...Step 9: Create the Multigroup by Auxiliary TC

Sort the bin by tape name and then by Auxiliary TC. Select all of the subclips, go to the Bin menu, and click Multigroup. A window pops up asking what to group by. Select Auxiliary TC. Avid will create a bunch of groups and one main multigroup. Scroll through the multigroup to make sure everything looks right and everything is in sync.

8.6 Project Organization

In each episode's project, the following folders are included. The episode's current *showbuild* is kept at the root level of the project in a bin called 101_Showbuild (for episode 101). There is a folder at the top of each project called 00_Old_Showbuilds in which you can put all old cuts of the showbuilds for the editors to reference if needed. After that, the following folders are in each episode's project:

- Source tapes folder: In the project, organize the source tapes by date so the editors have access to all the raw footage if they need it.
- Cast folder: This folder is all of the footage by cast member, and then by date, including all grouped footage for each cast member and a sequence for each shooting day for the cast member.
- Interview (intv) folder: This folder has a bin for each cast member. Within that bin is each grouped clip, organized by the date of each interview for that cast member.
- Editors folder: Each editor has a folder within this folder to work from, and this is where they keep their current cuts, work bins, render bins, etc.
- B roll folder: All B roll is organized into as many places as it fits, so that if one editor is looking under Car Footage and one editor is looking under Cast Member, they can both find what they are looking for. Organize the B roll by cast member, driving shots (by each different car), day and night shots, time lapses, and exteriors of city. All B roll is logged in the Name column in the bin. Here is an example of a clip name: EXT WS HIGH ANGLE NIGHT FREEWAY, BUSY, CARS DRIVING.
- Graphics (grfx) folder: Put any templates for graphics that the editors might need in here. This includes an example of the correct subtitles so the editors know what font and what size font to use for anything they need to subtitle. Also in here are the lower thirds for each character, the coming up graphic, and the time stamps that are often used. For example, each scene could be opened with a time stamp of an intersection where the scene takes place and the time of the scene. If these are created in Avid, create them and add the music that is agreed upon. Make sure the graphic is the correct duration so all the editor needs to do is copy it and change the time, if necessary. If it is a graphic you have from a source outside of Avid, import the graphic with the correct specifications (alpha channel, pixel shape, etc.) and cut it into a sequence with the correct music. Label it so the editor can find it, see how it looks in a cut, and

copy it to use it easily. Always include in the bin name if the graphic is final or temp so the editor knows what he is dealing with (e.g., COMING_UP_GFX_**FINAL** or TIME_STAMP_GFX_**TEMP**).

- Music folder: The company hired to do the music might give you a music library to use. If all of it is cleared, you can air it. Import the library to the Music work space on the Unity. All music is assigned a color. It is organized into folders by genre (e.g., drama, quirky, western, rock, electronic, etc.). Put the theme music for the show in a bin at the root level of the Music folder, and in the label indicate if it is final or temp, such as THEME_MUSIC_MIXED_**FINAL** or THEME_MUSIC_**TEMP**_V1_0714.

- SFX folder: All SFX are assigned a different color. Often the SFX comes from the music company and from the mix house. Import all SFX and organize them logically. They are organized into bins, like sirens, cell phones, ambience, etc. They will probably already be cleared to use and to air as is. If they are not cleared, it is helpful to color them differently so that they are easily found in the cuts. If they are not cleared SFX, when prepping for the mix they have to be separated out and replaced.

- VO folder: This is the folder that all VO goes into. If the editor has to record temp VO for the episode himself, make sure he has a VO work space on the Unity that he has write access to so he can record easily. Also, any VO done out of house by the professional voice-over artist will be imported and located here for the editor. Be sure to label if the VO is temp or final in the file name, such as JOHN_DOE_ TEASE_VO_TEMP_0815 (John Doe is the name of the VO artist, and 0815 is the date).

- Outputs folder: Put a copy of each completed output of the episode in this folder. An example of a bin that contains the output is EP_101_RC_OP_0814, which indicates episode 101, rough cut output, and the date. It is labeled like this so that when the notes come back, if they reference specific timecodes from the output, the editor can easily go to the output sequence and find what the note is referring to.

- Assistworks folder: This is a folder where all your work for the episode and the other assistants' work is placed so it is out of the editors' way. Always ask each editor if there is a certain way he prefers B roll to be organized or if he would like the project to be organized differently. That way, everything is organized to his liking, and everyone is happy.

8.7 Outputs

An assist bay could have an HDV deck, XDCAM deck, Digital Betacam deck, and DVD recorder. The online bay could have an HDCAM-SR deck. Some shows don't have any decks in the bays and instead have a machine room in which all of the decks are located and can be patched. In the assist bay there is often a router and several patch bays that allow you to choose which deck is going into the Avid or which deck the Avid is going out to.

8.8 Things to Check Before Outputting a QT or DVD

The sequence needs to be drop frame, if that is what you are working in. Tease tags out of the act to commercial are usually exactly 3 seconds, and there are exactly 5 seconds of black between acts. In some shows, no act can be shorter than 4 minutes, and it is preferable that the first act is longer than 8 minutes and the last act is longer than 5 minutes. Each show and network has different specifications. It is important to be aware of your show's specs and check all of this before output.

Always make sure you have the clip color of your sequence set to offline so that if any media is offline in the sequence you can find it easily because it shows up in red. You can re-create any title media that is offline, which perhaps was saved to a local C drive by accident, by setting an in-point and out-point around the offline media and going to the Clip menu. Select Re-create Title Media. You can add a slate, stating the show name, episode number, which cut it is (rough cut 1, fine cut 2), TRT, and the date. The slate goes on the sequence from 00;59;50;00 to 00;59;55;00, then 5 seconds of black, then the picture starts at 01;00;00;00. Again, this varies from network to network. For a show that is 16 × 9, you may need to add a 16:9 reformat letterbox onto the sequence if you are outputting to an SD 4 × 3 format.

You will also want to add visible TC in the middle top of the screen, with the background of the timecode slightly opaque. (DVD and QT outputs are SD, so you use the reformat 16:9 letterbox so that the show is the correct aspect ratio on an SD DVD and when outputting a 4 × 3 QT from an SD 30i NTSC project. The footage in Avid will be 16:9, if it was shot that way, which it would have been if you are finishing HD.) Render the sequence. (Not the TC generator or the 16:9 letterbox because these things show up on playback and in QTs without rendering. This will save time.)

8.9 QuickTimes

You can post cuts on your network's FTP site for producers and networks to view, as well as send them DVDs. There might be file size restrictions for the FTP site (400 MB), so make various QT tests using different settings to see what would be best. Some workable settings are shown in Figures 8.1 through 8.3.

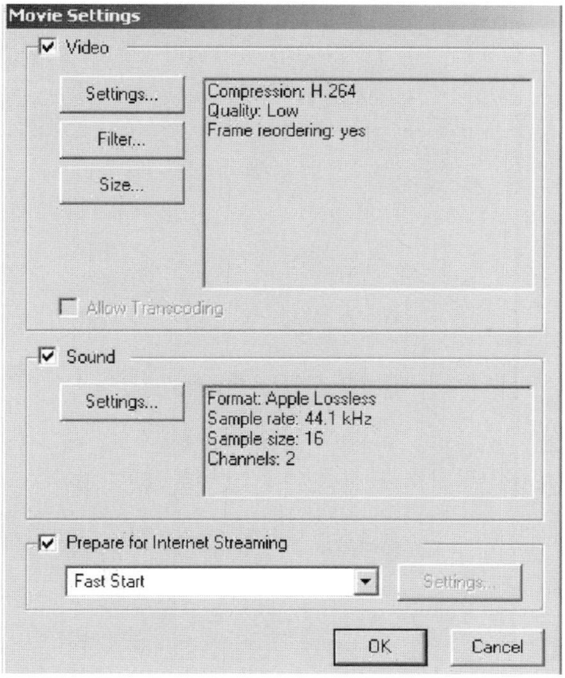

Figure 8.1 *Movie settings*

117

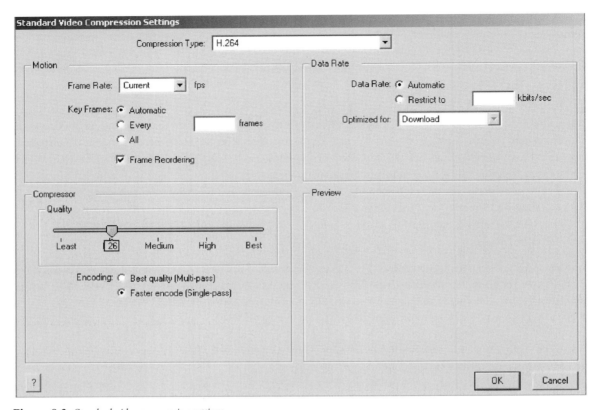

Figure 8.2 *Standard video compression settings*

Figure 8.3 *Sound settings*

For shows whose cuts vary between 44 and 49 minutes, these settings give a QT that is right around 380–390 MB, which is perfect for uploading to a network FTP.

8.10 DVD Outputs

Do all the same checks that are listed in the QT section. When the sequence is ready, patch the Avid to the DVD recorder, and the DVD recorder to the monitor, so you can watch what's going onto the DVD. Check levels going out of the Avid to the DVD recorder on a VCR that can be attached to the DVD recorder. This will show the audio levels. Adjust the audio levels on your Mackie (or comparable machine), and then hit record on the DVD recorder, play on the Avid sequence, and watch the output. After it is done, stop recording and finalize the DVD. QC the DVD and check both the sound and picture at the beginning, middle, and end of the episode. Then duplicate it in the DVD duplicator. Be sure to QC the duplicates as well.

8.11 Locking

Check the same things that you checked before DVD outputs (e.g., check to see if the sequence is drop frame). Tease tags out of the act to commercial specs. These numbers vary according to the show. The first frame of picture of the show is at 01;00;00;00. The entire show (six acts), for example, could be exactly 43;55 (this varies from network to network).

Some networks or shows will require that an extra scene be delivered with each episode to be used if the show airs internationally because the show length requirements may be longer in other countries. If there is an extra international scene, make sure that it is to the proper time as well. It will be located at the end of the episode sequence after several seconds of black, with its own slate.

8.12 Up-Rezzing

It is necessary to up-rez your show when onlining in-house because the offline edit is usually at a low resolution to save drive space. When up-rezzing, prep the sequence so that you only recapture the media used in the cut (including a defined amount of handles on each clip; 60 frame handles is a good reference). You do not want to up-rez any more media than needed. High-resolution media will take up a lot of space on your Unity. It is best to give the online

> **DEFINITION**
>
> Up-rezzing is taking the offline locked cut and recapturing the media at a higher resolution. This is the format required for finishing and delivering the show.

editors an up-rezzed reference picture because the image is clearer and therefore easier to read lips and check sync. An up-rezzed D-Beta may be requested for an SD show.

It is good to know that if this show were onlining out of house, instead of up-rezzing from a copy of the sequence, you would have to generate an EDL to give to the online house. (There are various forms of EDLs—C-sort and A-sort—and it all depends on the specifications that the online house gives you.)

8.13 Audio for OMF

Duplicate the locked sequence and copy it into a bin called EP101_LOCK_FOR_AUDIO. Delete all video from this sequence, leaving audio only. Then separate all of the audio tracks, splitting up production audio, music, VO, and SFX. Avid Nitris can play only 16 tracks of audio at a time, but when prepping for an OMF, the audio can spread to as many tracks as needed. Avid allows 24 tracks of audio to be in a sequence, even though only 16 will play at once. Try to get all of the production audio to tracks 1–4, SFX onto tracks 5–10, music onto tracks 11–18, and VO onto tracks 19–20. Sometimes production needs tracks 1–6, so SFX will not start until track 7, and so on. The goal is to use the least amount of tracks possible but not to mix production, SFX, or MX onto any one track of audio. Sometimes mix houses will like VO on the track below production instead of at the bottom. Many of these details may vary. It is important to be aware of the delivery requirements and prep everything as it is requested.

When the audio tracks are all organized, the audio sequence needs to be consolidated onto the Unity partition called OMF. This is because when the OMF is created, it is only taking media from what is needed. If it takes media from the source footage audio, usually the OMF ends up being a much bigger file than needed.

When the consolidation is done, unmount all Unity drives except for the project drive that has the assist project you are working in and the OMF drive. After all of these drives unmount, make sure the sequence can still read the audio from the OMF drive and that all are still online. Then you are ready to create the OMF. OMFs cannot be larger than 2 GB. For a 44-minute show, it can often be close to 2 GB. To ensure the file is not too big, you can do an OMF of each act separately. AAFs export more smoothly from Avid than OMFs. Basically, OMF is the old standard, and AAF is becoming the new standard. Use the settings shown in Figures 8.4 and 8.5 in the OMF window.

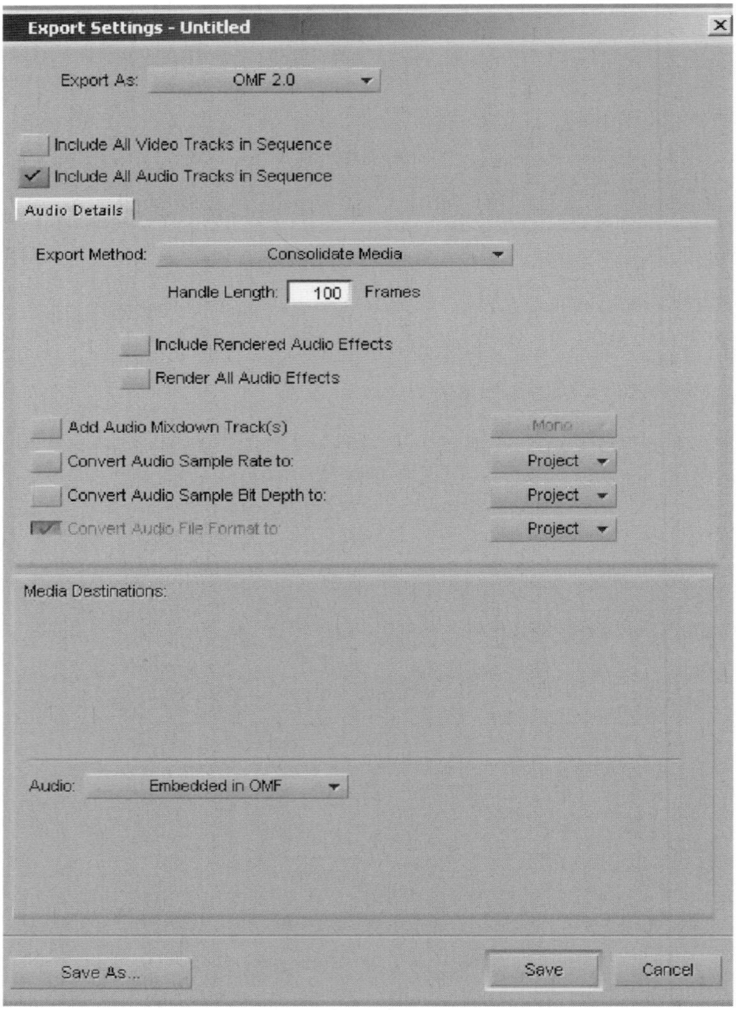

Figure 8.4 *Settings for OMF*

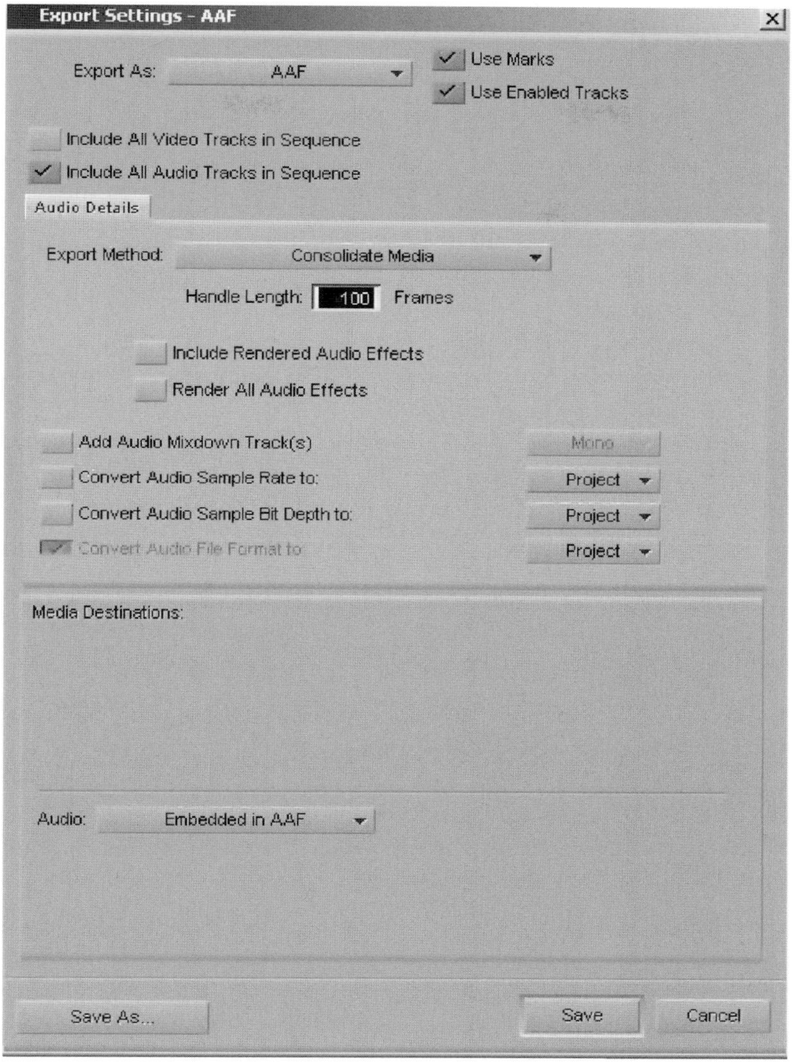

Figure 8.5 *Settings for AAF*

Set the file name to be the episode number and the act it is in, click Save, and it will export to the OMF (or AAF). Continue this process until you have done all the acts. When all of the acts are complete, burn a single-layer data DVD of all the OMFs to give to the mixing house. Along with the OMFs, the mixer needs a reference picture to mix to. If it is a QT, it needs visible timecode. It is good to give a reference HDCAM-SR tape of the up-rezzed, locked cut for an HD show.

8.14 Prepping for Online

There are a few more steps to take to prep for online. You need to organize the video tracks for the online editor. Every online editor likes things organized a bit differently, so make sure you ask how he would like things to be set up so it is all ready to go when online begins. One example is as follows:

- V1: All video except for interview footage.
- V2: Left empty for the online editor in case he needs it for blurs, FX, transitions, etc.
- V3: All interview footage. The online editor color corrects these differently from the rest of the footage, so he likes it all on its own track.
- V4: All subtitles. These subtitles need to be re-created in DNxHD 220 when you are in online. You will subtitle people who are not recorded well. For example, it is sometimes hard to hear everyone in intense cop scenes, fight scenes, or whispering scenes.
- V5: All lower thirds and graphics (GFX). These are GFX created out of house, so you just need to cut in the HD versions to replace the SD versions.
- V6: Time stamps that begin each act. These are Avid titles, so you need to re-create them in DNxHD 220 for online.

Marry the audio mixdown you did to the sequence, and put the offline video mixdown on V7 so that the online editor has the reference he needs. This sequence is then ready for the online editor, and you can use a copy of this sequence to output to HDCAM-SR for the mix house reference tape.

8.15 Assisting on FCP in Reality Television

Many reality shows today edit with FCP (Final Cut Pro), and even though the work flow remains basically the same as the Avid, the procedures for the system will differ and possibly entail another set of technical skills. A scenario for an FCP show could be as follows.

After a shoot, the production hands over XDCAM tapes to the assistants, who will then digitize the media through the Sony XDCAM decks using XDCAM Transfer. As soon as the assistant editors receive the tapes, they will name and number them. This is a critical convention. If this step were not performed, every tape would be named Untitled. Tape names are organized by the following:

- Shoot date: 0618
- Camera and tape number: 01
- If using the B camera: B01
- Show's two-letter initials: TS ("The Surprise")

This information would then be written on the tape as 0618B01TS.

For interview tapes, the same process is used, but the initials of the cast members are added to the end. For example, if the tape contains the actor John Doe, the initials JD would be added, and the tape would be labeled 0618A01TS-JD. If using the B camera, it would be denoted as 0618B01TS-JD.

8.16 Importing and Organizing the Project

When the tape is renamed, select all the clips in XDCAM Transfer (each clip represents each time the digital camera captured footage) and click Import. Assume the video format production shoot is MPEG HD, bit rate of 50 Mbps, frame rate of 59.94, 16 × 9 aspect ratio, and a frame size of 1920 × 1080.

In Figure 8.6, the XDCAM is importing the selected footage locally.

When the footage is imported locally, it is dragged over to the SAN (or XSAN, FCP's version of the Unity). Each holds 23 GB of information. It takes a long time to import 23 GB locally and to transfer the media to the server. Coverage from a daily shoot can average anywhere from 2 to 12 hours of footage on 10–30 tapes a day. These tapes could include reality footage from multiple cameras to interviews of the cast members. Handling this work flow on a daily basis can require four decks running with two assistants on two computers.

Figure 8.6 *XDCAM importing selected footage*

When the footage is transferred to the SAN at full-res (resolution), it then has to be compressed to an offline file size capable of being handled in FCP. The Cluster is a system used through Compressor over the SAN. It uses processing power from each computer that is connected to it. This is the system used to compress the files. It runs large processing tasks, such as compressing 23 GB full-res footage to 1 GB low-res footage. However, using the cluster during the day slows down the processing power and speed of each individual computer that is connected to the SAN. One tape being compressed over the cluster works well, but when you have 20-plus tapes to compress, it slows down your editor's computer and does not allow him to keep working. Because of this, digitizing, transferring, and compressing footage is usually done during the lead assistant's shift (probably at night). When the second assistant arrives, the lead assistant will hand over the remaining undigitized tapes to be organized into multiclips (group clips in Avid) and into B roll.

The assistant editor organizes the footage on the SAN starting in two ways: media then projects. Media is dailies, graphics, audio, QuickTimes, and photos. This raw material should not be altered in any way. The material that can be altered is placed in the Projects folder on the SAN. This includes multiclip projects, B roll, transcriptions, episode projects, and editor backup projects (see Figures 8.7 and 8.8).

While in dailies, the assistant editor has three main jobs: organize multiclips, B roll, and prep for interview transcriptions.

8.17 Multiclips

To organize the multiclips, the assistant editor should create a new project. Label it with the show's initials, the date, "Groups," and then the assistant's initials. This way everyone knows who set up which project. Create three folders: media, multiclips, and sequences (see Figure 8.9).

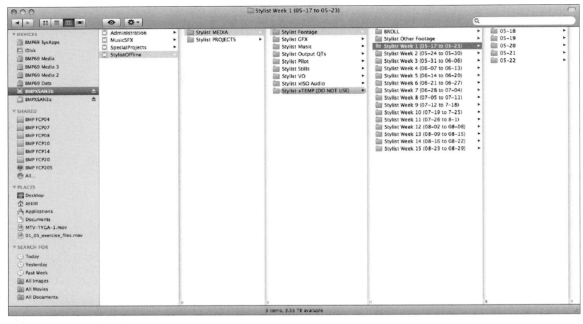

Figure 8.7 *Media folders* These media folders are not to be altered

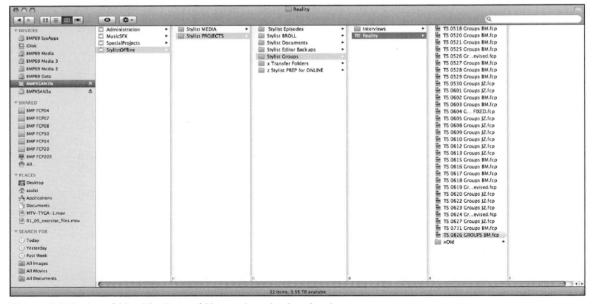

Figure 8.8 *Projects folders* The Projects folders can be updated or altered

From there, drag all the dailies into media. Then start with camera A footage, comparing it to cameras B, C, D, and E; media start; and media end. Any timecodes that overlap can be given a color to stand out (orange is the first color available in FCP). (There is software that can vastly speed the process of creating multiclips, like PluralEyes from Synthetik Software.) Then select all clips with overlapping TC and create a multiclip sequence. Using that sequence, check to make sure all the clips are in sync and the cameras are jam-synced. To check sync, solo the audio tracks from each camera and listen to make sure there is no echo (reverb sound). If there is an echo in the audio, you have to

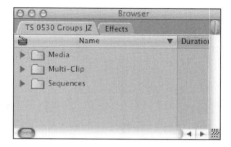

Figure 8.9 *Browser*

slip an individual track to line them up. When they are lined up, set in-points in the sequence on each individual clip at exactly the same point. Then create a multiclip using in-points or timecode (see Figures 8.10, 8.11, and 8.12).

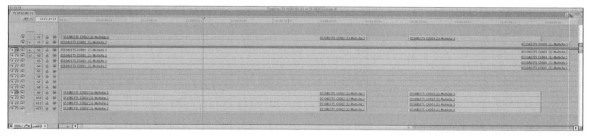

Figure 8.10 *Multiclip sequence*

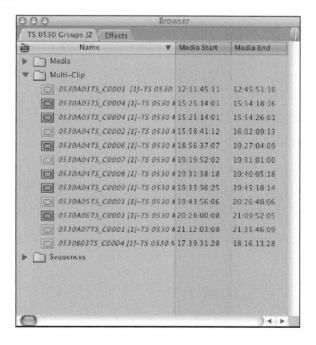

Figure 8.11 *Multiclip bin*

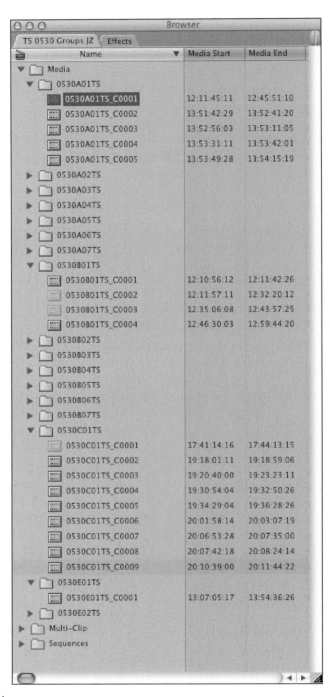

Figure 8.12 *Multiclip folders*

Look for matching or overlapping TC. V1 and V2 have the same TC. Drag the final multiclips (groups) into the proper folder (bin). Place the multiclip in the multiclip folder, and move on to the next set of clips. Color the next set red (next color available) to differentiate between what clips are used.

8.18 B Rolls

When all the dailies are digitized, the assistant sorts the B roll into major categories for the show. A logical method is to break down the B roll into day, dusk, and night shots. From there you can further build folders based on various footage that is covered—aerial shots, city locations, restaurants, cast vehicles and living areas, etc. (see Figures 8.13 and 8.14).

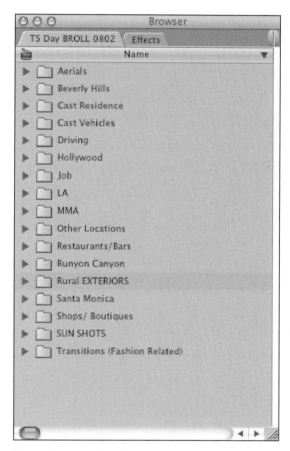

Figure 8.13 *B roll location*

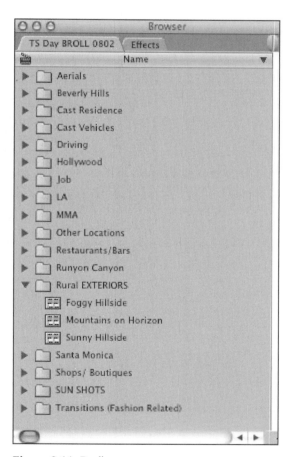

Figure 8.14 *B roll sequences*

It is a good idea for the assistant editor to generate and print a B roll list for production and for the editors so they have a quick reference of what was covered in their notebooks (see Figure 8.15).

BROLL DAY	BROLL DUSK	BROLL NIGHT
Aerials	**Aerials**	**Aerials**
Beverly Hills Aerials	Beverly Hills Aerial Dusk	City Night Aerial
City Aerials	LA Aerials - Dusk	Hollywood Night Aerial
Hollywood Aerials	Sun Aerials	LA Night Aerials
LA Aerials	Traffic Aerial - Dusk	Traffic Night Aerials
LA River Aerial		WB Night Aerial
Landing Aerial	**Beverly Hills**	
Mallibu Aerials	Beverly Hills Hotel & Strt -EXT	**Cast Residence**
Mansion Aerial	Rodeo Dr - EXT	Brett's Apt - EXT
Santa Monica Aerials	Rodeo Dr St Signs - EXT	
Traffic Aerials	Streets/People - EXT	**Cast Vehicles**
	Window Shopping - EXT	Gary's Truck
Cast Residence		
Brett's Apartment - EXT	**Resteraunts/Bars**	**Hollywood**
Brett's Apartment - INT	The Abby - EXT	Hollywood Streets - EXT
Eric's House		Kress - EXT
Gary's House	**Santa Monica**	
Janna's House	Santa Mocia Peer - EXT	**Jobs**
Janna's Neighborhood	Low Tide w/2 Seagulls	Alex Merez - Cemetary Time-lapse
Jen's House - EXT		Coach House-EXT
Julie's Apartment	**SUN SHOTS**	El Rey - EXT
Tara's Apartment	Alex Merez - Cemetary Time-lapse	El Rey - INT
	Mountains on Horizon	Soulja Boy-EXT
Resteraunts/Bars	Sun through Tree	Veronica's @Hight Profile-EXT
Boulevard Lounge - EXT	Sun TIME-LAPSE	
Catherine Malandrino - EXT		**LA**
Corner Cafe - EXT		LA Streets-EXT
Cuvee - EXT		
FABS - EXT		**Resteraunts**
Jack n Jill's Too-EXT		Boulevard Lounge - EXT
Jack n Jill's Too-INT		Lulu's-EXT
Lulu's-EXT		
Magnolia Grille - EXT		**SUN TIME-LAPSE**
Minestraio-EXT		Sun Time-Lapse
Pane Dolce - EXT		
Pane e Vino - EXT		**MOON SHOTS**
Snackbar - EXT		Focus through branches
The Abby - EXT		Moon Tilme-lapse
Beverly Hills		
Beverly Hills StRT/City-EXT		
Expensice Cars - EXT		
Rodeo Drive - EXT		
Rodeo Drive - INT		
Rodeo Drive People - EXT		
Rodeo Drive Street Signs-EXT		
The BLVD - EXT		

Figure 8.15 *B roll list*

8.19 SFX and MX

Many reality shows are given music from the music coordinator. Some of the music is in MP3 files and some is in AIFF. Convert all audio to AIFF before placing it on the SAN. A demo program called Switch converts audio files to the appropriate ones needed, as does iTunes, QuickTime, and Soundtrack Pro. FCP does not support MP3 audio and requires either WAV, AIFF, or SDII files. When the audio is on the SAN, it is then dragged into iTunes on an individual playlist and organized by artist, album and genre. From iTunes, export the playlist labeled by date, and import it to every editor's computer on iTunes. It references all the same media on the SAN. There is a great search feature in iTunes that you can use to look for a particular song or sound effects. When the desired audio is found, right click in iTunes to reveal it in Finder, and the file is shown. That file is then dragged into FCP.

8.20 Transcriptions

To send the filmed interviews to a transcriber, the assistant needs to compress the interview tapes into a small size so they can be uploaded to the website of the transcriber. The compression creates a large timecode stamp as a visual reference and guide. (Adobe also offers automated transcription using special software.) The transcriptions will then be sent back as Word documents with encoded timecode from each interview tape notated in the margin at regular intervals. This allows the easy identification of what was said at what time (see Figure 8.16).

Figure 8.16 *Transcription movie*

8.21 Story Stringout

When the assistant completes the prep of the material, it is passed on to the story editors. They view all the footage, multiclips, and nonmulticlips and look for story points to create the show. FCP is eminently affordable, so every staff member has access to the footage through SAN. The story sequence, or the stringout, is the guideline that the story department assembles from select material. It is the spine of the narrative and includes highlights of the shoot from which the editor will create the film. The show starts here. Some stringout sequences have been known to be more than 2 hours long for a 42-minute show!

On some series, the producers will view all the material and deliver a rough story line on paper. It is the assistant's job to find the footage through the timecode guidelines and create an assembly for the editor to cut (see Figure 8.17).

When the editor has completed his cut, he will hand it over to the assistant editor for an output. The cut time line will consist of many video and audio tracks. Note that V7 will probably contain all titles, lower thirds, and graphics (see Figure 8.18).

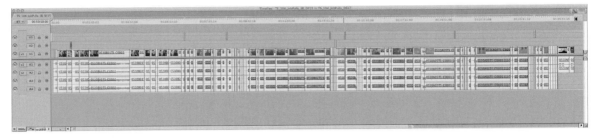

Figure 8.17 *Story stringout The different colors represent alternate multiclips*

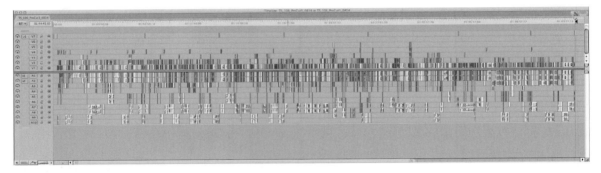

Figure 8.18 *Time line cuts*

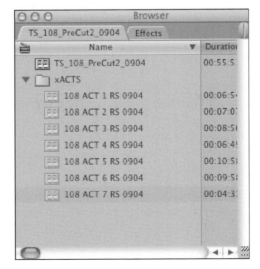

Figure 8.19 *Editor's cuts and the built sequence for an output*

8.22 Output

To complete an output, the assistant will receive the editor's cut either as a full sequence of the show with each act tied together, or he will receive each act as individual sequences. Whichever the form, the assistant will build the final sequence with a 5-second head slate for the show, the episode, the cut, the total run time (TRT), and the date it is shipped. That is followed by 5 seconds of black, and then picture starts at hour 1 (e.g., 1:00:00;00) (see Figure 8.19).

Labeling the cuts with the right information is important. It is equally important to remain consistent when naming projects. Here is some of the vital information that needs to be included:

- Give two initials for the show: TS
- Followed by the episode number: 108

- Which cut it is: PreCut2
- The date: 0904

Also include an underscore between each piece of information to prevent using spaces (e.g., TS_108_ PreCut2_0904). In general, editing systems, FTP sites, and storage systems like the SAN and the Avid Unity don't like file names with spaces.

Each act is timed, and proper title slates are created for the beginning of each act. The sequence is then rendered, and the audio is mixed down to only two tracks, 1L and 2R. When each act is timed (drop frame), the total running time (TRT) is added to the final slate, and the sequence is exported at its current settings (Offline RT HD 29.97) to a QuickTime movie. This QuickTime is then compressed through Compressor to an H.264 QT movie. The Compressor settings compress the QT and adds timecode in the upper right-hand corner. (In FCP 7, the new Share feature simplifies this process. It is automated, runs in the background, and automatically transfers the file to the FTP site of your choice.) The timecode is used as a reference when making notes about changes that need to be made on the show. That H.264 QT is then uploaded to the FTP (file transfer protocol) site. This site has an assigned login name and password for clients, producers, and executives so they can access the cut for viewing.

To create DVDs, another process is required. Because DVD Studio Pro cannot burn H.264 files, the assistant must take the H.264 QT movie and run it though Compressor again and have it create an audio file (AC3) and a video file (M2V). The assistant then drops those two files into DVD Studio Pro to create a DVD. This DVD is then duplicated and mailed to the executives. If the assistant is provided with data DVDs and he has Share (available in FCP7), he will be able to automatically create both an H.264 file for FTP and an SD DVD from a single sequence automatically and in the background. This speeds things up dramatically because he no longer needs to spend time exporting. This is preferable to wasting time and recompressing already compressed footage that creates very low quality visuals.

8.23 Online

When a show is finally locked, the assistant editor must format the sequence and prepare it for online. All reality footage, B roll, and interview backplates go on video tracks 1–3.

Any photos or still images go on V tracks 4–6, and GFX and titles go on V tracks 7–9. Video track 10 is used for slates only. This way you know exactly where each act starts and ends, which makes it easier for timing. To format the audio, the assistant puts all reality audio on audio tracks 1–4, interview or VO goes on tracks 5–6, all SFX (including bleeps for cursing) go on tracks 7–12, and all music

> **DEFINITION**
>
> During an interview process, interviewees are filmed against a green screen. Backgrounds (a forest, the pyramids of Giza, a nightscape), called backplates, can digitally replace the green screen.

goes on tracks 13–16. If there are more video or audio tracks needed, then everything is pushed up. But at *no time* do two different classifications (dialog, FX, MX) rest on the same track. This is done to keep the media organized for online and for the mix.

When the sequence is formatted, add the following:

- Bars and tone for 30 seconds
- 10 seconds of black
- 10 seconds of show slate
- 10 seconds of black

The first frame of footage starts at 1:00:00;00, then add the following:

- 10 seconds of black
- 10 seconds of act slate
- 10 seconds of black
- Start the next act

Now add tail slates for the end credits and dot.com SLATE.

The online editor will handle all main titles, titles, final GFX, and end credits (see Figure 8.20).

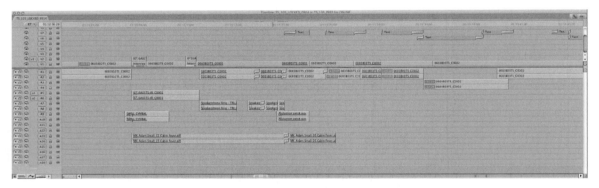

Figure 8.20 *Timeline with soundtracks organized and all video pulled down to V1 and V2*

Due to budgetary reasons, the assistant editor often has to help out in online. Take the offline media and create a batch list from the locked cut. The batch list carries each tape number and timecode needed for each cut. It tells you what media needs to be recaptured at full resolution and relinked to the locked cut. This batch list can now be handed over to the online editor. The assistant puts the required XDCAM tapes from the batch list into the XDCAM deck and allows the application to capture only the required TC for each cut. The assistant will then relink the high-resolution footage to the locked cut and sync check it with the video assembled master (VAM) created from the offline cut (basically a QuickTime movie used as a reference). This VAM is placed in one of the lower corners, and the assistant should go cut by cut to make sure each shot matches. In the screen grab shown in Figure 8.21, the VAM is on the top video level.

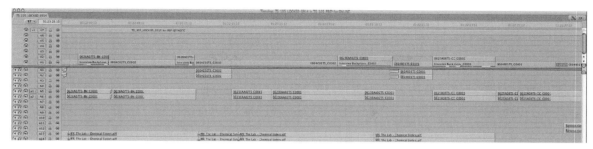

Figure 8.21 *VAM on V7 to check cuts*

The assistant editor then media manages the sequence at XDCAM HD422 1080i60 format. This will create an HD sequence that will be used to create a batch list that tells exactly what clips need to be redigitized for the locked cut (see Figure 8.22).

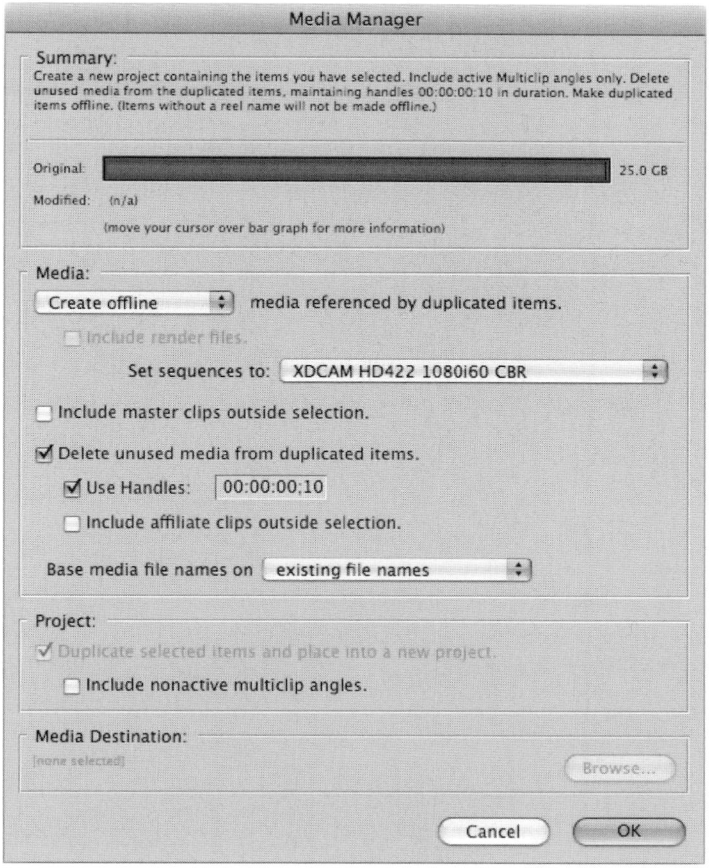

Figure 8.22 *Media manager settings*

Media managing creates a new project with the HD sequence and a list of all the master clips. Create a folder to put your reference QuickTime (VAM) in for sync (see Figure 8.23).

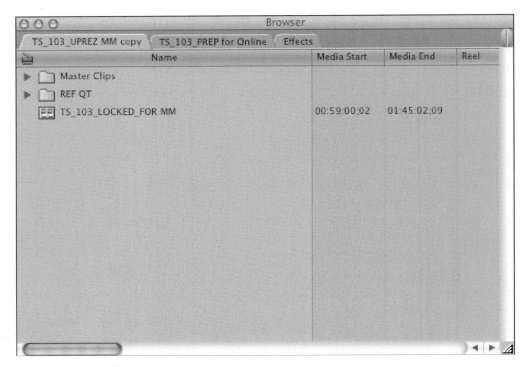

Figure 8.23 *Media manager browser*

The sequence creates a list of the master clips needed to be digitized at full-res for online. Use the XDCAM Transfer to digitize the needed clips back in, add the reference QT (VAM) to the top track of video, and check the sync (see Figures 8.24 and 8.25).

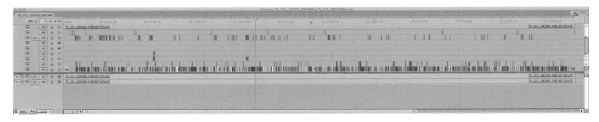

Figure 8.24 *HD sequence with mixed down tracks checked with VAM*

Figure 8.25 *VAM VAM can be seen in the lower right corner. This is a great way to double-check that all the cuts match*

8.24 Audio Prep for Online

If you turn the locked audio over to an outside mix house, they might require the OMF to be delivered with 10-second handles. These are very large handles, so the OMFs might have to be broken up by acts. Larry Jordan, author of several FCP handbooks, recommends using Automatic Duck, which removes many of these limits and simplifies the prep work. The OMF is then output from the formatted sequence with audio tracks in their proper places and delivered on an external hard drive. The assistant includes a reference QuickTime (chase cassette) and an audio guide track created by mixing the editor's tracks onto one track.

The assistant will also upload the final locked show to an FTP site that handles transcribing the show for closed caption.

8.25 In Summary

As you can see, the work flow (receiving dailies, importing, organizing, measuring, formatting, outputting, and locking) is similar on Final Cut Pro and Avid. However, each editing systems uses different terminology, methodology and the user interface will vary.

From features to television, from documentaries to reality, and from Avid to FCP, there are also many commonalities. The tools change, the language alters, the specs differ, but the overall tasks remain the same. With careful attention to minute details, an understanding of the functions of various editing programs, and a vigilant eye toward the needs of the editor, you can successfully become a worthy assistant.

All that remains for your education to be complete is a heightened awareness of the editorial department. This is probably the trickiest part to becoming a successful assistant editor in any venue, on any machine, in any country in the world.

Chapter 9

First Day Observations in the Editing Room

The ACE Internship Program selects interns and gives them the chance to observe the daily routines of an assistant editor. This is an opportunity to see firsthand the inner machinations of the assistant's tasks and how he juggles the work flow and problems that arise during the course of the day. Each show is at a different stage of postproduction, and even though everyone's daily experience is quite different, there is a commonality of work flow in every venue. We asked a few interns to write down and share their experiences, and what follows are excerpts from their first day's journal entries and a peek into the doors that were opened for them.

9.1 A Day on Episodic Television

... Laura Sempel (American Intern 2010)

Today was my first day in an episodic television editing room. I managed to arrive on a very good day! The editor had finished his editor's cut the day before, so he was making changes according to the notes the director had given him. The show is still missing a few scenes, so we will still be receiving dailies in the next few days. They will only have one day to cut in the last scene before the picture needs to be locked! It's amazing how quickly the world of television moves compared to features, and I think it's fair to assume that the end of the week may be extremely hectic.

The wonderful thing about being on this show during this week is that the assistant is leaving the show, and so he spent all day today giving the new assistant the rundown of the editorial process. So essentially it was as if he were training me as well to be the new assistant.

Going into this I knew hardly anything about TV, so some of the things I learned today may seem a little simple, but they were new to me. This show is broken up into five acts that are separated by commercials. The assistant separates the time lines by acts, so anything he needs to find or change is easily accessible. He puts the editor's cut into a new bin, and so the acts that are left in the project are relabeled as director's cut because that is what they are currently working on.

DOI: 10.1016/B978-0-240-81398-1.00009-2

The assistant gave the new assistant and me a tour of all of the project bins. He explained what was in each one of them, how he labels them, and why he does it that way. He showed me the forms that come with the dailies, such as the progress report, the sound report, as well as the camera report. It looks like all of these reports are emailed to him and are kept in files on his computer as opposed to a binder.

In terms of music and temp tracks, it appears that the editor likes to cut in his own temp track, and so the assistant just needs to keep the bins organized and accessible for him. The assistant also went over the way the show is delivered. He printed out a sheet that goes over everything that needs to be delivered along with the final cut. This includes paperwork as well as all of the elements and what format they need to be delivered in. He also printed me out a final continuity, a format sheet, a recap sheet, and an ADR list. Needless to say, all of these elements will be extremely helpful to refer to as templates when I have to make my own set of forms as an assistant!

I did manage to get a look at the continuity used for the editors cut. The concept of what it was made so much more sense when I was able to hold one in my hands and look it over.

Because the show is shot in New York and the visual effects are done out of house, they use a private Internet exchange program called D3. This way they can post QuickTimes of the episode, or just of specific scenes, for either the director or the producer to see. This makes it easier for someone to see the changes after they have given the editor their notes.

There was a break from the all the technical stuff, though, so don't think that I was just trapped in a room furiously writing down strange words like VAM and CTM all day! The editor wanted us to take a look at his editor's cut, so we watched it after lunch. Afterwards he came in and sat with the three of us and asked us what we thought about it. I, of course, remembered all the warnings and said very positive things about the episode. The editor seemed a little distracted, though, because there are a few story problems that he is aware of, and I'm afraid there isn't a whole lot that can be done about it. It's nothing major, and I think we were aware of it only because we were being asked about it.

The editor gave me a copy of the script for the episode to read tonight so I'll understand what's going on in the scenes where the footage is missing. Tomorrow is time for dailies! The assistant showed me how they process their dailies. Because the show is shot in New York, all of the dailies are digitized there and sent to Los Angeles on a FireWire drive. At the facility here, all of their media is stored on the Avid Unity system. This includes files for special effects, renders, media files, as well as all of the Avid project folders.

When a FireWire drive containing dailies is received, it contains five things: MX files of media, wave files of sound, a FLEX file, an ALE, and an Avid bin. The FLEX and ALE are delivered from telecine and allow the assistant to have a record of all of the footage that should be on the drive. The paperwork that comes with the drives is kept on the assistant's computer, except for the line script and the notes from the script supervisor. These forms are printed out and placed in the editor's binder so he has access to them as he is cutting the scene together.

Only one scene was received today, and it contained only three setups. It was a scene with two characters walking down a hallway having a conversation. I was extremely glad to see the dailies be processed because I realize how thorough an assistant needs to be while processing dailies. The assistant has a saying that he explained to me as "garbage in, garbage out." This means that if media is ingested into the system incorrectly, then it will be incorrect when it needs to be exported. He had a copy of the script supervisor's notes in front of him as he watched the dailies, and he checked each take off with a red pen to ensure that each take was, in fact, delivered.

When the assistant made sure that all of the takes were on the drive, he organized the clips by scene in a bin for the editor. This way all of the takes for scene 40 are in one row, below that are all the takes for scene 40A, and below that are all the takes for 40B, and so on. The assistant jokes about being extremely anal about all of his paperwork and starts a lot of sentences with, "It's probably not necessary, but I like to…". He keeps a database in FileMaker Pro of all the scenes in an episode that have been received, how long they are, how many takes there are, and what the script supervisor estimates the scene time should be.

Prior to arriving on this show I did not realize that the script supervisor keeps an estimate of how long each scene should be; when added up it gives an estimate of how long the show should be. At the moment with all of the scenes they've received, the estimated TRT for their show is seven minutes longer than what the editor has actually cut. The editor came into the assistant's room to ask him about the measurement of the episode, and when he informed him how short the show was running, the assistant asked, "So what does this mean?" The editor looked at him and simply said, "Trouble."

9.2 Different Venue in Episodic Television

… Andreas Arnheiter (International Intern 2010)

I had an awesome and really interesting day working with the assistant editor on this TV series. The whole editorial team enjoyed the pastry I brought from Switzerland, and they gave me a really warm welcome. Then the assistant and I jumped directly into our work. There are eight days of shooting for the current episode, and the PIX lock is in a couple of days. I wasn't aware that TV series are produced that fast! First we started getting the dailies ready for editing. The assistant usually prepares a small scene first, so when the editor comes in, there is a least one scene to edit.

Today we got almost three hours of footage! The director tends to do several takes in one shot, and because it is shot on video, there is always some time before the clap (slate). This might add to the amount of footage. The set is in New Jersey, and they load the footage and sound to the exchange server. In the morning, the assistant copied everything to the external hard drive. He also got all the reports and made duplicates, which he put into the editor's binder. When the editor arrived, the lights in the editing room were set and the Avid Media Composer was started and the binder was ready. The assistant told the editor which moments from the dailies she liked and also let her know that another editor—there are currently three editors and three assistants on this show—would help out with editing some scenes if she needed help. The really cool thing is that they all access the same server, and the editor gets the changes the assistant editor makes immediately and vice versa. That makes the work flow really easy!

After having lunch, we faced a problem; a wild audio line was missing. We had to call the sound facility in New York. They sent us the wrong file but eventually resent the correct one, and we were able to sync it by eye with the in-points. We continued to do the paperwork. All reports are sent first by fax. Later in the day we also get the same reports, tapes, and the audio backup by FedEx. In case we lose a file, we can recover it with these materials.

The rest of the afternoon consisted of the following tasks:

- Checked measurements, filled estimated times from facing pages and editorial time into the scene time log and sent it to the post supervisor so he could decide whether to report back the differing times to the producers.
- Prepared temporary background sound (music, SFX, dialog), chose the position of sound effects, and leveled the sound.
- The editor gave us two cuts and two music options, and we had to give her our opinion as to which we preferred.
- Checked the continuity breakdown and compared it with the shooting schedule to see which scenes we had already received and what we were still expecting.
- Made a to-do list for the next day.

Things that caught my attention today are grouping clips is awesome, communication with the editor is essential, a good bin order–view makes editing easier, adding color to the clips helps a great deal, setting locators and making notes is important, watching the scenes during dailies is vital, adding background SFX and being asked to evaluate cuts has been a really good education. The variety of tasks accomplished today led me to a far deeper understanding of the responsibilities of the assistant and his vital contribution in the editing suites.

9.3 A Day on a Feature

… Paul Penczner (American Intern 2010)

I was anticipating a difficult day where I would have to carefully maneuver as an intern in the cutting room of the first feature film that I had ever been involved with. I had been running through a few notes of advice I had been given; don't be too loud, don't be too small, ask laterally, be honest, avoid triangulation! But, as I stepped into the editing suites for the first time, all of those thoughts suddenly floated away and were replaced by overwhelming excitement.

The feature film is currently in production day 52 out of 70 shooting days.

Many people were out of the office today. This meant I got to ease into things and spend a lot of time with the assistant editor as he broke down the new Red Camera work flow that they are developing for this film. I will try to quickly go over here some of the things I learned today in as much as I can understand it so far.

The editing staff is currently four people. The first assistant is in charge of syncing the transcoded video footage to the raw audio, managing the final cut project file, and preparing sequences for edit and review. The second assistant is in charge of ingesting the material, managing the server, creating LTO tapes for archive, maintaining the digital database that combines all of the information from the paperwork from the set with the metadata from the footage, watching all of the dailies for quality control, and reformatting and preparing the drives and CF cards to be delivered back to the set to be shot on again. The post PA is in charge of moving the media back and forth and manually logging script notes, camera reports, and sound reports.

Dailies come in to the facility in a variety of media. Video comes in on CF cards, Red SSD, or Red HDD. The preference is to shoot most video on 16 GB CF cards because there is less risk of losing data if a single card fails because you can fit fewer takes onto it. The failure of a large hard drive with many more takes would mean a much greater loss. Audio comes in separately on a portable Lacie HDD.

The first thing we do is run a checksum program that copies source material from our media onto the server. After all the files are written, the checksum reads through all of the data to look for any potential discrepancies between the files sitting on the drive or card and the server. Now that they are sitting on the server we can access the R3Ds for transcode. Before we run the transcode, the first assistant first consults the script supervisor notes for takes that the director has asked to be deleted for one reason or another. The remaining takes are for print and are then transcoded to Apple Pro Res LT for the second assistant to start organizing. The first assistant then plays each clip that comes in to see if there are any irregularities in the footage.

Simultaneously, the first assistant will be entering the footage data into a digital database created through FileMaker Pro. This database automates a variety of fields of information that are derived from the metadata coming from the camera. Additionally, through a terminal command, the assistant automates frame grabs from the QuickTime proxy files by building a line of code that extracts a single frame from the centermost frame in a clip. For example, in a clip of 24 frames, the code would know to grab frame 12 and place it in a field for that page in the database. This little trick was the first in a series of code lines and terminal commands that the assistant showed me to quickly navigate and automate much of the tasks that would otherwise take too long to do manually as an assistant.

The assistant also reviewed scenarios where hard drives have corrupted or are missing directories that would cause hard drives to appear empty when they have been shot on. This can sometimes happen if a hard drive is ejected from the camera without being safely shut down. The data is usually still sitting on the drive, and so we use a command built by the Red company called RedUndead that rebuilds the directory of the file system to allow access to these files.

We discussed the conforming process that they are preparing so that when the picture is locked they can send a 2K sequence to the DI for the online. Through RocketCine-X we can manually look up and load the corresponding R3D files that match the ProRes clips in our sequence and then export those R3Ds as DPX sequences made from single frame DPX files. But the assistant is building a program that utilizes the EDL with the database that he has been creating to automate that process in RocketCine-X in a way that essentially rebuilds a 2K final cut sequence shot for shot.

I also realize that everything here is not necessarily universal to all feature films. In the world of digital post, tapeless work flows are still like the Wild West. Most importantly, I think that I am understanding the depth of control one can have over their machine if they can develop an understanding of the code behind all of the video software. Though most assistants rarely use terminal commands, they are empowering and kind of neat to know.

It's an exciting challenge for me because I see postproduction as ever changing. The hope is by opening your work flow to new ways of thinking and processing film in post, films can really move the ball forward in creating better systems for editing. I can see already that all of us in post are striving for the same things—faster ingestion periods giving more time for the editor to be creative, and easier outputs.

9.4 A Day on Reality

... Nompi Vilakaze (International Intern 2010)

I now understand what is meant by "the editor cuts, and the assistant editor does everything else." Shadowing the assistant was a true lesson in this. I came to realize what responsibility she carries on this reality show. Everybody from the editors, to story producers, to the postproduction supervisor wanted something from her. She is the first one to arrive on the premises and the last one to leave. Her day, my day, began at 9:00 a.m. and ended at 8:00 p.m. She booted up all the machines and logged everybody on. She dealt with people's requests, such as monitors that did not work, offline media, virus scans, sending the PA to buy DVDs and labels, and onlining a sizzle. A sizzle is about two minutes long and is used by the production company to get funding for the pilot. I watched as she disconnected this sequence from the server so that the media was offline, and she decomposed it and batch captured it at high rez at 1:1. I also watched as she put together an OMF sequence. They use AAF because it's more compatible with the DS Nitris. This had to go to the mix house because one of the characters pronounced a word incorrectly. Because an ADR line was not possible, she had to find different takes of the shot where the word was said correctly. She later emailed the file over to the mix house.

In all the episodes of this show, they have an international add-on. This consists of extra cut scenes that are dropped in at the end of the finished show and can be inserted in the international version. It's called a snap in. After lunch, the assistant helped the online editor draw a schematic for his online suite because he was not happy with the way it was wired. Their tech support came in, and the assistant had to make sure that the bay would be correctly wired according to the specs required by the online editor. For technical problems, I learned the assistant becomes the go-to person. She manages the Unity and gives people read or write access and decides what they need to see and what they don't need to see. It was also interesting to see how she dealt with different personalities. Mostly everybody was great, but there was an occasion where she had to navigate a certain challenging personality. I'm learning.

9.5 In Summary

These interns experienced a variety of technological tasks, organizational insights, and social skills at work on their very first day in the cutting rooms! It is important to arrive in the cutting rooms with a basic knowledge of the tools and a willingness to learn on the job. Having a hands-on experience completes your education and is one of the best ways to observe the kind of decorum that is expected of you when you join the workforce.

Part 2

Protocol

Chapter 10

The Unwritten Rules of the Editing Room

Therefore, however you want people to treat you, so treat them.
The Golden Rule, adapted from Matthew 7:12

Talent is cheaper than table salt.
What separates the talented individual from the
successful one is a lot of hard work.
Stephen King

Now that you have learned about your assisting duties, there are certain social skills you must develop for use in the cutting room. These skills involve common-sense rules about manners and protocol. They are as important to your career as your technical skill level and should be honed with equal vigor.

How to anticipate needs, read peoples' emotional states, and contribute an energetic, positive ambience to the editing room are skills that will be learned with time. But there are several social skills that can be accomplished immediately. Your technical skills coupled with a finely tuned personality will be the formula for success in the film industry. Here are a few guidelines.

10.1 Be on Time (15 Minutes Early)

One of the first rules of etiquette in the film industry is that you are never late for your call time. This applies to the editing room as well. It is a sign of respect when you arrive on time. Plan your day so that you arrive 15 minutes before you are expected. Before your first day on the job, do a dry run to time how long it takes to arrive at your destination during rush hour traffic. Know how to get to the studio, where to park, and how long it takes to get from the parking lot to the cutting rooms. This is important for interviews as well.

DOI: 10.1016/B978-0-240-81398-1.00010-9

Being on time will be important throughout your career. You should try not to keep anyone waiting, let alone your boss. So get in the habit of arriving early.

10.2 Make the Coffee

Make the coffee in the morning when you arrive, even if you do not drink it. If you do not know how to brew it, learn. The editors had to make the coffee when they were assistants, and now it is your turn. Take this opportunity to please your editor and postproduction visitors. Think of it as solicitous rather than a servile act.

10.3 Unlock the Editing Rooms

Make sure you open all the doors to each cutting. It is more pleasant for the editor to find his door open and the lights on when he arrives in the morning. Make note of the lights that the editor prefers to have turned on to start the day. Check all voice mails. Check all emails. Make sure your flex file (the ALE is embedded in the flex file) has arrived if you are in dailies. Respond to important messages left by the production and postproduction departments. Check the call sheet to make sure all of the newly scheduled meetings that might include your editor are flagged. Sometimes there are changes made to the time and place of the tone meeting, SFX–MX spottings, or lock dates. Inform your editor with a brief note regarding any changes in the days' activities.

10.4 Boot Up

Boot up all the computers and editing systems upon arrival. Take the time to straighten up if there is debris left over from the previous day's activities. This process takes only five minutes or so and will start your editor's day off on a pleasant note.

Make sure the machine settings are in the editor's preferred mode—his personal settings are up, the monitors are in the correct aspect ratio, the soundboard is back to the proper levels, and the room is good to go!

The assistant often has work to do on the editor's system. When your tasks are complete, make sure to put the pens you have used back in the holder, place the wrist support back in its normal position, adjust the chair to its regular height, remove your coffee cup or can of soda, and leave the room tidy, if not tidier, than when you entered it.

10.5 Prepare for the Day

Be aware of any scheduled events for the day (e.g., if there is to be an output that day, make sure you have blank DVDs, labels, a current continuity, and the delivery addresses and instructions). If a sound effects spotting is to take place in your cutting room at 9:00 a.m., arrive at 8:30 a.m. As discussed earlier, you will need to get the coffee brewing, provide the right amount of chairs, present copies of the necessary paperwork for distribution, open and display the timecode window, and cue up the spotting version of the show *before* everyone enters your cutting room. Now everyone will arrive to the quiet ambience of a smooth-running editing room. The assistant editor has created this inviting atmosphere and will be appreciated. That is how you **shine**.

10.6 Informative Messages and Post-it Notes

Editors appreciate it when assistants leave notes about the work they finished the previous night. It is also good to set up a system whereby the editor is informed about how many hours of dailies to expect for that day. Between these brief notes and Post-it messages, the assistant can inform the editor about everything that affects the cutting rooms.

10.7 Grooming

This seems obvious, but there are actually people who come to work in dire need of a shower. Wearing stained, wrinkled clothing sends a bad message; high heels and strong perfume is inappropriate. Tight, revealing clothing is the wrong way to bring attention to yourself. Save the cleavage, ladies, for the wrap party!

10.8 Know the Phones

Learn how to transfer and receive conference calls correctly. It is one of the assistant editor's tasks to set up the phones, the answering machine, and voice mail passwords. Think of the phone as one more piece of machinery for which you are responsible.

Make a list of postproduction numbers and extensions to place next to your editor's phone so that he does not have to waste time searching through the production crew list for contact information. All the editor really wants to think about is story telling, and, "How am I going to make this scene work?"

10.9 Ask Down, Not Up

If you have questions about a task or need technical assistance, always ask laterally or down. Ask another assistant editor, the tech assigned to your show, Google and troubleshoot on the Internet, or refer to your editing system manual. Try not to ask up. However, if the question pertains to your editor's personal preferences or prioritizing of the workday, you *should* ask the editor for clarification. Do not be afraid to ask questions to which only your editor will have the answer.

- When would the editor like to do an output?
- Would he like the dialog brought in on two tracks?
- When would he like to send a copy of the show to the composer?
- What scene would he like to start editing first?
- Does he want the main title to be attached to the cut for output?
- Does he want visible timecode on the output?

These are the kind of questions you have to ask your editor. Other questions about distribution lists, formats, addresses, phone numbers, duplication, auxiliary timecodes, and specs should be posed to your post producer, post supervisor, or fellow assistant editors before you trouble your film editor.

Only after all avenues have led to a dead end should you seek counsel from your editor. Let the editor know you've called these many people, talked to these many techs, and that you have run out of ideas. Your editor will appreciate that you've done due diligence. When you do choose to ask the editor, wait for a break in his schedule. If he is in the middle of cutting a scene, do not disturb him. If your editor does not take breaks, jot a note on a Post-it and ask for a moment of his time. Quietly leave it on his desk without causing him to stop working. It is also good to compile your list of questions and cause as few interruptions as possible.

If there is a technical difficulty (e.g., the Unity or SAN needs to be maintained) that requires all editing machines to be shut down, do your homework and be prepared with a solution before presenting it to your editor. Know the hours that the tech is available, and ask your editor which night he would prefer to leave early.

Think before you ask questions. So many questions can be answered with just a little forethought. If you are in doubt about certain chores and whether they need to be done, it is sometimes easier to just *do them*. It might takes less time and cause less aggravation than figuring out whom to ask.

Remember to carry a notebook and pen with you at all times. When you ask your editor a question, you can write the answer down and not have to ask a second time. People say there are no stupid questions, but questions asked twice are a dangerous negation of that philosophy.

These chores are all a part of being a successful assistant editor. When you do these tasks efficiently and cheerfully, you will **shine** and be a cut above all the other assistant editors who are competing for the same position. You will also evolve into an editor who knows how to please the next level of colleagues—directors and producers.

Chapter 11

Personality

There are careers that have definitive road maps that help chart your journey to success. You take X many years for study, pass X amount of exams, and begin your career in an entry-level position. Getting into the world of film editing is not quite as defined. There are no tests, no formal sets of requirements, and no guarantees that you will be promoted.

Your path to success includes two complementary attributes. The first is your array of honed technical skills, and the second is an engaging personality. Both assistant editors and editors must run the room with a quiet confidence, take notes graciously, and remain loyal, cheerful, and passionate. As you begin your career, you need to iron out any personality quirks or negativity that might get in your way. It might make the difference between getting hired or even fired.

11.1 Have a *Yes* Attitude

An overall positive attitude toward your work and relationships in the cutting room is an essential personality attribute. We call this the *yes* attitude. The editor is responsible for cutting the film. The assistant editor is responsible for *everything* else—from supplying the room to onlining the film, from ordering lunches to overnighting the cut anywhere in the world, from taking curt orders from rude associates to placating stressed employers.

The assistant needs myriad skills that include an understanding of technology, creativity, and psychology. Along with these basic skills is the need for a positive *Yes I can!* attitude, which will help keep the cutting room a harmonious place. The room is filled with many large personalities, and the assistant must maintain his equanimity at all times. The editor might emote, the director might stomp, the producer might rant, but the assistant must remain the essence of patience and fortitude.

When a request is made of you, your response should range from, "Yes, I will do that—right away," to "Yes, I haven't done that before, but I will find out and get it done—right away." This is when your network of fellow assistants comes into play. For example, if you are asked to apply auxiliary timecode to the dailies and you have not done it before, call your assistant friends, and they will talk you through the process. When the

DOI: 10.1016/B978-0-240-81398-1.00011-0

> **TIP**
>
> Editors are very good at reading expressions, physical reactions, and tone—we do this for a living. Make sure you respond to *all* requested tasks with a cheerful countenance. We will know how you feel about doing it. No loud sighs, no shrugging the shoulders, no averted eyes with frowns—just an affirmative response.

> **TIP**
>
> Try to get back to your editor to let him know the status of the task. This way the editor does not have to ask you, "How's that auxiliary timecode coming along?"

editor asks for things that are not usually requested, your attitude must be willing and helpful. Let your editor know that you will take care of it completely. The editor has now given you the assignment; he crosses it off *his* list and will expect *you* to finish the task.

We have mentioned that the assistant editor should have a notebook and pen with him at all times. This is especially true when you are called into the editor's cutting room. When you arrive ready to take notes, it will instill confidence in the fact that you, his assistant, are prepared and competent and that the task will most likely be accomplished. Try to complete all tasks daily, and if one has not been finished, it should go to the top of your list for the next day. The editor should be informed that you are still on it.

When you have been asked to telephone someone, call him during standard working hours—9:00 a.m. to 6:00 p.m. Avoid phone tag by not calling someone during his lunch hour. When you make contact, it is polite to begin the conversation by asking, "Is this a good time?" or "Do you have a moment?" This provides the opportunity for him to ask you to call back at a more convenient time if he is in the middle of something. When you leave a message, make sure it is informational. If you do not hear back, follow it up with an email, and cc your post producer when necessary. It is a good troubleshooting habit to find out everyone's home and cell numbers for when you are unsuccessful at reaching them at work. After you have called all of their numbers, left messages with your questions, and emailed those same questions, you have done due diligence.

At the beginning of your voice mail message, state your name and number slowly. Repeat the number. This way, if he finishes listening to your message and missed your phone number, he can go back to the beginning of the message and retrieve it quickly. Always leave an informational message that is a brief summary of the subject matter that needs to be discussed. When the message contains the question you need to have answered, he can call you with an answer and leave an informational message *for you* if you are unavailable. Try to make his life a little bit easier by repeating your phone number at the end of the message. If you have received no answer by that afternoon, try again. Keep calling until you are successful and have at least confirmed he has have received your message. Update your editor. If your editor has to ask you the status of his request, an answer of "I left a message" will not be enough.

11.2 Make Eye Contact

Look people in the face and make eye contact with them. This is key to a communicative relationship. When speaking with your editor or any visitor in your cutting room, stop what you're doing, turn to face him, and make eye contact. The back of a head in response to "good morning!" or "how many reels of dailies do we have today?" starts the day off badly. Be polite. When you are swamped with the daily rituals of the cutting room, you must still take the time to say, "Forgive me, I have so much to do, I have to get back to it." This provides the opportunity for the editor to respond with, "Of course, sorry to interrupt."

11.3 Admit Mistakes

When a mistake has been made, a brief apology or acknowledgement of the error goes a long way to defusing the situation. For example, saying "I'm sorry" and "Oh, no! Let me fix that right now!" is a good way to let your editor know that you understand the error was grave. It will immediately reduce the annoyance level. It also lets the editor know that you are the sort of person who will take responsibility for an error, and it affords him the opportunity to say, "That's okay, these things happen." This social interplay applies to *all* situations. Without these conciliatory interchanges, the editor's confidence in you will begin to diminish.

11.4 Be Honest

When something goes wrong, let the editor know what has happened and that you are taking care of it. Trying to hide a problem will backfire.

When your editor needs you to do something you are not familiar with, be honest and say, "I haven't done that before, but give me a few minutes and I'll find out." You must then do whatever it takes to come back with the correct answers. That is a great assistant.

You are not expected to know everything at the beginning of your career or current project. The editor chose to take a chance on you based on your personality—he assumes that your learning curve will be steep. Your social skills will make up for myriad newbie errors.

11.5 Be Proactive

Stephen Lovejoy, A.C.E. made a great comparison of an assistant editor to the character Radar in the film *M.A.S.H.* In the television show, Radar worked for the commanding officer, and he was always two to five steps ahead of him. Usually the joke was that he would answer the commanding officer before the question had been completed. That's what a great assistant does. Anticipate what's coming next. The assistant that can anticipate is worth his weight in gold. Be proactive at all times.

When an editor says to you, "phew, it's hot in here," you need to get up out of your seat and check the thermostat by the time he finishes his sentence. The nonproactive person will remain seated and say, "Do you want me to check the thermostat?" By then the editor has already stopped editing and changed the thermostat setting himself. Take these hints as a clue for you to get up and do something. Do not sit in your seat and say, "Let me do that for you." Actions speak louder than words. Get up, volunteer, do it. And do it with a smile.

11.6 Leave Your Problems at Home

It is so nice to spend the day in the cutting room with someone who has an energetic and sunny attitude. It helps to have a sense of humor. If you are having a rough time in your personal life, it is best not to bring your problems to work with you. When your editor asks you in the morning, "How was your evening?"

choose your response with care. Try to make it have a positive spin. If you are depressed, upset, and angry, you might have a hard time stretching to a response of "great, terrific," or "happy." But you must try. You can say, "I have had better nights, but I'm okay." The editor does not really have the time to listen to the story about your cat needing surgery or that your boyfriend did not show up for your birthday party. The workplace is not a confessional, it is your professional life. After you have built a special relationship with your editor, you might share more personal information. Remember, we are *colleagues*, not *friends*. During the making of a film, we are lulled into the false belief that we are now working with friends. This is a misnomer. We can count on one hand the amount of true friends we have made in Hollywood over the course of three decades.

11.7 Crying

Crying while watching a sad scene is acceptable. Crying in reaction to having made a mistake is inappropriate. Excuse yourself from the room, find a private place, and pull yourself together. This goes for men as well as women.

In addition to crying, there are other behaviors that have no place in the cutting room. Sitting on producers' laps, off-color jokes, and a bad temperament will only backfire over the course of time. Behave professionally at all times.

11.8 Arguing

Remember the old axiom that the customer is always right? This holds true in the film industry as well. When asked to bring a second chair into the cutting room, and you do, and the editor says, "Where's the third chair?" what should your response be? That's right! "No problem, I will go get it." It accomplishes nothing to point out your editor's mistake. Just go find another chair. This will apply to you as you move up in the ranks. As an editor, there will be situations in which the director or producer insists that you made a change in the picture that he did not ask for. Remain calm and put the film back to the way he now would like to see it. No arguments, do not even skip a beat, just make the change. You could spend a few moments correcting him, proving he is wrong, but you will accomplish nothing except creating ill will. Just let it go and move on. Practice taking the higher road.

Be careful how you phrase your answers. The tone, body language, and words you choose will affect the ambience of the room. Use diplomacy in all your dealings.

11.9 Lodging Complaints

When dealing with difficult situations, we all need to let off some steam. What will serve you best in the long run is to choose carefully how you react and with whom you discuss these complaints. You should not complain about your editor to someone involved in the film. You can call a friend, you can tell another assistant, but never complain up, never complain down, and *never* complain to the rest of the film crew or anyone in post. If you have a very strong complaint to lodge, go to your editor and say, "Can we have a chat?" When something is disturbing you, discuss it with him face to face. We had an assistant editor who preferred to email us when he was disturbed about something. This is also fine. One of the problems with complaining is that one day you might say something to an ambitious, mean-spirited, or jealous associate, and he could use it against you.

For example, an Academy Award winning editor once complained to the A.P. about a director he worked with for more than 10 years. The A.P. took that complaint to the director, and the editor got fired on the spot.

The world of postproduction in Hollywood might seem immense at first, but it will become quite small in time. Your reputation will follow you throughout your career, and it begins on your very first job. Remember that it is often your *reputation* as well as your *personality* that makes editors, directors, and producers hire you on their next project.

11.10 Gossiping

Eleanor Roosevelt said, "Great minds discuss ideas, average minds discuss events, small minds discuss people." There is no benefit to gossiping. Avoid as many dramas as possible. Inevitably, there will be situations that are emotionally charged and you will be tempted to enter the fray. Sometimes a colleague will want you to join in a negative discussion about someone. Gracefully extricate yourself from the situation by leaving the room to complete your work. A good response to gossip is "hmmm." That is it. If an assistant says "I cannot believe so-and-so is doing this to so-and-so," respond simply with "hmmm." If you must engage more than that, go the therapist route and say, "Wow, that is interesting" or "Don't you just hate it when that happens? Oh, I hear my phone." And off you go. It validates their dismay, it is empathetic, and it does not commit you to an opinion. Remain as neutral as possible. Joining in the fray will only hurt you over the long haul and bring so much negativity into your life.

We must admit there have been times when we have gone against our own rules and said nasty things about a coworker. Word always gets back to him and causes problems. It is too high a price to pay for a momentary release of anger.

Remember this: you are there to work, not socialize. Be professional and keep your emotions to a minimum in the cutting room. Maintain your equanimity.

11.11 Noise and Personal Hygiene

Be aware of noise levels. It is very disturbing for an editor to listen to unnecessary noise around the editing rooms when he is trying to concentrate. Editors do not want to listen to people eating, talking on cell phones, filing nails, chewing gum, tapping pens, or cracking their knuckles.

Grooming is another innocuous but annoying habit that should not happen in the editor's cutting room. Brushing hair, putting on makeup, or dental flossing should be done in the privacy of the bathroom.

If this sounds at all tyrannical, we're sorry. The expulsion of these habits will serve you well in becoming a successful assistant. You will find that directors and producers have equal or more intolerance for idiosyncratic behavior.

> I worked with a director on a pilot, and when he fired the director of photography, I asked him what was the determining factor for making this bold decision in the middle of the shoot. He said it was mainly due to the amount of time delays caused by the DP, and then he admitted, "and I hated how he was always munching food so loudly in video village."
>
> —ljc

11.12 Creating Ambience Levels

Go through the room as quietly as a mouse. Do not make waves or ripples. You might be the most skilled assistant editor in the world, but if you are too big for the room, it can be disruptive. Several years ago we interviewed a marvelous candidate for the ACE Internship Program who was skilled, educated, and perfect for the program, except for one minor thing. She was overwhelmingly talkative, loud, and effusive. The editor does not want to compete for the airwaves in the cutting room. Be careful to not be smarter and cleverer than the editors themselves. It's hard to be with that personality for 12 hours a day. It will make the editor very uncomfortable about how to deal with an assistant who does not know his place.

Generally we have found that every assistant falls into one of two categories: a bit too quiet and reserved, or a bit too loud and verbose. Understand the difference between humble and weak, assertive and aggressive, solicitous and subservient. Recognize yourself when we critique certain characteristics that are unsuccessful in the editing room. Ask yourself, "Is that me? What should I do to change it?" Make a mental note and remember to work on improving your behavior to suit your work environment.

You have to read the room and evaluate the personalities of your coworkers. The cast of characters and personalities changes from show to show. What might have worked with one editor might not work with the next. We need to function in editorial with both functional and dysfunctional people. After we've groomed our personalities or improved how well we handle our different bosses, we still have to evaluate ourselves throughout our career. There is always room for improvement in the cutting rooms, and making sure that the ambience in your cutting room is pleasant and inviting is part of the job. Your progress will be a testament to how well one can adapt.

After you have all these skills sets, the way you **shine** is by being this wonderful person. We share cutting rooms for 12 or more hours a day, longer than any other waking activity. We must look forward to seeing each other, in the good times and the bad.

One of the hardest messages to get across to novice assistants is that their education and skills is not enough to get the job. It is so very hard to examine your own personality, put your finger on your shortcomings, and amend a lifetime of behavior. But you must! Getting hired, fired, and rehired is all about your skills *and personality*.

Chapter 12

Navigating the Room

How to navigate your way through the editing room is a skill that should be part of the assistant editor's job description. It will serve you well when you learn to read the room's atmosphere and figure out when to keep your head down.

Working in close quarters creates the need for a social dance. When choreographed well, the editing room functions smoothly. It takes just one participant to tip the scales away from an amiable atmosphere. Figuring out the politics of seating arrangements, how to enter the cutting room, how long you should stay, when to give an opinion, and when to answer the telephone, are decisions that need to be made in a split second. The editing room is filled with egos, including your own. Through time, you will navigate these deep waters without a ripple. For now, we can offer up a few guidelines to help you avoid some of the pitfalls.

12.1 Entering the Room

Be aware of your editor's preference on how you should enter his room. Some editors like their assistant to knock and then enter without pausing for a verbal invitation. This helps warn him that someone is coming in without having to stop cutting. When the editor is cutting a scene, he is zoned into another world, and for him to stop and say "come in" might cause him to lose his creative flow. Always ask your editor what works best for him. You cannot assume that what worked for your last editor will work for the next one. Remember that when you enter the room, you enter someone's private domain. Use common courtesy.

12.2 Know When to Leave the Room

Recognize the physical cues that tell you the conversation is over. Some of these are averted eyes, multiple sighs, shifting in the chair, and moving toward the door. These are clues you must pick up and then find a way to gracefully exit the cutting room. When an assistant editor cannot sense something as simple as when to leave an editing room, it is an indication that some other personality attributes might also be lacking. Editors look for these signs and make decisions about hiring based on these subtle nonverbal communications.

DOI: 10.1016/B978-0-240-81398-1.00012-2

When the editor engages in polite conversation, remember to keep your answers brief. If he asks, "How are you?" do not give the full 10-minute answer. Long, involved stories are not okay. Remember, the editor has dailies to cut, a schedule to keep, and all he really wants to do is start editing.

12.3 Answering the Phones

You are representing the editor, the cutting room, and the production when you answer the phone. It is polite to identify the name of the show and your name. One preference is, "Editing, this is Mary," or perhaps, "*The Competition*, Mary speaking." Again, you can ask your editor how he would you like you to answer the phone.

Whether speaking to the PA or the executive producer, we expect you to speak in a respectful manner. Treat everyone with an equal amount of kindness and consideration. If someone has made a mistake, there is no excuse for you to raise your voice. Be positive, courteous, and helpful. It is always a pleasure when we talk to the crew or production and they say, "Oh, we love your assistant." That is the sort of feedback we like and expect.

If your editor walks into your room and you are on the phone, ask that person, "Can you hold on a second?" Put your hand over your mouthpiece and say, "I'm talking to the executive producer about the output; do you need me right now or should I finish up?" This gives your editor the chance to prioritize for you. No matter how important the other person on the phone is, the assistant editor should always consider the needs of the editor first. If you are on a personal call, it is prudent to end the phone conversation and give the editor your undivided attention. Hold your personal calls to a minimum and take care of private matters during your lunch break.

The assistant is often asked to do many things by many people at the same time. Prioritizing these requests is learned with experience, but if you find yourself caught in the middle, ask your editor to help prioritize for you.

12.4 Reading the Room

The editor has the enormous responsibility of weaving the best possible story from the material that has been shot. In scenes that have little or no dialog, the story is told with the use of the characters' facial expressions and body language. Their feelings, thoughts, and intentions come to life with the use of images only. Just as an editor plays the emotions of the scene by reading their faces, the assistant must do the same reading of faces in the editing room. You have to know when your director is displeased or when your editor is grumpy or when to order lunch because someone is having a blood sugar problem. You have to know when to be quiet and when to speak, how to modulate your voice, and when to offer refreshment. You have to know your place, when to be there, and when to leave.

Remain quiet and attentive until you are asked to join in. When you do speak, what you say will be evaluated carefully, so choose your words well. The stakes will be higher as your career progresses, and if you have not learned from some of these guidelines, being replaced (fired) or not hired can be the result.

Be sensitive to all the nuances of protocol and behavior in the cutting room. It is a special skill to be able to maintain this delicate balance, and this skill will help when you become an editor. As the editor, you handle the personalities of your executive producer, director, line producer, and coproducer, sometimes all at the same time. As the assistant editor, you will often take notes for your editor and be in the room with the producers. You will witness these social politics firsthand; this producer wants to trim four frames, the other producer wants to add four frames, the writer wants to lift the entire scene. It can become a bit harried. The requests, ideas, and notes will come flying at the editor quickly; pay attention to how he handles all these instructions and makes the changes at the same time.

As editors, we try to balance these highly charged sessions by doing *all* the notes as quickly as possible. If there are conflicting notes, a copy of the scene is made so that each person can look at his requested change. Through the course of your career, you will be dealing with the psychology of people and their relationships in the room. The assistant needs to learn how to show respect for the other person's space, develop an understanding of the pecking order, and learn to read nuances.

12.5 Taking Notes

One great asset for an assistant to cultivate is to be a great note taker. Sometimes notes are flying at you so fast it is hard to keep up. Producers don't want to take the time to reiterate their thoughts. If you miss a note, you must have the courage to speak up and ask for clarification. This might annoy some people, but your editor will be supportive and appreciate your efforts when it comes time to execute the changes. Take this chore very seriously. Write notes with concise language and legible handwriting. There is nothing worse than having an assistant hand you notes you cannot read, are incomplete, or are inaccurate. An assistant is worth his weight in gold when his notes are great. Sometimes an editor will take notes along with the assistant and compare them, making sure nothing has been overlooked.

If your handwriting is challenging to read, offer to type the notes after the screening, or use a laptop. This way, you can type the notes as you go onto the continuity on your laptop, thereby preempting the need to write down the scene numbers. Then all the assistant needs to do is print it out. There is a great responsibility attached to this task, whichever system you choose.

> Practice writing numbers clearly. Some numbers are especially easy to mix up; 1 and 7, 3 and 8, and 4 and 9 are clearly red flag numbers. This will apply to scene numbers, key code, and telephone numbers. My numbering was atrocious when I began assisting, and after botching an optical count sheet that had lengthy key numbers, I learned the hard way that I had to perfect the way I wrote numbers.
>
> —ljc

If the assistant does not take good notes, the editor will most likely opt to exclude him from this intimate process. However, if you do take good notes, your editor will want you to be in the room during a screening, which is a great learning experience. It helps you understand how different creative input contributes to the evolution of the film. It keeps you abreast of the changes that affect your work. For example, if a scene is lifted, you will need to denote that on the continuity.

One valuable lesson you will take from this experience is that you will see how editors must always respond with a positive attitude toward the requested change, regardless of whether he agrees or disagrees. You, the assistant, must be equally open to every note given to you by everyone you work with. It is an invaluable experience for your future as an editor.

12.6 Giving Your Opinion on a Scene

It is very exciting to be called into your editor's cutting room to give your opinion on a scene. Initially, you might think this is your opportunity to show how smart you are and how your knowledge of editing can help. Beware! Think before you speak.

Confident editors want to know what did or did not work in the scene, but there are some editors who do not react well to a negative critique. An editor may want to hear how much you liked the scene and that you are impressed with what he has done with the dailies. It will be up to you to evaluate both the situation and the temperament of the individual editor. This will determine how safe you are.

There is a protocol on how you should respond in this situation. We suggest you start with an overview of the positive elements of the scenes. For example, "I liked the part where they first embraced," or "The ending made me cry," or "The gymnastics scene was seamless. I couldn't tell the stunt doubles from the actors." This affirms the editor's hard work and sets the tone. There is *always* something positive to say—"I was so engaged," "That was a compelling moment," or "It works for me." If you are hard pressed to find something nice to say, at least begin your comments with some sort of validation, such as "I watched the dailies on this scene and I am amazed at what you have done!" Remember that the editor would not be showing you the scene if he thought it was in bad shape.

Be diplomatic at all times. Remember when giving notes to the editor one-on-one that he wants responses to these kinds of questions: "Did this work for you? Did that seem slow? Was that funny? What bumped you? Do you think there were too many cuts? Do you think the close-up reaction should be earlier?" He does not want to be told *how* to fix it, but rather *what* needs fixing.

We are not suggesting that you lie. The editor will see through that, and it will be an awkward moment for both of you. You need to be tactful. Find the language that will gently present your thoughts. For example, if you feel there is a squeaky part in the scene, you can ask to see the sequence again. This will buy you the time to collect your thoughts, identify where the problem is, and make a suggestion that will not be insulting or offensive to the editor. Saying *cutty* is a no-no. Instead, say, "This part was a bit fast for me." If there are awkward moments in the scene, you can say, "Something bumped me here…not sure what." The editor will know by this statement that the problematic parts of the scene have been identified and are probably in line with his own assessment. One way to approach how you give notes is to phrase your response as a question. Sometimes a simple "hmmm…" is enough for the editor to know that something needs work. On the other hand, be careful when you give a note that the editor deems inappropriate or uneducated or lacking in depth. He might not ask for your notes again. Know your editor well before you give a negative opinion, and you will avoid getting burned.

Of course, if you truly love the scene and have no notes, say it! Eventually, when the editor trusts your opinions, your judgment, and your loyalty, you will be able to give more in-depth notes. Quite frankly, your input will become invaluable.

12.7 Triangulation

During the director's and producer's cuts, the assistant editor is sometimes called in to give an opinion on a sequence. In this situation, be *very* careful. You are entering shark-infested waters. There are egos in the room that need to be protected, preserved, and pampered. First, your allegiance is to your editor. If you know how your editor likes the scene cut, and now you see that it is cut the way the director prefers it, and you are asked which way you like it more, you are in a no-win situation called triangulation.

If you get the nod from the editor allowing you to answer, think twice. Ask to see the way it was or to see it again. This will buy you time to collect your thoughts. Or dive right in and say you loved the way the editor had it the first time (know that this director might not hire you, but your editor will!). If you do like the new version, you can say there were wonderful parts to both versions.

The assistant editor must never side with the person opposed to the editor. It is the editor who hired you, to whom you owe your job, and hopefully who will take you on to the next project. Do not

> **TIP**
>
> When the editor, director, and producer call you in to the cutting room to give an opinion, you will know by your editor's physical cues (widened or averted eyes, angry stare, tilt of the head, etc.) whether he even wants you to answer the question. Discuss with your editor, in advance of this situation, what he feels would be appropriate to say. Prearrange nonverbal signs so that you will know exactly when to speak and when to avoid giving an unwanted opinion. Politically you could affect your editor's job if you walk into that room and make a comment that offends the director, producer, or editor. You want to be very, very careful not to get embroiled in discussions or arguments that take place in the editing room.

make the mistake of furthering your career by aligning with a director and placing a knife in your editor's back. That is *not* the way to move up, and the director will see right through it and think less of you. If he does not think less of you, is this really the type of person with whom you want to work?

If you are caught in the crossfire of triangulation, Chris Cooke, A.C.E. suggests the following technique. You state what you see are the differences. You might say, "The new cutaways to the CU of John as he drives are effective and beautifully shot even though the performance is a bit broad. In the earlier version without the CUs, I missed seeing John during the chase. So, the question is: is his bad performance hurting it enough to make that shift? I don't know." Basically what you do is throw it up in the air. What you are really doing is mediating. You're taking two different points of view and you are restating them in a calm and controlled manner and then these people can say, "Well you didn't do us any good. Get out!" At least you're safe because you didn't take sides. Or maybe they will say, "Well yeah, that's really an interesting point of view. Maybe we can just use the CU once or twice in that scene."

You have provided exactly what was needed in that room. You have pointed out what bumped you without choosing sides. It is important to realize the value of your virgin eyes in that room. They need a response from an objective viewer who has not labored for hours on the scene. Remember, identify the problem, but do not provide the solution. That is *their* job.

I had an assistant once who was called in by the director to see the chase scene. My assistant watched me edit and refine this scene for weeks. When the director and I finished adding his touches, he asked my assistant to come view the scene and afterwards asked, "What do you think?" He said, "Oh I like it! It is so much better!" He innocently meant to be encouraging and helpful. I felt it was tantamount to saying, "The editor's version was bad, and the director's version is good." The irony was that the director and I had only added a couple of CU shots of the actor's eyes in the rearview mirror, and the rest of the car chase was virtually the same. If my assistant had said, "Looks good!" or "The scene is riveting," there would have been no hurt feelings. The point is, avoid making comparisons of versions when possible. It is a common pitfall and serves to make the editor feel betrayed.

I talked with my assistant about this incident a few weeks later, after I had cooled off, and expressed my feelings. He apologized profusely. His intent was never to devalue my work but to simply be supportive. I cared deeply for this young assistant editor, and I would work with him again in a heartbeat, but we had to learn this lesson together the hard way.

—ljc

The editor does not really want the assistant to be the deciding vote in the cutting room. Unless you are there to say how brilliant he is, your best choice is to leave the room as quickly as possible.

12.8 Email Etiquette

Emails can be a bit tricky. To begin with, there is a hierarchy to which you must be sensitive. Always list the names in the cc bar according to their titles and in descending order. The executive producer should be before the line producer, the head of the department should precede his staff, etc. This is a subtle yet necessary nod to their hard-earned positions.

When an email is sent to ask for SFX, MX, spec sheets, or stock, it is not necessary to cc the post supervisor. The response is more likely to be positive and informal because your colleague knows that no one is listening. This will keep the communication friendly. It leads to more productive interchanges and better relationships. When and if you do not receive positive responses, that is the time to start cc'ing the head of your department. A paper trail is a good way to cover your ass (CYA) when problems arise.

There will always be politics in your cutting room. Trying to remain uninvolved is tricky but a good survival technique to master. If you find yourself in a contentious situation, remember to take the higher road. Be kind, and know that the patience and forgiveness you practice today will serve you well in the future.

Part 3

Make the Cut

Chapter 13

Approaching Your Career

If you would hit the mark, you must aim a little above it: Every arrow that flies feels the attraction of earth.

Henry Wadsworth Longfellow

If one advances confidently in the direction of his dreams, and endeavors to live the life which he has imagined, he will meet with a success unexpected in common hours.

Henry David Thoreau

Imagine, if you would, a photograph of 1000 doors slightly ajar, just enough room to get your foot in, each one representing an assistant editor job. A large majority of these jobs will go to assistant editors who are already well-established in the film industry (*slam!*) and a large portion to the friends and relatives of producers, directors, and editorial staff (*slam!*). Of the remaining doors still ajar, the newly arrived assistant will have to compete with fellow film school students, some of whom have graduated from high-profile schools that offer multiple networking opportunities (*slam!*). You can see how the remaining opportunities, the doors that might be open to you, are limited. You have to find your way inside one of these doors by honing as many technical and social skills as possible and by joining the Motion Picture Editors Guild, Local 700, if you wish to enter the Hollywood work force.

Jobs in Hollywood are either union or nonunion. When an assistant editor gets into the union, he will be able to work both in union and nonunion jobs. High-profile features and episodic television are union. Therefore, to have as many options as possible, you must position yourself to be eligible for union jobs by getting into the Editors Guild as soon as you can.

As we have discussed, personality quirks might lead to some of the remaining doors being shut. The personalities that will be less successful are the class clown, the wallflower with low energy, the loquacious person

DOI: 10.1016/B978-0-240-81398-1.00013-4

who is too big for the room, and the negative nay-sayers whose first response is always "no!". If your personality fits into one of these categories, recognize it and *change* it! The objective is to have as many doors open to you as possible so that you will have the greatest opportunity to succeed.

13.1 Get into a Cutting Room

If you have already written to your favorite five and no one has responded, do not despair. Write again, but recognize the fine line that separates tenacity from stalking. Sometimes an editor's response is delayed only because he is very busy and intends to get back to you when his schedule is clear. If after a few months and a few tries there are no replies, choose five more editors to write to. One day, an editor will write back. Promise.

Your task is to gain entry into one of those cutting room doors. When you make your list of favorite editors, it is best to make sure they are *local*. If you are living in Chicago, Sydney, or London, there are editors to contact there. Personalize your messages! Let the editors know you have watched their films carefully. Whenever an editor receives an email from someone looking for work and sees that the assistant has sent this same letter to multiple recipients, he is not inclined to respond. Lynzee Klingman, A.C.E. said that while she was sitting on a panel for Editfest in Los Angeles she received a fan letter and was so impressed that she hired him!

The point is to meet the editor and his assistants, see their cutting rooms, and to begin the networking process. You are looking for a mentor as well as assistant editor colleagues with whom you might work in the future. When you are invited to an editing room, make the most of it. Look at the assistant's paperwork, his wall charts, project windows, scene bins, and notebooks. Take notes. Offer to help—proactively—if the opportunity presents itself. If you see that the coffee pot is nearly empty, ask if you might wash it out for the assistant and get a fresh pot going. Hopefully, when the assistant editor needs to hire a second assistant editor, he will remember you.

> I remember when I was the apprentice editor on *Fun with Dick and Jane* (with Jane Fonda and George Segal). Danny Greene, A.C.E. was the editor, and we were working next door to *All the President's Men* on the Columbia lot. I saw Lou Lombardo, A.C.E. (one of *my* favorite five) every day. He was good friends with Marion Segal, who was also cutting *Fun with Dick and Jane*. Louie would stop by at the end of the day and give Marion some pointers while looking over her shoulder on the Moviola, and I would try to listen in the adjacent room to his pearls of wisdom. When I read in the trades the following year that Louie was starting a film at Universal Studios (*Which Way Is Up*), I called him out of the blue, asked if he needed an assistant, and much to my surprise he said, "Yes darlin'—come on down!" I was asked to work with Louie on his next film as well (*Up in Smoke*). I learned half of all I know about editing by his side.
>
> —ljc

So give it a go—sometimes you get lucky. You must have the drive, do the homework, make the calls, and opportunity will knock on your door. Remember that you have to *help* the Fates be on your side.

Arranging to meet your favorite editors is only the first step in the larger plan. What you really want to accomplish during your visit to one of your fave five is the opportunity to meet and befriend their assistant editors.

13.2 Develop a Relationship with the Post Staff

In television, both the editor and assistant are sometimes offered work by the coproducer, head of postproduction for the studio, and post supervisors, as well as editors and directors.

> I worked with executive producer Paul Stupin on *Dawson's Creek* and *Beautiful People*. When he offered me a seat on the first season of *In Plain Sight*, I turned it down because I preferred to not work on Final Cut Pro. I went on to do *The Memory Keeper's Daughter* with Mick Jackson, and then a nonunion feature with David Hollander. When the movie was complete, my funds were low and I needed a union job quickly (my health insurance had lapsed). I knew Paul Stupin needed to fill two editing chairs for the second season of *In Plain Sight*, so I called him, left messages, and did not hear back. I knew I had offended him by turning down the first season offer. I called the coproducer, Drew Matich, and asked for his help. I will be forever grateful to Drew for smoothing out the bumpy path back into Paul's graces and pushing for me to be hired.
>
> —ljc

When you are on a television show, both the editor and assistant should take great care to cooperate with the entire editorial department, which consists of the coproducer, associate producer, post supervisor, post coordinator, and post PA. A symbiotic relationship will develop. Your coproducer can advocate for the editing staff when dealing with production. Having a great coproducer as your advocate can be the difference between being happy in your work or feeling taken advantage of.

Assistant editors sometimes find themselves between a rock and a hard place when it comes to pleasing both the coproducer and the editor. Conflicting requests might be made by both of your bosses simultaneously. We think the best way to handle this is to let the coproducer know that you would be happy to do whatever it is he asks of you and that you need to run it by your editor. Then let your editor prioritize for you. All the tasks will be addressed, and both parties will be pleased.

13.3 Find a Mentor

Choosing a mentor will be a valuable part of your education in the film industry. Sometimes a mentor chooses you. For us, the most important quality in a mentor is his willingness to share his thoughts about editing—style, momentum, tricks, and storytelling techniques. It is essential that your mentor encourages you to cut—every day—and that he gives you notes, has you make the changes, and then reviews the scene with you. It is most important that you respect your mentor's ideas.

> I sat behind one editor for months, assisting him on a Kem, and it was staggering to me that he categorically made cuts that were diametrically opposed to my sensibilities. Clearly I needed to find a new editor whom I could learn from and admire.
>
> —ljc

The opportunity for an assistant to be mentored has declined due to technology, budgets, time restraints, and the need to downsize the staff. However, most editors love to mentor and are often the kindest and most approachable members of the film industry. Editing often keeps us isolated, but we love to chat when the work is complete. There are so many talented editors to choose from, most of whom would welcome the attention and opportunity to teach. You must look for and find an editor who is willing to go the extra mile for you!

13.4 Keep a Journal

Now that you have started your networking process, it is wise to keep a journal and an account of all the people you have contacted. Keep track of their pertinent contact information, including spouse's and children's names and birthdays. Note the name of the film and the date you visited. This way you will know when an appropriate amount of time has passed and you can ask to revisit their cutting rooms.

> I have notebooks filled with names of PAs who are now executive producers, apprentice editors who are now film editors, and line producers who are now executive show runners. Their contact information might have changed, but when I interview with them now, I am able to remind them of our past contact, who, what, when, and where. It is a great ice breaker.
>
> —ljc

TIP

When you are invited to a cutting room, bring some donuts or treats for the editorial staff. They may protest about diets and say, "You shouldn't have," but the box will be empty by the time you leave. They will more likely remember you because you have done something unique and generous. However, do not go overboard with expensive offerings because this will negate your good intentions and cause discomfort on their part.

We also recommend keeping a daily account of what you have learned while visiting any cutting room. Your notebook will help remind you of how to perform certain tasks when faced with doing them alone for the first time on your first job. It will also help organize what functions need to still be learned. This journal will ultimately be your time line as you progress on your upwardly mobile path. When several years have passed, you will look at these journals and marvel at how far you have come. It will also be the source of much amusement as you realize how green you were at the very beginning of your career.

Remember that you must have a notebook and pen ready wherever you show up. Take notes when watching an assistant work or when you are just chatting with an editor. It sends out a clear message that you are ready for *anything* and that what is being imparted to you is *important*. The editor will feel that what he said has *reached* you.

13.5 One-Year Plan

One way to ensure success is to have a plan. Envision where you would like to be in your career at the end of one year. You are currently at point A, and you want to be at point B by the end of year one, so work the plan backwards.

Here is a list of goals for you to accomplish by the end of your first year:

1.   Work 100 nonunion days.
2.   Visit the Editors Guild and Complete paperwork and classes to get on the union roster.
3.   Compile a list of contacts and broaden your base of contacts.
4.   Hone your editing machine skills, and improve your knowledge and understanding of VFX.
5.   Position yourself for a union job.

When you first arrive in Los Angeles, go the to the Editors Guild and start your application process. Fill out the preliminary paperwork so that when you are eligible, the process is in the works. It is possible to be in the union within the first year of coming to Hollywood.

You are eligible to join the union when you have worked 100 days on a nonunion show or in a post facility (in the vault—shipping and receiving). These 100 days will get your name on the roster and allow you to take a union job. You will acquire your roster days on reality shows, independent features, documentaries, or trailer houses. Some of the websites to visit to find these jobs are as follows:

- mandy.com
- realitystaff.com
- indeed.com
- simplyhired.com
- entertainmentcareers.net
- indeedjobalert.com

There are new sites to explore all the time, and you must keep abreast of the latest ones. There are also trade papers (*The Hollywood Reporter* and *Variety*) that list films in production and future projects. You can purchase production reports, like *Production Weekly*, which are weekly or monthly updates of all sorts of projects, along with crew names and contact numbers.

Nonunion reality shows are great training grounds for entering the world of filmmaking. Many budding film editors begin their careers there, and some choose to remain—the pay can be good, the opportunities for advancement are abundant, and there is a wave of new production all the time as the genre increases in popularity.

There is also an opportunity to get your days on a documentary or at a trailer house. Exploring these venues can result in realizing that you love one of these niches.

Whichever path you take, your goal is to get 100 days of employment with a paycheck stub as proof. The job title must be assistant editor, apprentice editor, vault, or editorial assistant. With these paycheck stubs and a letter from one or two producers, you will be eligible for the union roster and able to accept a union job. Finish your application process at the Editors Guild, which consists of more paperwork and a class that is offered by the union office. When you are on the roster, the first union job you take will get you into the union! After beginning your job and paying your membership fee, your bank of hours will begin to add up, and you will be eligible to receive medical insurance after working for about six months. Your pension fund starts to grow on your first day.

13.6 Gracefully Leaving Your Nonunion Job

When you are eligible to get on the roster, you will be tempted to leave your nonunion job. Do not leave abruptly. This first venue that offered you work has trained you and has been a generous home for you, so it deserves a bit of loyalty. It has been your foot in the door to an incredibly difficult industry. It is wise to treat such opportunities fairly. They provide a training ground for the next generation. It is good to leave that path intact so that you can return if you need a job again in the future. Give at least two weeks' notice and offer a replacement suggestion. You should also stay to train the new person, making the transition painless for the employer.

Replacing yourself also provides an opportunity for you to give a break to one of the new kids in town. Make yourself available (for free) to help the new assistant. Even if it means working before and after hours, you owe your previous employer a seamless transition to his new employee. Be on good terms with all of your past employers, and they will want to hire you again. They will also be listed on your resume and might get a call regarding your work habits. Remember, your reputation follows you wherever you land. The world of postproduction is much smaller than you think, and word of mouth carries great weight. Ethics counts in how you handle your decisions about leaving a show.

SHINE NOTE

It is *always* a good idea to write thank-you notes to all the people who have helped you. It makes them feel appreciated and special, and they will remember that about you. It is another way to stay in contact with them without asking them for any favors or a job. The assistants who stay in touch with us and/or send us thank-you notes are often the ones we hire or recommend to other editors. It is another way to **shine**.

13.7 When to Look for Work

It is best to look for work while you are still working on a show. Calls made to people on your contact list during your tenure on a film are more readily received. They will not feel that you write to them only when you need a job, and you also appear more successful if you are working. Their estimation of your value increases.

Nobody likes to look for work. It is hard to make calls, send out resumes, or ask for favors. However, it *must* be done throughout your career, so it's best to be good at it. Make contacting people throughout the year a fun, social thing—not a chore. Email your contacts to say hello and give an update about your current job; inquire about how his life and job are going, and comment on his last terrific show. Making these calls is part of *landing* your next gig in advance of *needing* it.

13.8 Choose Your Genre: From Features to Television

After you have gotten into the union, you will be able to choose your genre. Features, television (1 hour, sitcom, long form), documentaries, reality, trailers, and music videos are some of your choices. It is important to choose a path, begin your network of contacts, refine your skills that apply to your chosen genre, and grow your resume.

The film industry is highly compartmentalized. The players involved in features or television are often pigeonholed, allowing very little cross-traffic. Television producers are wary of hiring feature people because they might lack the speed necessary to keep up with a 7-day shoot. Feature producers are opposed to hiring television people for fear they lack the talent, the manners, and the breadth of ability for the large screen. Breaking into *any* field you choose takes time.

Choosing your path allows you to dedicate your time to a specific genre. Each time you change venues, you must network with entirely new people. So choose one and get started. Know that you can change your mind later.

When you have chosen your genre, you should choose who you would like to spend time with in a cutting room. Sometimes this choice will be made for you based simply on who invites you to their cutting room. Ultimately, this will be how you position yourself to be considered for a gig. When a door opens, you have the opportunity to show the editorial staff how hard you work and how easy it is to have you around. You will **shine**! The editor and assistant will hopefully want to take you with them on the next film. If you were to change your genre at this point, you would have to start at an entry-level position again and make new contacts.

Sometimes the worlds overlap; your feature editor does a miniseries, or your television editor is offered a feature, and you follow *his* career path. That works, too. It is possible to change genres once, maybe twice, in a career. Remember that it is only time you have lost in the change of venues.

When considering which genre is right for you and how quickly you might move up to editor, consider the lifestyles that are inherent to that genre, such as the salary, the duration of the gig, whether you leave home to go on location, and the amount of time it takes to move up to editor. Table 13.1 shows estimates for these factors.

Table 13.1 *Genre characteristics*

	Features	*Television*	*Documentaries*	*Reality*
Salary	Highest[a]	Mid–high[b]	Low[c]	Mid–high[d]
Duration	2–24 months	3–10 months	2–6 months	2–10 months
Location shoot	Most likely	Unlikely	Unlikely	No
Upward mobility	5–10 years	3–5 years	1 year	2–3 years
Turnover speed	Many months	1 month	1 month	2–3 weeks
Key				

[a]Assistant: Union scale[d] plus $1000–$3000 per week; Editor: Union scale[d] plus $1000–$10,000 per week
[b]Assistant: Union scale[d] plus $100 per week; Editor: Union scale[d] plus $500 per week
[c]Assistant: Nonunion, $800–$1000 per week; Editor: Nonunion, $1500–$1750 per week
[d]The union scale varies annually. Go to its website at www.editorsguild.com.
Note: Documentaries and reality television are mostly nonunion. Unlike union jobs, you will have to pay for your own health insurance and pension plan.

You can see that the genre you choose comes with inherent lifestyle differences. Also, there is no guarantee that you will be offered an editing position. Skills, having a mentor to advocate for you, your personality, the Fates, and successful films are the guiding factors in the equation. Some of these factors are within your control (skills, finding a mentor, personality), but many are not, so make sure you **shine** in all the categories you can.

In television, there are many opportunities to show the editors, post producers, and executive producers that you have talent beyond your assistant tasks. You can cut in the opening credits, placing them artfully over the first scene of the first act. You can cut a recap of the previous episode's highlights. You can cut a gag reel for the wrap party. You can cut in sound effects, the temp score, and needle drops. Hopefully your editor will have you cut scenes, maybe whole acts. If your editing is well-received by the executives, the editor will most likely sing your praises, thereby increasing the producer's confidence level in your work and status. If, and this is the *big* if, the show is successful (remaining on the air for two or more seasons), your chances for moving up to editor increase exponentially if the editor and producers have been impressed with your work. There are usually two to three editors on episodic television, and one of their seats might open up due to scheduling conflicts, quitting, leaving to do a feature, or not being asked back. If you have already made a mark for yourself, the producer is often inclined to promote from within the ranks.

When opportunity knocks on your door, you must be prepared to perform on a high level. Too many times we've seen assistants have an opportunity to edit and, unfortunately, fail. In the interest of editing a wonderful scene, they tend to fall behind on the workload and their speed becomes an issue. Sometimes their handling of the personalities in the room, the producers or the director, lacks the grace that experience brings, and their communication skills might not be finely honed. Sometimes it is simply due to the fact that their ability to edit needs to be further tuned.

Our advice to all assistants is to cut, cut, cut—every kind of scene possible. Edit a chase, poker game, basketball championship, love scene, montage, two-person argument, three-person dialog scene. Whether your editor asks you to cut these or not, it is in your own best interest to take the time to edit all sorts of scenes. Sometimes you will get feedback, but if not, all you have to do is compare your version to the editor's cut of the scene and ultimately to the final locked. You will have an intimate knowledge of the dailies, understand the problems with the coverage, and be aware of the best eye candy that the director provided. Comparing the cuts should give you insight into your missed moments or the editing patterns chosen by the editor that avoid the pitfalls you were unable to circumnavigate on your own.

In features, there are sometimes fewer opportunities to **shine** because the novice assistant will be on the lowest rung of the ladder. You will start at the apprentice editor level or as the second assistant editor. Your time will be spent doing whatever the first assistant assigns to you. It is usually the first assistant editor who will be given the opportunity to be promoted. You must be patient, work diligently, and wait for your turn. You can still help with the gag reel and edit scenes after hours. Eventually, the first assistant will get a break, and you will inherit the editor. Hopefully he will like your work, give you suggestions, and begin to think of you as a wonderful first assistant *and* accomplished editor. This might take years, or you could be lucky and move up quickly. Sometimes a grateful and generous editor will offer you a coeditor credit. And finally, your hard work will pay off and your dreams will be realized—your editor recommends you for a gig!

Because the duration of time in the cutting room on a feature is longer than in other venues, the length of time you spend cutting and recutting the same film is much greater than anywhere else. There are plus and minus sides to this. You might tire of the story after an extended length of time. The personal relationships in the cutting room might be wearing thin. If you go away on location, you might miss your family, friends, and your hometown's familiar comforts. Distance puts a certain amount of stress on your intimate relationships.

On the plus side, features tell rich, wonderful stories, the direction is stylized, the photography is stunning, and the film makes you proud to be a part of its creation. The length of time spent with your editor and director can lead to lifelong career associations.

The speed of each phase of filmmaking is different in features. The shooting schedule is much longer, and there are often fewer dailies per day. The post schedules of features vary greatly, and more than one editor is often brought on to complete the editing phase quickly. As the release date approaches, the pressure increases, and you might find yourself working 16-hour days as well as weekends. Because your life revolves around finishing this film, it becomes essential to be surrounded by people with whom you can laugh, eat, and work amiably for extended periods of time.

Most low-budget features have only one editor and one assistant editor. The larger the budget of a feature, the larger the staff employed. If there are visual effects in the film, there might be an assistant editor dedicated to working on those scenes along with the VFX editor during the shooting of the show. Your knowledge of the tools to create VFX will serve you well and might facilitate your upward mobility.

Moving up to editor in features generally takes a longer period of time than in television. It will take many films, and therefore many years, to prove your worth to your editor. If you are lucky enough to stay with one editor who works frequently with a prolific director, your rise to editing might take less time. The editor will need to be your advocate, and he will need to convince the director (and sometimes the producer) that it is worth taking a chance on you. Given the critical convergence of all the factors—available position, an editor advocating for you, the director agreeing to give you a break—*you must be ready when opportunity knocks.*

There is so much money involved in the production of a feature that the responsibility of editing the film carries great weight. There are not many studios that will take a chance on a novice editor with that much at stake.

On episodic television, you complete up to 24 *little movies* during a year. It's the same technical process in both venues—from dailies to the online or negative cut. The amount of time allotted for each step differs, budgets vary widely, the staffing is different, but the process is the same. The technical differences you will encounter (a film finish instead of a video finish) can be prepared for as the situation arises. The post facilities, your colleagues, and the heads of postproduction are all willing to give you advice and guidance if you need it.

There are no rules governing the staffing of a cutting room. Before the advent of technology in the 1990s and the influx of digital editing as the norm, the rule of thumb was one editor, one assistant. By the mid-1990s, it was clear that the editorial process had been streamlined and that the three staff editors could share two assistants. We call this a *3–2 show.* Some television productions still hire a 3–3 staff by choice. These shows are usually VFX heavy or high profile enough to warrant a larger budget. Some producers must hire three assistants because of the governing Editors Guild rules about independent productions.

An assistant must have special aptitudes to perform well on a 3–2 show. You are often required to please three editors and a coproducer at the *same* time. The tactics we discussed earlier work best. Let each person know you have a conflict, and let your editors prioritize for you. If the three editors are in disagreement and each needs help simultaneously, it is best to let the coproducer help make the decisions. It will get easier during the course of the season, and eventually you will be able to prioritize on your own.

On the first season of *Make It or Break It*, a 3–2 needle drop show, we were fortunate enough to have two assistants, Melissa Brown and Tim Brinker, who were so congenial, compatible, and generous that they made the three editors feel like we *each* had two assistants instead of two-thirds of one assistant.

—ljc

SHINE NOTE

Be *extra* nice in the cutting room—offer your editor a random cup of tea, a chocolate bar when his energy is waning, and stock the fridge with his favorite drinks. This ability to make each editor feel taken care of is one more way to **shine**. When an editor is pleased with an assistant, he will be inclined to nurture him on his road to editing and do what he can to make sure the assistant is successful.

The rules of etiquette become enormously important in the feature cutting room. Just as five-star hotels provide niceties, such as after-dinner mints on the pillow, fluffy bathrobes on wooden hangers, and polite, solicitous hosts, the manners and customs on a feature offer similar treatment for the editor. Unfortunately, these practices have not been instilled in the behavior of the majority of the postproduction staff in television. It is more like a Motel 6. There are so few assistants left in television who were trained with these standards. Your success in television will increase tenfold if you bring with you the etiquette suggested in this book. Make your editing room, whether feature or television, a five-star hotel, and you will **shine**.

Chapter 14

Plan Ahead and Move Up

You have joined the union, landed yourself a job within the genre of your choice, and are successfully making contacts. You continue to keep a journal and hone your skills as an assistant editor. You have moved from point A to point B. During the second year of your career, you have gone through the process of dailies to online many times on a television show and once or twice on a feature. You are confident. You are paid great sums of money, and you have medical insurance and a pension plan. It is time to start planning part C of your career path for the next couple of years. If you stay the course, you will move that much closer to the day you move up to editor.

14.1 Three-Year Plan

Hopefully, you still enjoy the genre in which you have chosen to start your career. It is not uncommon to be curious about the other paths you have yet to explore. If you prefer to work in a different venue, now is the time to make the change to the other genre. New contacts have to be made to crossover. More donuts need to be bought. The final goal during this time period is to find yourself assisting on a show that allows you to become ready to move up to editor if the opportunity should arise. Changing venues might delay this upward mobility, so think carefully before you make the move.

Perhaps you are happy on features but wish you had some experience on dramatic television. It is *always* a good thing to have a season of TV under your belt. If you are working on a television show and want to explore features, it is best to try to switch as soon as possible. Sometimes it is harder to land a feature gig when you have been working on TV than it is to get a TV job after working on features. This is true for the assistant as well as the editor. Remember to look for work while you are still employed!

Here is a list of some goals to reach by the end of your third year:

- Work on a union job.
- Hone your assisting skills.
- Cut every day.

DOI: 10.1016/B978-0-240-81398-1.00014-6

- Work for an editor who is supportive of your editing goals.
- Expand your network base and meet directors.
- Work on a show that will lead to an editing position.

Because you are in the union and receiving those wonderful paychecks for the first time in your life, you might be tempted to buy lots of expensive toys. Cars. Cha-ching! Another monthly bill comes in. Entertainment centers filled with 60-inch LED screens and multiple channels of high-def reception. Cha-ching! Label clothing, fashionable adornments, furniture, vacation resorts, and restaurant and club hopping. Cha-ching, ching, ching! This is a big mistake. All of these toys will go on your credit card, and you will be in debt before you can say, "in sync." Your career choices will now be incredibly limited.

14.2 Money Management

When you have credit card debt, you limit your choices as to what jobs to take because your decisions are based on financial needs. With golden handcuffs—possessions and debt—you will not be free to turn down a job, or stay out of work to look for that right position in the genre of your choice, or make it through the months of unemployment that generally follow each gig.

As soon as you start to earn a good salary, pay off your student loans and car payment as quickly as possible. It is expensive money. It is also important that you start an individual retirement account (IRA) because the pension fund from the union will not be substantial enough to support you in retirement. Putting away at least $42 a week adds up to $2000 per year and will have exponential returns for you when you reach retirement age.

To help you budget, a good rule of thumb is provided in Table 14.1.

Table 14.1 *Planning a budget*

First week salary	Should equal your monthly rent
Second week salary	Goes to bills
40% of third week salary	Pays off student loans and car payment
20% of third week salary	Put in savings account for when you are unemployed
20% of third week salary	Automatically deposit into IRA
20% of third week salary	Put in savings account to buy a house (if you have debt from student or car loans, this percentage of salary should be applied to the loan payments until they are gone)
Fourth week salary	Fun money: Toys and vacations (the more you *save* of this money, the greater number of career choices you will have)

If you are able to follow these general rules of banking your salary, you will have the best control over your career path. Money should not be the deciding factor for the job you choose. Remember, there will be unemployment between gigs, and you must have a nest egg to survive these times. Your savings will free you to take the time to network with colleagues, to look for work, and *wait* for the job you really want. It is essential to have savings for hiatus so that you can stay your course.

Amortize your salary to make sure you are not overextending yourself. For example, if you work on a television show with a full season of 22 episodes, you will probably average 10 months of work, with a 2-month hiatus. To know how much your amortized monthly salary is, divide your annual income by 12 months. Now you can approximate how much you can afford to pay for rent. Your hiatus will be much less stressful if you are prepared for downtime. You will be able to *choose* when to take your next gig.

> **SHINE NOTE**
>
> Always volunteer for extracurricular activities and partake in social functions with the Editors Guild and ACE. You must *participate!* This is one of the secrets to being a successful assistant editor.

14.3 Perform at Your Highest Level

Stephen Lovejoy, A.C.E. shared this wisdom at the Internship Lecture Series in 2009:

> These are the standards you need to set for yourself in this business. What happens is that when you get into a working environment you are going to have a few other assistants that do not abide by these rules. Do not become like them. Avoid becoming the lazy assistant or the assistant who only does something when asked instead of anticipating what to do. I've seen this decline in standards happen time after time. Never allow yourself to adopt that negative attitude. If you have an internal desire for excellence you are an invaluable asset to the editor. If you don't possess it, I don't have time to teach it to you. When I was growing up people really cared about their quality of work and how they treated people. A lot of that has disappeared from our society and our world altogether so when you meet people with that burning desire to be the best they can possibly be—just give me that person. I can do something with that person.

One assistant in the audience asked, "How do those crappy assistants get hired in the first place?" Stephen responded, "In terms of the business, there are hundreds of movies that are made every year that never appear in major markets. There is a whole industry that produces them and distributes mediocre product. Because of movies of lesser budgets and quality, people get used to assistants who are kind of lazy and do not wish to excel. There are a lot of people who are threatened by excellence."

Allow yourself to follow the higher road of standards. Regardless of the venue, the budget, or the scope of the film, do what you really love to do and **shine** in your job.

14.4 Edit Every Day

The best deposit you can make in the bank of your career is to edit everyday. It is the only way that you will be prepared to *make the cut* when the time comes to move up to editor. Even when the editor has *not* asked you to cut, you should take the time to cut as many scenes as possible. Every day. We know you are tired, dailies can be challenging, multitasking and assisting multiple editors is exhausting. It is difficult to retain enough energy at the end of a 10-hour day to begin cutting a scene. We suggest that you come in at the crack of dawn when the editing rooms are empty and quiet. This way you will not be distracted or called upon to answer phones or perform workday chores.

Show your scenes to your editor. Ask for notes and make the changes. Practice makes perfect! If you find yourself in a job where the editors are not willing to mentor you, reevaluate your current job and ask yourself whether your three-year plan is moving forward.

In some cases, it is hard to determine what your chances are of getting moved up to editor, but there are some universal factors that must be in place, including having honed your editing skills while still assisting.

14.5 Upward Mobility

There are several key people involved in moving you up. They are your editor, the coproducer, and the executive producers. You need the support of all of them. During the time that you have assisted on your current show, you have cut recaps, gag reels, and countless scenes. You have developed relationships and laid the groundwork for moving up to editor.

If you have been assisting on a show for three or four years and you know you will not be moved up when a seat becomes available, then you must reevaluate whether to stay with the editor who hired you or whether to stay with the show at all. However, try not to burn bridges if you do leave.

To successfully move up to editor, you should find a new job that offers a more supportive crew who can help you advance. It is also important that there is an editor there willing to mentor you, as well as the possibility of an editing seat opening up. It is often hard to find these safe situations. Do your homework before taking another job, and make sure it is an environment in which you can **shine**. Ask other assistant editors, film editors, and mentors for advice, and soundboard your ideas with them.

14.6 Cementing Relationships

During the course of your career, there will be long-term relationships that develop between you and your editors, other assistants, and hopefully producers and directors. When you find one of the good guys, cherish him. There are a lot of bad guys out there. Our world of postproduction is truly a small family, and we must take care of one another. Never leave a show without giving advance notice, and always suggest and train a replacement for yourself.

On every film, you should take the opportunity to meet as many new people as possible. If your cutting rooms are on the studio lot, there are editors and assistants downstairs, upstairs, and in the neighboring bungalow. Wander down the halls, check out the nameplates, and look them up on IMDb. Introduce yourself. Or better yet, ask your editor to introduce you. Keep broadening your base of contacts and make new friends. There is nothing like networking to guarantee that you will find work all the time.

During your tenure on a show, try to make sure that at least two of your bosses would want to hire you again—the producers, other editors, or someone on the postproduction staff. But always remember that your primary responsibility is to be the best assistant editor possible and to keep your editor happy.

14.7 Gracefully Leaving Your Union Job

Leaving is *always* an issue, especially when you've been a great asset to the show. There are a few good excuses that will not burn bridges or cause your boss to be angry:

- Moving up to editor: Any opportunity to move up to editor is generally understood and sanctioned by all editors and producers.
- Leaving for a feature: It is understood in television that an opportunity to work on a feature is desirable. Understand, though, that each time you leave TV to take a feature, your reputation will follow you, and people will be less willing to hire you in television again.
- Leaving for a longer gig: If your show is ending soon, and you are offered a job that will last longer, your editor will understand if you choose to leave. Most editors do not want to lose their assistant midstream—training a new person is time consuming and hard work—so you need to help out as much as possible during this transition and make sure that no one feels abandoned or annoyed.
- Personal issues: Leaving a position due to personal issues will not burn bridges. However, if you have prior commitments already on your calendar that occur during the course of the shoot, let your employers know in advance. A wedding and honeymoon, new baby, or health issues can be worked around, but full disclosure at the start of the project is necessary.

> **TIP**
>
> The Editors Guild does not have maternity leave for either parent, so oftentimes we have to consider when would be best to start a family. In network television, there is still a fall season that starts around July and ends between March and May, so there are a few months between May and July when hiatus babies are born! In cable TV and features, there is no fall season per se, so scheduling a family is more challenging.

If you have positioned yourself carefully, edited your heart out, networked with others and developed solid relationships, and been lucky enough to be on a successful TV show, your chances for being promoted by the end of your third or fourth year are good. If your goals are set high, then you should certainly be editing by the end of five years. With a little bit of luck, you will be on your way!

Chapter 15

On the Brink of Editing

It is possible for you to move up from assistant editor to editor on a television series as quickly as five years after the day you set foot in Hollywood! Some people even land a job as an editor on a student film, documentary, or independent feature right away. This is rare but not impossible.

> I got my break to move up to editor on a movie of the week, *Thou Shalt Not Commit Adultery*, when I was 24, just three years after moving to Hollywood. Understand, though, that prior to this opportunity I had worked my butt off. I cut film every chance I had, found several mentors, and worked outrageous hours. I was primed and ready to cut when Bud Isaacs, A.C.E., the editor, had to leave the film for health reasons. Bud recommended that I be moved up to editor during his absence. The director, Delbert Mann (*Separate Tables*, *Marty*), asked me to cut a reel (about 10 minutes of screen time) for the following morning. He liked what he saw, and I got the gig plus a great credit for my resume!
>
> —ljc

When you set your goals, set the bar high. You just might surprise yourself and accomplish everything you hoped for. Do not be disappointed if your plans take longer than scheduled. Reevaluate the path your career takes at all times and make the necessary adjustments to reach your goals.

15.1 Five-Year Plan

At the end of your first five years of being an assistant editor (or maybe even 10 years, if you've chosen features), you should be ready to advance to editing. Before opportunity knocks, you will have accomplished the following:

- Already been promised that the next available editing seat will be yours
- Expanded your network (it now includes producers and directors)
- Advanced your skill set to include heavy VFX
- Studied the editing styles of many editors and be able to emulate various styles
- Edited projects during hiatus and received credit

DOI: 10.1016/B978-0-240-81398-1.00015-8

15.2 That Promised Seat

There is no guarantee that your TV show will get the *back nine* (a pickup of nine more episodes to add to the original network order for a pilot and 12 episodes). If you have the misfortune to be on a show that is not renewed or gets canceled midseason, you have to start your journey to move up to editor on the next show. Making friends, winning support, and clearing the path becomes your mantra. Choosing the right TV show becomes a talent. You will either follow your editor or the producers of the recently canceled show. Maybe they are one and the same. During your tenure with these colleagues, you must always let it be known that you want to move up to editor, show that you are willing to go the extra mile whenever asked, and remind them that you hope you will be considered for the next available seat. Remember, all the people involved in post *must* want to see you succeed. Continue to take every opportunity to cut—scenes, gag reels, titles, montages. Do their notes and changes with enthusiasm, and remain passionate about each project.

Sometimes, one of the editors will leave the show early to cut a pilot or a feature. You can go with the editor to his next gig, which is probably *his* preference, or you can stay on the show, and if asked, cut his episode. The politics of this decision is tricky and can be evaluated in a case by case scenario. Moving up to editor is what you have been working for, so we suggest you take the opportunity to edit if it presents itself!

Be prepared at the beginning of your editing career to move up and then back down to assistant while in this transitional stage.

> After cutting my first MOW, I had to go back to assisting on a feature, *Divine Madness*, directed by Michael Ritchie. Glenn Farr, A.C.E. had to leave the show early, and he promoted Alan Balsam, the first assistant, to editor. When Alan had to leave, I was moved up to editor for the second time in my career, before Glenn came back to finish up. My next gig was *Zorro, the Gay Blade*, directed by Peter Medak. The first film editor, Ray Lovejoy (*2001: A Space Odyssey, The Shining*), was from England, and the production needed a standby American editor. While on location, I assisted Ray and I was moved up to editor for the third time in my career when we returned to Los Angeles. When that film was completed, I decided I would try to not go back to assisting. I turned down several assisting jobs and waited for an editing offer. Ray Lovejoy was kind enough to convince Peter Medak to hire me again on his next gig. I had to wait seven months, but it paid off, and Peter hired me on his next project, a movie of the week. I never looked back!
>
> —ljc

If you have remained on a successful show for the last three years and not one editor has left, you must evaluate whether it is worth your time to remain on this show. If the producers have moved up the other assistant instead of you or brought in an editor from outside to fill in the vacant slot, read the writing on the wall. Changing shows at this point might put you behind your schedule, but you need to look for another job where you *can* move up to editor successfully.

15.3 Expanding Your Network

By now, your network of editors, assistants, and postproducers has expanded. To move up to editor on television, you must also have access to the heads of postproduction of the major studios. Contact them all, or better yet, go and see them, and send them your new resume that reflects your credits as an editor.

When you do make the move up to editor, it is important that your networking now include as many directors as possible. They will remember having worked with you as an assistant, and it is to your benefit to let them know how well you have progressed and that one day you hope to get to work with them as their editor.

Your network should also include producers and co-producers for television. With a good reference from your editor, they will most likely hire you. They want an editor who will work their heart out for them, stay late willingly without demanding much overtime, and possibly bring a youthful point of view to the show. Start to cultivate these relationships as soon as you can.

15.4 Advanced Skills

You will impress your producers and directors when you have a broad base of knowledge about the latest digital technologies. You will be able to utilize these skills as an assistant and when you become an editor. It's an exciting, changing world in post, and there are countless opportunities to take seminars and classes.

15.5 Editing Styles

Watch the way your editor cuts a scene. Notice if he prelaps or postlaps (L-shaped cuts that allow audio to start before or after the visual edit), how often and when he uses the master, and when he chooses to score a scene and where he likes to start the cue. You can learn so much from recognizing these editing patterns. If you are able to recognize how your editor likes to cut, then you will be able to emulate his style when you cut a scene for him. After receiving change notes from him, make a mental note about how to apply these suggestions to the next scene you cut. The next set of change notes will be a much smaller list!

One of my all-time favorite scenes is the train wreck in the film *The Fugitive*. I asked Richard Nord, A.C.E., one of the six editors on the movie (Don Brochu, David Finfer, Dean Goodhill, Dov Hoenig, A.C.E., and Dennis Virkler, A.C.E.), which editor had cut this exciting scene. He said that almost every editor on the show had taken a pass at one time or another! I was amazed. The entire movie had a seamless, unified flow and style. The combined efforts of many editors and the overall look of the show must end up being uniform.

—ljc

In addition to learning the style of editing that your current editor has, you should become familiar with the body of work of your original five favorites. You will learn some wonderful techniques to add to your bag of tricks!

15.6 Edit During Hiatus

If you have done everything we have discussed so far to prepare for the day you get the opportunity to cut, there is still one more step you should take. During hiatus you must find independent editing jobs. Look for webisodes, training videos, documentaries, student films, music videos, or your own films to cut. That way, when your editor or post producer tries to advocate for you and get you moved up, there will be more editing credits on your resume with which to impress the executives.

The temptation to go on vacation or just relax during hiatus is tremendous. Remember that you are making a deposit in the bank of *your* career when you continue to pursue jobs that will help expedite the realization of your dreams.

15.7 Remaining an Assistant

There is *nothing* wrong with wanting to stay an assistant. If your reputation is solid, the advantage of staying an assistant editor is that you will always be in high demand and have a steady income. You can pick and choose the shows and people with whom you would like to work.

15.8 In Conclusion

There are multiple venues that will teach you the nuts and bolts of assistant editing as well as editing. There are Avid and FCP training courses given worldwide. There are free seminars, extension classes, and the lecture series offered annually through A.C.E. Through these classes and lectures, you will meet fellow assistants and film editors, all of whom are willing to discuss their career paths, open their editing rooms to you, and encourage you with their tales of how they got started in the business. These are opportunities to network, which is an essential part of starting your career. Be proactive about meeting people and learning new skills by checking the Editors Guild and A.C.E websites. Subscribe to *The CinemaEditor* magazine!

Participate. Be Helpful. Be Cheerful.

You will be remembered that way.

If you follow all the steps we have enumerated, we can assure you that you will eventually have an opportunity to become a film editor. If you stay in your hometown, from San Francisco to New York, Sydney to Rome, London to Cape Town, Beijing to Mumbai, the same rules still apply. Cut, cut, cut. Stay your course. Work hard and **shine**.

It is ultimately *you* who has the power to make the cut.

Part 4

Commonality

Chapter 16

Editors Panel Discussion

Destiny is no matter of chance. It is a matter of choice. It is not a thing to be waited for, it is a thing to be achieved.

William Jennings Bryan

There is a passion for perfection which you will rarely see fully developed; but you may note this fact, that in successful lives it is never wholly lacking.

Bliss Carman

When a group of film editors gather, there is an old joke. If asked their opinion, four editors will have five opinions. But when it comes to their career paths traveled, or the expected etiquette of the cutting room, or the passion to succeed as a film editor, there is a commonality to each of our stories that binds us as a community—the search for excellence, the commitment to the truth of the scene, and an incredible love for the craft of editing.

American Cinema Editors has an internship program during which a panel of A.C.E. editors share their stories with an audience of aspiring editors and assistant editors. The subjects that the panelists touch upon can be recognized as some of the themes we have shared with you throughout this book.

The following excerpts include comments by the following editors:

- Matt Chesse, A.C.E.
- Lori Jane Coleman, A.C.E.
- Diana Friedberg, A.C.E.
- Alan Heim, A.C.E.
- Mark Helfrich, A.C.E.
- Stephen Lovejoy, A.C.E.
- Sabrina Plisco, A.C.E.
- Troy Takaki, A.C.E.

© 2010 Elsevier Inc. All rights reserved.
DOI: 10.1016/B978-0-240-81398-1.00016-X

```
TIP

Recognize your own personal-
ity in the following discussions.
When we talk about events that
have alienated us from cer-
tain types of assistant editors,
ask yourself, "Is that me? Do I
do that?" Realize that you are
capable of fixing these quirks
or traits. Be absolutely honest
with yourself.
```

Lori

When hiring your editorial staff, what sort of traits do you look for?

Stephen

I hardly ever hire anybody that hasn't worked for me or for some-body I know in the past. It's really tough to evaluate somebody in 5 or 10 minutes. Of course, they're putting their best foot forward and their resume can say they've worked on many things. So when I call people I ask who is hot, who is good, and who have they discovered.

Lori

So word-of-mouth is key for you?

Stephen

Yes, it's really the thing that works the best. I look for somebody that obviously has done the job. It is more their approach that is important. We're telling a story here and I want the assistant to be as involved as they can possibly be. I've had assistants who have liked to cut and I like that. I like to interface and discuss cuts with them and help them understand the cutting process too.

Lori

What I look for is someone with whom I feel comfortable. Someone I look forward to seeing every day.

Mark

I'm completely reliant on my assistants because I know next to nothing about technical things. Because if you do know it, like if you admit you can type, you're going to have to type. My assistants do all the technical stuff. I don't know how to input. I don't know how to output. I'm not really proud of that but it's a fact. And it's changing all the time. I'm really reliant on their technical know-how. That knowledge and a good person-ality is what count the most. And be a nonsmoker. You can smell smokers, when they come in. If somebody is overperfumed—it's just as bad.

Lori

So personal hygiene *can* be an issue. When interviewing, we look at personal habits as well.

Mark

A couple of months ago I edited a music video and the producer hired the assistant and assured me the guy was great, he'd done commercials. I said, "Great, how hard can it be?" It should have taken two days to cut this piece and finish it but unfortunately this well-meaning assistant was wrong in everything that he did. Every technical thing that he could have screwed up, he screwed up. I didn't know until later that he had screwed up and I ended up working for two weeks on a music video that should have taken two days. Finally I was able to fire him because I said I could not take it anymore. I told the producer, "Just give me somebody who can output this thing." So they did and then they went to do the online, and nothing matched the master HD. What they ended up having to do was to eyeball every single shot and it took three days to conform at an astronomical cost. So that one assistant cost this company hundreds of thousands of dollars—and will never again work in this town.

But seriously—if by some chance somebody asks if you know how to do something, and you don't want to lose the job, and you really think that you can do it, then tell them you can do it and go home that night and find out how to do it. I'm not against saying, "Sure I can do that," but you have to have the confidence to know you can get the task accomplished. We don't expect you to have all the experience in the world from the get-go, but you have to be confident to know you're not going to screw up. You get one shot at some of these things and then you're blacklisted. You also don't want to say you don't know how to do that or "I've never done it before" when it could be learned. I'm not telling you to lie—but what I'm saying is—you've just got to know that you *can* do what you're offering to do.

Alan

When I started, if I didn't know something, I would call a friend and they would tell me how to do it. That's what a network is about and that's really important if you don't know how to do something. You better either read the manual really fast or call somebody up. Know somebody to call.

Mark

But you want to jump on that opportunity. If you're being offered a job and you feel that you can do it, then accept. If you feel you can't, you might just want to save yourself for the next time. Say, "I don't know that system, but I'm going to learn it."

Alan

I'd like to say one more thing on this topic. I was a sound effects editor in New York and one day a guy I'd gone to school with called me and said, "Can you edit picture?" I said, "Can I edit picture!" I had never edited picture, except at school where I was pretty good at it, but this was a real job. It was a real job in St. Louis, Missouri on an industrial film, a political film actually. And I had never done this in my life. I was terrified. I was absolutely terrified. So I called my psychiatrist, I had one then, and I sat down with her. And she said, "You know, if you're really as scared as you say you are, you better not take it."

So I walked across the street, because they were across the street, and I said, "You know, I really don't want to miss this opportunity, I absolutely can do this." Again, I relied on my friends in New York. I knew I could call them, and I did the job. I ended up doing a couple more films for this company. At one point the director I worked with—we were quite friendly after the first film—and I were having a drink one night, and he said, "When you started, when you came out to St. Louis, you were really pretty green weren't you?" And I said, "How'd you know?" He said, "Well you kept throwing the picture into the sound head." You have to understand that in those days, sound and picture were separate. They looked different. Sound looked like audio tape and the sound was brown and the picture had picture on it. But because I was so used to working with sound, it just seemed second nature to me. Eventually I stopped doing that, I guess!

Stephen

When I got my job on *Tales from the Crypt*, the postproduction supervisor hired me unaware that only the night before, I'd been in a room learning the Montage editing system. Somebody had showed me how to do a splice in and splice out, and that's all I knew walking in the door for the interview. But by the time I needed to know, I'd figured it out, because I could get on the phone and call friends.

Lori

The idea is not to pass up opportunities but not to be too cocky. My first job back after seven years of raising my kids was on *Beverly Hills, 90210*. The producer, Chuck Rosin, was a friend of mine—we'd gone to high school together—so I was sort of safe. They asked, "This show is digital, have you learned digital?" "Sure." "Can you use a Montage?" "No problem." "Good, you start on Monday." This was a Friday. That weekend I went into the cutting rooms and worked that Montage to death, cutting every way imaginable until the machine crashed. I didn't know how to fix it, so I went home. But on Monday I had this incredible assistant, Dan Valverde (currently an editor on *Damages*), talk me through the remaining problems. The Montage editing machine was just another tool to learn—I knew how to edit. You have to take some chances. And work your little tushies off.

Sabrina

That's really the bottom line, just know the parameters of what you know, what you don't know, what you're willing to do, and what you're not willing to do. I had a chat with my old assistant about this and he said, "You know the most valuable piece of information I have as an assistant is—I don't know everything, but I can find out. That's the most important thing." And with the network, with the Internet, with everything that's out there, there are ways to find out.

Matt

I actually lost a great assistant because she sort of stopped having the eye of the tiger, which I think you need to have when you're an assistant. You can tell when somebody is really into it and really fired up. The first film we worked on together, she did a great job, had my back and I just never worried about it. Then we moved on to another film a year later and she was organizing the project and the dailies and there was a sort of lack of pickup going on. I asked about it and she said, "It'll be okay, it'll be okay." I started to get this very soft impression about her and by the end of the job she had let a visual effect go into the movie that she had miscalled the numbers on. The key code reader from the movie wasn't accurate and she didn't double-check those when she loaded them. We wound up with this very expensive visual effect that didn't match what I'd cut. Once it was baked in there, there was no way to go back. I would never have changed assistants, but this one mistake really hurt. What it came down to was that she was tired of doing the job she was being hired for and really wanted to edit. Whatever the reason, I wound up getting burned and we had to have a big talk about it. She moved on and became an editor and that was great for her but it was frustrating for me to be stuck with somebody who had lost her edge.

It's a big responsibility to be first assistant or second assistant. You touch a lot of things that nobody else touches. If you're not holding up your end of the bargain, you can really cause a lot of havoc. It's not to be taken lightly and it's not all about learning and being green. A lot of it is about applying yourself, holding up your end of the bargain. Editors don't have the time to double-check the assistant's work, you're busy cutting the movie.

Lori

Many assistants get to that point at the end of their assisting career and they're not willing to work as hard. They get a chip on their shoulder. This becomes very difficult for an editor to work with because he knows they want to move on and he can feel their frustration. It burns the editor and possibly his relationship with the director, or the producer. It's a reflection upon the assistant. The assistant is the final safety net in that editing room when dailies are wrong, when numbers are wrong, when visual effects come in, when things don't get shipped, when playback is not on the stage—all the things that the assistant is responsible for. The assistant is the final safety net. Truly. The last stop. It's too late by the time the editor sees it. The editor trusts the assistant.

Mark

Assistants are like the ambassador for the editor, especially in studio situations. The people in the studio get to know your assistants, your apprentices, your runner. They hardly ever come into the editing room and meet you or talk to you but they're talking to your assistants and your crew all the time. So then the studio will say, "Oh, we love to work with Mark Helfrich," but what they mean is, they love to work with Mark Helfrich's crew because they don't even know who I am! So that's why it's important to have a really good crew. I have to like them, they have to be smart and have good taste.

Troy

We will hire our assistants over and over if they have good attitude. One of my assistants is a really good friend of my director and of mine, and on the last movie, he stopped giving his all. Because we were friends, I'd walk in and I'd say, "Okay, stop the DVD, I've made a change, start the output again." And he'd say, "What, why'd you do that?" His attitude was, "Troy is my friend and I can roll my eyes at him." I'm never allowed to roll my eyes at my director when he walks in and says, "I've changed my mind, let's put the sound effect back." I say, "Okay, sound effect's back." And the sound effect is back.

Everybody has to be having fun and have his heart in it. You can never think that you're such good friends with the director or the editor that you're allowed to roll your eyes at them and complain. You're never allowed to be late, complain, or disrupt. All of those things are just so important to everything working correctly when everybody is overwhelmed by the workload.

Stephen

That's why working with friends doesn't work, by and large.

Lori

Sometimes colleagues do become true friends, but you can't confuse the boundaries while you are on the job.

On another topic, how does the editor know whether everyone on his team is doing his job, especially the second or third assistant?

Sabrina

I actually deal with everybody when I run the ship. I look to my first. I dialog with my first constantly because I want to know everything that is going on. I even want to know where the runner is going, but that is whom I am. I practically posted my last show. Even the post people at Disney said, "Well we didn't do this because you did it all." I probably work a little bit differently than most people because I keep my door open. I want to know what is going on all day long with everybody *and* I get my work done. I feel like I can keep the machine running smoothly if I know everything.

Matt

It kind of helps morale to connect with everybody that you are working with, so that nobody is serving you in a way that feels different or distant. If they know who you are and that they are working for you and you have an open room, then they want to do a good job. The first assistant will usually tell you if there is a weak link. Often the post supervisor fills other positions by recommending somebody for the job. I think this is good idea because if somebody screws up, it is going to fall back in the post supervisor's lap. So, sometimes part of the team is assembled and maintained by the post supervisor. Usually, if something goes wrong, they turn on someone—there's always a scapegoat. The first assistant carries a lot of that responsibility.

Sabrina

I worked at two different studios during the last couple of years and each ran things so differently. On *Charlotte's Web* we had a post supervisor who was literally right next door to me and she handled a lot of stuff. But on *Chihuahua* with Disney, the post super was someone up in a tall building that had five shows and so literally, *I* was the post super. Every studio and setup is different and every show has its own way of running things.

Matt

Generally, I try to keep a small team because it makes it easier. Less people work harder and as a result there is better communication. The Bond movie that I worked on (*Quantum of Solace*) definitely had more floors and more people. The more delegations, the further it gets away from the creative cut in the Avid and your being in control. If you can, try and keep it tight.

Mark

Usually I'll hire the first assistant and I'll let the first assistant hire everybody under him or her because that's who they like to work with and that's cool with me. The responsibility of the first assistant is to not let me down with the crew. If you're working on a feature for nine months or a year, then you are going to get to know them, no matter what, even if it is just during lunch.

I've had bad experiences with assistants on past films. My wife called me once and one of the runners or assistants answered the phone and she said to me, "Who was *that* on the phone? They don't have very good phone etiquette. They sound dead and bored." I had to go and take care of that problem and speak to that person. "Wake up!"

Lori

Would you give that task to your first assistant or would you go to the person directly?

Mark

No, I'd tell my first assistant. Tell her to wake up. But I've always had good luck giving that responsibility to my assistant because they're really the ones running the show.

Lori

It's quite different in every room. The television show I am working on now, I didn't get to pick the first assistant that came on. He was chosen because he knows Final Cut Pro and I was asked by the coproducer, "How is it going?" and I said, "He is very proficient on Final Cut Pro." Efficiency is one thing but it is challenging because he has none of the etiquette and knows little about the unwritten rules in the cutting room.

Troy

And the opposite of that can happen too. I was starting this pilot and I called and said I have to cut on Avid and they said, "Nope, it's going to be on Final Cut Pro." "Are you sure it can't be on Avid?" "No, it's got to be on Final Cut Pro." I was talking to Joe Dervan, head of post, and I hang up the phone and I thought about it for a couple days. I called back and I said, "I will cut on Final Cut Pro." They said, "This is what you'll do, you'll cut on Final Cut Pro, we'll get you a really good assistant, a Final Cut Pro assistant. We'll get you really good machines, it's going to be great." I hung up the phone, called back a few days later and said, "I will cut it on Final Cut Pro, but I am bringing *my* assistant, even though he doesn't know Final Cut Pro, and you are training him and me." I would much rather have a great assistant that knows me and knows how I work that will learn Final Cut Pro, than someone who knows Final Cut Pro and I have to train to be a great assistant.

Lori

If, as an assistant, you are assigned to an editor, it is advisable for the assistant to go to that person and say, "I realize I've been assigned to you and that might be an issue. And I just want you to know that I'm on your team. I work for you. You let me know—how do you like your dailies, what makes you happy, do you take your coffee black? What can I do to make this okay?"

Mark

…and "Am I talking too much?"

Lori

…and "Is there anything you want to tell me because I would like to know how to make it work here."

Troy

Some of my best assistants have been given to me by the studios and just because they are given to you, doesn't mean you are going to have a conflict and want to fire them.

Sabrina

I think a lot of it has to do with personality. If you are assigned somebody, it just means that you didn't get to meet or chat with them in advance, to see if there is that connection.

Lori

I know as an editor, I've been put on shows and not hired by the executive producer and I had to win over the coproducer who had nothing to do with my hiring. You have to win them over and it is uphill. You just work twice as hard.

Mark

The oddest instance of not hiring an assistant or a crew happens when you are asked to take over a film. They've fired the editor and they want to bring you in to save the picture. I've done a few of those. Once I inherited the entire crew. The editor had gone, but I was left with his team. I said, "That's fine, they know where everything is, they know all the dailies, I'll be fine." It was fine, technically, and we were all feeling very comfortable. We learn that what's said in the editing room should stay in the editing room and you can say things to your assistant and vice versa and it will never go further than that. There is an unstated trust among your team. Quite often I will watch dailies and I'll laugh out loud because they are so bad or I'll say, "What the hell is he thinking?" I can say that to my crew, but I wouldn't say it to the director or the actors. In the editing room, you're constantly making fun of performances and all that stuff.

Troy

They are very funny until we get a hold of them.

Mark

In one instance I probably crossed the line and the trust was breached. The crew and I were looking at a cut of a scene that the original editor had done and in the middle of it I just let out this guttural moan, like "Oh, this is so terrible!" And I thought everybody agreed with me. But there was a turncoat whose allegiance was with the original editor. Somehow that got back to the original editor. As a result, the oddest thing happened. I got a letter from the original editor that read, "I hear that you don't think much of my cutting." I was so embarrassed that this had got out, but I was also furious that it had gone beyond the walls of the cutting room. We found the leak and the case was closed. He was "taken for a short ride." I made up with the editor but that was very embarrassing for me. I should have been more careful because it wasn't my original crew. But hey, I had already been on the show for about two months and thought that by that time they were my crew, but it wasn't the case.

Matt

The crew that I worked with on the Bond movie, I inherited from the *Golden Compass* and they had been through three editors in a very intense, short period of time. They had to change their allegiances and support for three different people who thought they were all going to come in and finish the picture—and then didn't. And then the first editor came back at the end and I think it was quite a dance. They really had to get into step with it all. They were great. They were road tested. I loved that British crew. They had that diplomacy to make it all happen in the end. I inherited them part and parcel from *Golden Compass* and they were totally trashed from that film but we kind of revived them and gave them a transfusion.

Lori

What advice would you give to those who are new to the whole assistant editor position, because you all seem to keep the same assistants? What kind of actions do they need to take besides doing a great job and standing out, going above and beyond? Do you have any other bits of advice?

Matt

I've hired from resumes, maybe five times out of eight movies that I've done. I've gone with totally cold calls from resumes and sat down, met three or four people and made a decision. I was looking for an assistant once when I got this really nice thank you letter. I liked the stationary and this young woman had really nice handwriting. I felt she just separated herself from the pack.

I've had really good luck with resumes and recommendations and just picking people. When I got to London for the Bond movie, I had about a week to pick the entire crew from top to bottom including sound people. I probably met with about 20 assistants who all wanted to be the first assistant. I got all of the editors they'd just worked with writing me letters of recommendation for them and calling on the phone. It was quite the derby of personalities, but I worked it out. I would say that the resumes and sitting down and having a meeting works, definitely.

Alan

What is good is to be yourself. Because we are editors, we read performance and so, just be honest when you interview.

Matt

Don't lay it on too thick.

Alan

And the pretty writing is nice. Somebody's got to do it, I sure can't.

Matt

And having good recommendations, too. Have people that know and trust you on your resume because I call all those people for references.

Mark

Even if they have worked with another editor and they are not on the resume, I will call the editor and say, "So what do you know about this guy?" If they *are* on it as references, then you know the person is going to say "Oh yeah, they are great." But call the person who is not on there and get the real feedback. But that said, you could have had a bad year and a bad experience with somebody many years ago, so you can't just judge a person by one job or one thing. It's the impression that you make when you meet that's important.

Lori

Would you say that being calm and confident is an asset?

Mark

Yes and do not be meek.

Matt

You don't want to be overwhelming, but you want to show that you are committed, that you have the eye of the tiger. It's a fine line.

Lori

There are big personalities, which are wonderful and you'd love to go drinking with them, but not when it's a 12-hour job. I tell myself constantly to remain calm, cool, and collected and sometimes I forget and I get very bubbly and happy but I know I have to keep check and say "Chill, don't get excited." It's very hard. Then there are some people who are so quiet that they have to be told to energize and give more. That's okay too. But that is what we gauge in the interview process and we are assuming that you are proficient and that you know the job.

Matt

I've got this pile of resumes to sort through and I almost always assume that skillwise, since they got to this point, everyone is on a level playing field. But it is in the interview process that the decision is made. It's really about the tone of the voice and the connection and even more, it's about the vibe.

Lori

Has anybody actually fired an assistant editor?

Mark

I did, just recently. That was my first and only. And I didn't do it, I had my producer do it. Actually it was opportune because there was only money in the budget for him to work three days. After a week, the guy was still screwing up and they were going to keep him on even longer.

Lori

Did he ever admit that he made a mistake?

Mark

He didn't even know he did. And to this day, I don't think he knows how badly he screwed up unless the producer called him afterwards and said, "You owe us money" or something. Because I wanted him gone, I talked to the producer and said, "I know you don't have any more money for him, so maybe you can tell him—I'm sorry but we don't have any more money for you, but thanks anyway." They got rid of him and found somebody who was willing to work for free who was perfect. He had to spend the next week trying to decipher and figure out what was wrong.

Lori

The producer made me fire my assistant on a pilot when he gave a wrong measurement to the network and it was a big to-do. We had to take out time, rather than put in time. It was horrible and I felt awful about it. Usually I just make the decision that we will not work together on the next project.

Troy

I've had to fire two people. I fired one assistant who basically had a bad attitude. He would complain and he was mean to the PA. I can't stand when a first assistant is mean to anybody else on the crew. He was annoying me quite a bit, and I would not have hired him again. We had a screening for the director's friends and family. After the screening everybody went to dinner. At one end of the table a discussion started about the changes we needed to make and suggestions were put forward about trying certain things. The director's friend, the post supervisor, was talking about these things that needed to be done and it involved a lot of assistant work. The assistant said to the post supervisor, "You better shut your mouth or I'll punch you in the nose." That night the supervisor called the director and said, "Can you believe the assistant editor said this?" The director came to us and said, "You have to fire him," and we were actually happy about that. We had to go and fire him.

The other person that I had to fire was a PA whom my assistant had hired and recommended as a great guy. He came in and just had this weird, low energy to him. His desk was in the same room as the director's assistant's desk and the director came to me and said, "You have to get rid of this guy. He's just got bad juju, basically. He is spoiling and messing up my creative force." You want to know something, it was true. You can't have somebody in the room who has a bad vibe. There was nothing wrong with this guy, it wasn't like he was weird or racist or anything—he just had this bad vibe. I had to agree with the director, he was like a bad apple in our room. You just can't have somebody like that around.

Alan

You also said something important—don't treat the people who work under you badly. There are ways to get things done without treating people like crap. And it gets picked up on and it makes the editing room an uncomfortable place. And as you might be able to tell, we like to be comfortable in the editing room, we really do. Once, I was doing this enormous industrial, political film, and I had about five or six assistants and I had hired a friend of mine to be the coeditor. It was cinema verité. The director was shooting in Pennsylvania and sending me all this film and there was just tons of it. In came thousands and thousands of feet of film, beautifully shot, with no identifying marks that you could tell. I mean it had to be sent to forensics to sync up. A slate on a cinema verité film was often two people who would take two pieces of paper and you couldn't hear anything.

Then the director showed up and he took a dislike—immense dislike—to my coeditor. It took me a while to figure out what it was and it turned out to be a very personal issue. He said to me, "I can't work with this guy. I just can't work with him and I think we have to fire him." And he said, "I'll do it" and I said, "No, I hired him and it's only right that I speak to him about this and, you know, work it out." So I said to my coeditor, "Let's go to lunch" and he said "Yeah." Well, before having lunch, we went to the men's room. We were standing there next to each other and he said to me, "You know, I'm really very uncomfortable since this guy showed up on the show, since the director showed up" and I said, "Funny thing you should mention that…" and so I was taken off the hook on this one.

The second one was much more awkward because I had hired a really good editor to work with me on *Lenny*, which was one of the first films I did. [Robert] Fosse and I decided we were getting near the end and we really needed some help and I gave him a very complex scene to cut. He's a good editor. And he did an absolutely terrible job. It was Friday and he went off to his weekend home and Fosse and I looked at the cut, well actually we looked at it before he disappeared, and Fosse said, "Well, he just doesn't have it. He's not working out." And I had to agree. So Bob [Fosse] said, "But don't worry about it. I'll come in Monday morning and I'll take care of it. Because I don't want to spoil his weekend." This is the way Bob put it. And I didn't really want to spoil his weekend either. So Monday, of course, Fosse didn't show up and he said, "Well wait, I'll come in tomorrow and I'll do it." And I said, "No you won't." And so I did it. I fired my friend. And in both cases, I mean these were both not colleagues, they were friends. And it's awkward—it's always awkward. I have only fired two people and they were both editors. I have never fired an assistant. I think I am too intimidated.

Mark

Too dependent.

Alan

That's it.

Sabrina

I've never had to fire an assistant, but I got to a point where I wouldn't rehire an assistant. It was because he got to the point where we had been working together for quite a while and he was letting his personal life interfere too much with the job. It was ruining his life and I could see it. It just wasn't servicing the job or the situation and I ended up having to take the fall for it. It was sad to see how hard a time he was having, and as much as I kept trying to talk to him, it just didn't get any better. It's the only time I have ever seen this attitude. We finished that job, but I just couldn't go back there anymore.

Lori

Did you ever tell him?

Sabrina

Absolutely. Constantly. "This is beyond reason, this can't happen anymore."

Lori

He didn't hear you. You really drew the lines.

Sabrina

Twice a day, I gave him parameters of what was acceptable to me but he was just out of control.

Lori

That's sad, but it does happen. I had an assistant once who gave me detailed accounts of the progress of her cat and his surgery. I grew tired of it quickly and didn't know how to distance myself from the situation without hurting her feelings. It's best to keep the personal issues at home and keep a professional presence in the cutting room.

Mark

Keep it interesting. Don't be dull.

Lori

Would you like to share your worst nightmare of an assistant?

Alan

Overall I really have been very lucky in my choice of apprentices and assistants and for the most part I've been incredibly happy. And if I worked enough to keep people busy, which I've been doing the last couple of years, people stay with me and they cut with me and I then sort of push them out into the world. I try and get them jobs. I'm sharing a credit with my former assistant on the film I've just finished and he's been absolutely wonderful and he will be a great editor.

Lori

Do you let your assistants cut?

Troy

I beg my assistants to cut but they rarely do. I'm like, "Please, please cut." We're in a situation these days where we have multiple machines and as long as their work is done, they're often sitting there goofing off on the Internet for several hours during the day. After dailies come in and before I go home they have the opportunity to cut scenes and I ask them to and they just don't. It shocks me.

Lori

Do you ask them when you interview them if they're going to want to cut?

Troy

I've had the same assistant for years and he's great so I'll keep hiring him because I love him but it just shocks me that he does not want to cut.

Matt

I think there are a couple of kinds of assistants—some who really want to be editors and some who just want to be great first assistants.

Lori

And that's okay too.

Matt

Absolutely and I think there's room for both of them. I have both currently. One likes to maintain the mother ship and be in charge of everything and that's his happiness. My second assistant really wants to get her hands on footage. I let her break up my dailies into strings and cut lines of dialog over and over again and that makes her really familiar with the dailies. If I see something coming up that I'm under pressure to do, I'll let her do a version of that and then I'll bring it in, see what she did and we talk about it. Somehow a little bit of her contribution usually winds up in the film in some form or another. We have discussions about how she approached the cut and we throw it back and forth and it's very positive and open. I don't press the other gent to cut. He's very blissful in his position.

What you don't want is to have a first assistant or anyone in the cutting room who is aggressive, who's kind of wrestling your mouse and comes into your cutting room without being invited, "Hey I worked on something, what do you think of this?" People who are coming on too strong definitely can spook you. I think there's a fine line. There has to be a give and take. You have to be comfortable with your assistants.

Lori

Definitely, presentation is so important. There's a question that many young women ask—when is a good time to have a baby? For a woman it's very hard because it takes you out of the race.

Alan

Well, there is a problem. My assistant on *The Notebook*, who was going to be my assistant on *Alpha Dog*, was pregnant when we began *The Notebook*, and about the time when we finished shooting, she just couldn't stay awake. One day we were running some film with the director and she said, "Excuse me for a minute," and she walked out and when Nick and I got up and walked out into the outer office, she was sleeping on the couch. We looked at each other and I said, "I guess she really should leave now because it's not good for her." She wanted to hang in and stay as long as she possibly could. We had discussions about it. I just didn't think it was good for the baby in the womb to hear the language of the movie, which was terrible! I would buy her musical records like Mozart and the kid seems to be fine now! That's how I ended up with the assistant that I've been working with for the last 2 1/2 years. He was available and I liked him from meeting him on a different film and he took over her place. So she stopped working for about 3 years. Now she's back, but it does take a while to work your way back into the system again.

Troy

These days I'm cutting features and I get sent away for months and months at a time. I was in Australia for five months and my family only came for three weeks of those five months, so I didn't get to see very much of them during that time. Now it looks like I'm being sent to New York for a year. Because they don't want to go to New York for a year, I'll see them for the summer, on Thanksgiving, and I'll fly home for some weekends. It does get very tough.

Matt

Conversely, I was just in London for a year and got to take my two kids because they're too young to object and we had a great time. It was a wonderful opportunity. And they were right with me and I was able to get home for bedtime and tuck them in and then go back to work on the tube.

Lori

But you can only do that for a while. Later on they dig in and want to stay in their school and be with their friends.

Troy

My 7-year-old said, "I don't want to come to New York, daddy." And I'm saying, "You're 7, come on."

Alan

You have to do it until they start grade school. It's a pain in the neck. It goes both ways though. At one point my ex-wife went to law school and during her last year she asked me if I would just stay home for a year. So I turned down work and I just stayed home. For a year. I had been traveling different places, so she was left with most of the raising of our daughter when she was very small. It just seemed fair that I do that. Besides which, it was New York, there wasn't very much work…

Diana

It is possible to keep working while raising a family. I somehow managed to follow my career path while bringing up the kids. You have to just pick the venues where you will not be working long hours into the night—and this did happen on many an occasion, even double jobbing day and night when funds were needed. But with careful planning of the children's schedules and keeping them as busy as possible in the afternoons with extracurricular activities, you can be both professional and parent. Also I have for a long while had my own editing equipment with a cutting room set up in my home. With the introduction of FCP and digital editing and portable hard drives, there is certainly much more flexibility in being able to work out of one's home.

Steve

If you work for a studio, they want to see you in the chair. They're paying the money and they want to say, "Oh look, okay he's in, he's on the clock, he's working." The truth is, if you work at home, they get way more out of you because you get up, you get a cup of coffee, and you're in your shorts and your T-shirt and you go to work. You don't spend 25 minutes getting ready and an hour driving somewhere.

Lori

And when you can't sleep at night, you get out of bed and you go back to cutting.

Steve

I'm sure it's happened to everybody, where you're working on something, it isn't quite right, and you get an idea and would love to be able to get up and go to the machine and see if it can work. It's happened to me on Final Cut projects where I've gotten up to go in to my cutting room and my wife will say, "What are you doing? It's four o'clock in the morning." When the idea hits you, you have the opportunity to play with it.

Sabrina

On my last show they were filming in Mexico and I stayed here in Los Angeles with my crew on the lot. In order to keep the visual effects schedule on time and on budget, I had to fly once a month to location and set certain sequences for the director to turn over and get into the big visual effects pipeline. We had a little laptop system that I wheeled in this little backpack. I shipped a monitor and some speakers down to Mexico and it sat in the director's trailer. When I arrived, I had a whole Avid in my backpack with all the media that I had in Los Angeles. All I had to do at night whenever I got into an Internet zone was just email the file back to my assistant. They could then spit out the sequence I'd just worked out with the director. My assistant could walk it across the walkway to the producers at the lot and they could all sign off on the visual effects.

Well I did this trip to Mexico once and when I came back, I thought, "Why am I coming in to the office every day?" I live a good hour and a half drive away from the cutting room so I started cutting at home a couple of days a week. I saved 2 1/2 to 3 hours driving every day twice a week. I could sit at home without distractions of phone calls or people talking. Besides, I have a great window with a great view! I got a ton done and it just gave me a life back, too. I really appreciated that and realized where we're all headed. It gave me so much more flexibility than I had ever had on another show. That was pretty great.

Lori

I like going in to the studio and seeing a bunch of friends and chatting with everybody down the hall. But it would be nice sometimes to take dailies home. On a recent show Nancy Morrison sometimes took dailies home with her. We were cutting on Final Cut Pro and found it actually relinked well. She has two little ones who get out of school early in the day, and that's good for her. I wish that had been possible when my children were little. I think it is the future trend for postproduction.

Let's change course here now. How did you get that first cutting gig? How did you switch from being an assistant to editor? Who was that someone who took a chance on you?

Sabrina

I didn't go quite the normal route because I started in northern California where I cut something right off the bat. But it didn't count and I then had to move to Los Angeles and get an assisting job. I did this for a couple of years and then I became Debbie Neil Fischer's assistant on *Fried Green Tomatoes*. I had started work being an editor and I knew that is what I was going to do. The second I was done with my assisting work, and in those days we were on film, I would be in Debbie's room, right there, working side by side. And she let me. And the director got to be very aware of that, too. It got to the point where nothing would happen without my input as well. He started asking me to cut scenes for *Fried Green Tomatoes*, even though I was hired as an assistant. At the very end they called me in to look at the credits and they had surprised me with a single card, associate editor credit. That director, John Avnet, then turned around and gave me my first editing gig on a TV movie the next year.

Lori

The Fates were with you at that point—a combination of a great mentor in Debbie, and a receptive director. But you were fully prepared when opportunity knocked.

Mark

I didn't want to wait for opportunity to knock. My first job after I moved out to Los Angeles was as a PA on *Rock 'n' Roll High School*. I delivered the film to the cutting room and after production ceased, I hung out in the cutting room and became an assistant editor. There were two editors and they needed two assistants. I assisted for free for a couple of months and then I went to the producer and said, "You need me, please pay me." And so they paid me $100 a week and I was very happy. While assisting, they needed a trailer for the film, so the other assistant and myself volunteered to edit it. And because this was Roger Corman, no budget kind of filmmaking, they said, "Sure you can do it. We're not going to pay you though." We were more than overjoyed to make a black and white dupe of the feature that was still being cut and come up with a trailer. And that was my first professional editing gig. Of course right after that I wanted to edit a feature, but I had to assist a couple more times.

I went over to Cannon Films, which was also a very low-budget, Israeli-run organization and assisted on a couple more films. While assisting on *The Last American Virgin*, I said, "I really want to cut, whatever the next film is, I want to be the editor. Please let me be the editor." They said, "Well how do we know you can edit?" And I said, "I can, I'll edit a trailer." They said, "Okay, you edit a trailer." They had a film they had just bought, a Mexican film, which at that time was called *The Treasure of the Four Balls*. And so, I took this movie and I cut the fastest-moving action trailer you have ever seen. I flopped shots and sped them up and played them backwards and added every trick in the book to make it look like the most exciting film ever since *Indiana Jones*. It turned out great and everybody said, "This is much better than the movie"—and it was. And in fact, the trailer got reviewed in the *New York Times*. "This trailer's fantastic. Oh, and by the way, the movie is nothing like the trailer." The fact that the trailer got a rave review was my proof that I could edit. I got to coedit the next feature with Michael Duffy, who was one of the editors there. And so my first feature I got to edit was *Revenge of the Ninja*. There was no going back after that. I was anxious to cut and I kept saying, "I can do it," and I would volunteer and would do it.

Troy

I was assisting on *Tales from the Crypt* and one of the editors was interviewing for directing jobs on a TV show. It was the first day of dailies and he came in and put dailies in and left for the interview. The second day of dailies came in and he didn't even come in that day. He called and said, "I have meetings, you can edit it." It was only a five-day shoot on *Tales from the Crypt* and he came in, probably about two hours that entire week. And by the end of the week, he had this directing job and he quit editing. Steven Hopkins, who had directed it, came in and we finished the episode. That was my first thing that I edited.

Lori

Did they have to get permission from Steven or the producers to move you up?

Troy

We didn't get permission from anybody [for this episode]. It was one of those things where nobody was admitting it was happening. Michael didn't call up and say, "I'm not coming in because I'm interviewing for a different job and by the way Troy is cutting the dailies." It just happened that the week ended and the director's cut was coming up and there was no editor and I cut all the footage. Steven came in and said, "Oh, so what are we doing here?" We worked together and it worked out well. In fact, Steven went to the producers and tried to get me hired as an editor and they wouldn't do it. So, by the next season an editor had left at some point in the middle of the season and I did one episode on the third season, too.

Matt

I was a commercial assistant and I had tried my hand at everything. Back in the days before Final Cut, if you had the keys to an Avid or access to a facility that had an Avid, it made you pretty popular in town. So you could take on a lot of projects. Because I was single at the time, I spent most of my free time, nights and weekends, just cutting anything anybody had that I could get my hands on—people's reels, actor's reels. This is actually really good training. They have specific demands like "I want to make it look like I am playing opposite this guy" or "Make it look like I am shooting at the star." So you have to go in and take the bit that they did on some TV show and rearrange it so it looks like they are having eye contact with the main actor even though they aren't.

I was working for Angus Wall, who has now moved into features, but was then cutting commercials. He had just cut *Benjamin Button* and I had to cut his hairdresser's wedding video. Editors get asked, when cutting your hair, "Oh hey, I just got all this footage from my wedding video and it would be really great if I could get somebody to put it together." And Angus said, "Oh, I'll take care of it," and he dropped off a truckload of VHS tapes and said to me, "You do it." I put a lot of time into that and learned a lot from cutting that wedding video.

Marc Forster and a friend of mine wrote a script, *Everything Put Together*, about SIDS, and they gave it to me to read. I just saw the potential of the movie and knew what it should feel like if they shot it right. I knew how it should play and I told him, "I really want to do this and I have an Avid and 'I got the skills to pay the bills'—let's do this." So my friend told his partner, "You know, my friend can cut this and he has an Avid" and they said, "Really? He has an Avid? Well, we don't have any money left for the post, so let's see what he's like. What's his vibe like?" So Marc brought in a reel of a friend who was an actress and a bunch of dailies to add to her reel. We then worked together and I put in some music and we put some titles on it. We spent about a half a day together and he said, "Well you seem like a good guy and you have this nice facility and it's really comfortable and there's snacks in the kitchen and I can hang out here while you cut my movie." Then I said, "Okay great, let's do it."

So that began a very long process of working on the Avid when there wasn't a commercial being cut. Often we would get bumped. I would say, "Come in at nine," and then a dog food commercial would arrive and our day on the Avid would go away. So he would come back at nine at night and I would stay and cut till six in the morning, and then I would clean up the room and be an assistant the next day. Eventually we got a virtual movie that was in the Avid that we had cut with no help from anybody—I was my own assistant. I really busted my ass for him on this project. And then we heard, "We love the movie, bring it to Sundance," but it was stuck in the computer. I then had to pull it out and bring it to all these finishing houses that I had established relationships with as an assistant commercial editor. All those people that I connected with who were colorists and mixers said, "Bring it here and we'll finish it." I got an online editor to do our titles and all of our graphics. I fronted the entire post of the movie to get it up to Sundance without a nickel from the producers. I just did it all with favors. By the time we got to Sundance, Marc and I were kind of the last men standing and he said, "You know, you've really proven yourself." Luckily for me, I hitched my wagon to the right star and it really paid off. He parlayed that into *Monster's Ball* and we haven't stopped working together since.

Lori

What a wonderful success story.

Matt

Well, it's rare that somebody will stick with you. Normally you get that phone call that sounds like, "I get to do a studio movie. Thanks so much for the freebee and I'll call you on the next one. I'm going to get you back." And they don't do that. My director stood up to the studio and said, "You liked my first movie, which is why you hired me, and if you don't use my cinematographer and my editor, I can't promise that I will give you the same product, because those guys had a lot to do with it." And they said, "Really?" and he replied, "Yeah, really. I produced something with these guys and I am comfortable with them and that's my vision. And if you want me to stay, I can promise I will do a great job with them, but if you stick me with those other guys—I'll do my best, but I don't know what's going to happen." And they said, "Well, we can always fire the editor. We'll let him take a shot." So they brought me on and it went well.

Lori

It worked. It is rare for the director to fight for both the cinematographer and the editor. Usually the cinematographer wins.

Matt

It's been the three of us for eight movies now.

Sabrina

It's also rare that you stay on the same schedule, too. Just keeping the same schedule is very rare with directors.

Matt

You never know whom the freebee is really for. You don't know who's watching you or who you're impressing. It could a producer, a director, a post supervisor, but if you are dropping off film, you just don't know where it's going to lead. And if you are doing your best at all times and trying to impress people, they are going to notice you and somebody's going to pick you up. They are going to see you've got that quality.

Lori

You're always on your game.

Matt

Yeah, you've got to pick, *try* to pick your projects well, so you don't have your time wasted on a freebee for someone. Freebees don't go away. When they don't have the money to pay you, they will not leave you alone.

Lori

You still have to do those because you won't know if they are going to lead somewhere.

Matt

But any aspiring Sundance director could become Marc Forster, so you just have to do your best.

Troy

The hardest movies that I ever worked on are the free movies. They're so much harder than the normal movies.

Matt

I worked on a 60-second commercial for six months one time. Because they didn't have any money, they just kept coming around. Why would they go away if it doesn't cost them anything?

Lori

Pro bono films can be so much more demanding. I did an ERA [equal rights amendment] documentary once, I started getting a terrible toothache and I needed a root canal. I told the director/producer, "I have to leave… I have to go to the dentist." And she said, "No, you have to stay," and I said, "but…"

Matt

"But you're not paying me."

Lori

"…you have to let me go…"

Matt

"We've given you a great opportunity."

Lori

It was a great opportunity and I believed in the subject matter, but the director/producer was just horrible. I was doing it as favor to her husband, a director I hoped to work with.

Stephen

I came to work here in Hollywood and in those days there were apprentices. When you were an apprentice, you worked in the shipping room and you basically carried film around to rooms, because there were screenings there all the time and you just tried to meet people. You would try and find an assistant that you got on with and you would say, "When are you doing dailies?" and they would usually reply, "Be here tomorrow morning at six o'clock." You would go and in a very short amount of time, you would learn where he picked up the tracks and where he picked up the picture and you would start doing that chore and show initiative. Pretty soon you would say, "You can come in an hour later, I'll do all the dailies for you." And you were just thrilled to be able to do that.

After learning those skills, I got hired. I got invited to go up to this room where they were doing this film called *Winning*. It was a Paul Newman feature and at that time, etiquette between apprentices and assistants and editors was very different. If you were an apprentice, you almost never made eye contact with the editor. You didn't speak directly to him, but I didn't know that. I came into this big room and it's full of people and the editor is sitting at a Moviola and behind him is a little 16 mm trim bin with the top down, and I look around the room and go over and flop myself down right in back of him and say, "Oh hi, how are you?" He turned around, put his glasses down and gave me the evil eye. I just flashed him my best smile. He could easily have picked me up and thrown me out of the room, but luckily it did not happen.

Paul Newman wanted to see all 300 thousand feet of some race footage so they hired a bunch of editors and they hired an apprentice. And the editor said, "Get the love kid that's running around here." I was hired to empty ashtrays and make coffee and that was supposed to be my job. But I had a certain sort of sixth sense about film that I had learned when I was in college and so I was keen to follow my instincts. We had a couple of people who would work all night when the other editors weren't around and I would just watch how they laid stuff out. Somebody would say, "I need a red car with a green number going left to right on camera four." And I would go in and look for it. "I think I found the shot." They were impressed that I had the initiative to go in and find the material. I watched them splicing and I'd go by and think, "Oh hell, I can do that, no problem." Then one day we were rushing for a screening which was 45 minutes away, and this editor, who is the main editor, is getting up screaming, "Gordon, where's Gordon? Jesus Christ, I've got to make these changes. Where's Gordon?" And I walked by and I sat down in the chair and I said, "I'll do it." I was pretty sure I could do it or I could figure it out. I was fortunate because the editor responded to that initiative and he guided me, "No, no, not there, cut here," That was my first little interchange with him. About a month later, everybody that had been on the show left, and I was the last one standing. I became his assistant on that feature. He would constantly give me film and say, "Go cut it." It became that kind of relationship.

When that film ended, the editor went on to a TV show, *Marcus Welby, MD*, and then his assistant died. Ed said, "I want Lovejoy." He moved me up and I became his assistant in television. The worse the footage was, the more excited he would get and I thought, "I want to be like him. I want to get excited about this stuff." It set off a spark in me, to strive for internal excellence. That's where it came from; it came from that experience with him.

One day he gave me three pieces of film to cut and I came in at four o'clock in the morning to get it done before dailies would start. I struggled to get the shots to cut together. He sat across the room, looked back, put his glasses down and said, "Jesus Christ, what the _____ are you doing over there?" And I said, "Well, I can't—and the thing—and…" He walked over and ran it [the film] and ran it again and said, "Mark," and "Take this piece back and move this up there and extend these three frames." Before he had sat down, just 20 feet away, I'd made the cut and put it in the machine and run it and said, "G–d damn…" He asked, "What is your problem?" I replied, "I worked on that for 2 1/2 hours and you fixed it in 15 seconds." And he pulled his glasses down and said to me, "That's 35 years and 15 seconds."

Lori

That's awesome. I love that "35 years and 15 seconds."

Diana

In 1986 I moved to Los Angeles from South Africa with my family where I had worked as a film editor on many feature films and had cut countless hours of television programming from episodic to documentaries. My network of contacts in the industry in Hollywood was minimal and without local credits, finding work as an editor was proving extremely difficult. With two small hungry children, I was desperate to get my foot in the door of an editing room. Someone I knew was working on a feature film, *The Man Who Broke a Thousand Chains* directed by Danny Mann for HBO. She mentioned that the editor, Walt Hanneman, A.C.E. was looking for an apprentice editor and suggested I apply for the job. The film starred Val Kilmer, Charles Durning, Kyra Sedgwick, Elisha Cook, and Sonya Braga and promised to be a worthwhile project even though the work was that of an apprentice and entailed rolling and boxing the 35 mm trims—they were still working with 35 mm film and cutting on a Moviola. I went for the interview and got the job.

The first strange thing that happened when I went into the cutting room on the first day was that I took one look at Walt's first assistant and could not believe my eyes. Rewind my life almost 20 years to 1969. The scene—Pinewood Studios, London, editing room of a movie of the week called *The Gaunt Woman* for

Universal Studios directed by Boris Sagal and starring Lorne Green and Rachel Roberts. I am there as an intern sitting in a corner observing the workings of editor Archie Ludsky's cutting room. The second assistant on that film in London was Brian Frost. Fast forward. Almost 2 decades later. Walt's current first assistant in Hollywood is Brian. Here we were, working side by side in Hollywood on the same film. Serendipity or the Fates sure must have had a hand in this one! You just never know who you will be teamed with again in postproduction. It is a small industry.

Shortly after I started working on the show, Walt learned that I had a great deal of editing experience and gave me sequences to edit. The producer–writer also asked me to cut together a lyrical montage for the end of the show, which he loved. Then as fate would have it, Walt took ill and had to leave the film. The first assistant and I were then offered the editor's seat and together we completed the show. We all ended up sharing [the] editor's credit. It turned out to be a great movie and one I am very proud of having worked on.

This is really how I got my foot in the door in Hollywood. Sometimes you just have to swallow your pride and keep your eyes on the prize. Always be humble and know that you have to shine no matter what the circumstance.

Lori

What a great tale Diana. Great fortitude.

Alan

I started working in New York, which is another world and was another world when I started there. It wasn't as formal in that you didn't have to spend a particular amount of time in a category. There maybe were no categories. And I was never an assistant, I was a sound effects editor. And when I did have the chance to be an assistant at a commercial house, I hated it. So I went back to working in a music editing place and I did sound effects for several movies for Sydney Lumet. Sydney asked me if I wanted to edit his next movie. And what that meant was that Sydney would stand right behind you and tell you exactly what he wanted. But I figured yeah, I really want to do that because I was a little bored with sound editing. Before that happened, I got a call—I was doing the sound effects for the original film of *The Producers* and the editor and Mel Brooks did not get along for one moment. Ralph Rosenbloom was the editor and when he left, I took over the film. There was very little to do on it, of course in sound effects, but there was one sequence in the middle that never got a laugh. And Mel said, "Okay, you come in on Monday, we'll work together and we'll get that working" and I said, "You know, you worked on this with Ralph for quite a while. Why don't you let me take a shot at it?" and he said "Okay." So, I went in, looked at the dailies and discovered that only one big master shot was used in the scene. When I started editing it, I discovered there were close-ups and two shots and all kinds of treasures. And then I started cutting this scene together and discovered that Ralph had basically put the scene together the same way. And Mel had taken it apart. When you had film, you could see the splices and the old marks, so my splices were very similar to Ralph's—a third of a second this way or that. And when we screened the movie, Mel came in and looked at the scene and I guess he figured that if two editors said it was funnier this way, he'd go for that. I don't know, he never complained. And we had a screening shortly thereafter and the audience laughed so hard at the section, that they couldn't hear the dialog in large part. And I thought, "Oh boy, I really love this." I mean, you could take material and you can manipulate people, you can make them laugh, you can make them cry, *you* can do it. I didn't know I had those abilities. Once I did, I didn't want to go back to being a sound editor anymore. And then I did a couple of films for Sydney Lumet and he was over my shoulder and I learned an enormous amount about performance and things. That was how I got started. A few years later Sydney asked me to do *Network* and I was afraid he wanted to be over my shoulder again and I wasn't going to do that, but it was on a tight schedule and he left me alone and we had a great time.

Lori

Thank you Alan. Thank you Mark, Matt, Stephen, Sabrina, Troy, and Diana! There is so much to learn from all of you. Thank you for sharing!

The messages from our esteemed colleagues are clear as a bell. When you dedicate yourself to succeeding in your chosen field of endeavor, anything is possible! Follow your dreams. Make them a reality.

The world you desired can be won. It exists, it is real, it is possible, it is yours.

Ayn Rand

Make the cut.

Glossary

A

AD

Assistant director. The person in charge of the shooting schedule, directing the extras, keeping the actors on time, and the right hand man to the director.

ADR

Automatic dialog replacement (looping). This is done on a looping (recording) stage to rerecord dialog after the film is completely shot to replace unusable original sound, change performance, or add new dialog.

ALTS

Alternate takes.

AUDIO LAYBACK

After the movie is mixed on the dub stage, the tracks are applied to the film in an optical track (in film) or to the audio tracks on the video master (CTM).

B

BACK NINE

The last nine episodes of a TV show ordered for pickup by the network.

BACK 12

The last 12 episodes of a TV show ordered for pickup by the network.

BACKPLATE

A still photograph used as the background for live action.

BG

Background. Either the ambient sound on location, or the actors who are extras on a film set.

BROADCAST STANDARDS

See *Standards and Practices*.

BUMPERS

A short piece of video shown on television shows during commercial breaks that identifies the show and tells the audience that the show will return shortly.

BURN-IN

The process of adding live or still visuals to a blank screen (i.e., TV set, computer) after completion of the film.

C

CALIBRATE

To determine, check, or rectify the graduation of different equipment ensuring they are all lined up and give the same readings.

DOI: 10.1016/B978-0-240-81398-1.00023-7

CALL SHEET

A sheet of paper issued to the cast and crew of a film production, created by an assistant director, informing them where and when they should report for a particular day of shooting. Call sheets also include other useful information, such as contact information (i.e., phone numbers of crew members and other contacts), the schedule for the day, which scenes and script pages are being shot, and the address of the shoot location. Additionally, call sheets may contain information about cast transportation arrangements, parking instructions, and safety notes.

CHASE CASSETTE

An ouput (copy) of the completed show that will be used by the online editor as a viewing reference.

CHEAT SHEET

A list of necessary information.

CHECKING BLACKS

Before digitizing footage, the levels of brightness are checked. One looks at the color bars, a standardized set of graduated vertical colors that are recorded to a precise standard onto a videotape.

CLEANING THE TRACKS

The process of preparing tracks for onlining and mixing by removing jump cuts, add edits, extraneous sounds, and separating dialog, sound effects and music onto dedicated tracks.

CLONE

A digital tape, such as D1 or D2, that is copied to another digital tape. There is no loss of picture quality because the process is digital and the copy is identical to the original.

CONTINUITY

A list of the scenes in the film, with scene numbers and short scene descriptions.

COVER SHEETS

A cover page with relevant information that explains what a document is about or explains briefly about the accompanying film material.

D

DAT

Digital audio tape. A small cassette tape onto which two tracks of audio can be recorded. Because of the digital nature of the recording, tapes can be copied countless times without loss of quality.

DEFAULT SETTINGS

Inherent settings to which a computer will return.

DIGITAL INTERMEDIATE (DI)

After the negative is conformed and cut to match the picture edits, a digital copy called the DI is made. This allows the process of color correction, titling, and VFX to be done in the digital world before the final print is struck.

DROP FRAME TIME CODE

A time code in which certain numbers are periodically skipped (two frame numbers at every minute except the 10th) to make the numbers exactly match real (clock) time. The actual picture frames are not dropped; only numbers are skipped. Drop frame time code adds 3 seconds and 18 frames each hour over nondrop frame time code.

DUPLICATE
A copy of a shot or a sequence.

E

EDITOR'S PREFERENCES
Settings that can be programmed into the computer and keyboard that reflect the personal choices of the editor. They reflect the way he would like to edit with regard to making shortcuts or other commands to ease his working process.

EVENT
In digital editing, a visual or sound change in your timeline or edl.

F

FLEX FILE
A computer file that contains all the relevant data concerning the dailies that is needed to import material into the computer.

FORMAT SHEET
The paperwork that the network provides with commercial blacks and ID's filled in, and blanks for the assistant editor to complete with regard to the amount of time for each act, the recap, and the total running time.

FX
An abbreviation for effects, such as sound effects.

G

GROUP CLIPS
This form of syncing dailies, also known as multicam, is used when a scene is shot with several cameras following the same action. All the coverage is synced up and laid in on the time line on different tracks at matching timecodes. In this way, all the different camera shots can be played together in sync, which makes it possible to view all of the action from all angles simultaneously.

J

JUMP CUT
A cut where the out and in footage are both from the same take, but there are frames missing in-between.

L

LAYBACK
See *audio layback*.

LICENSE
The rights for use for any given materials, such as music, product placement, lyrics, etc.

LIFT
A scene that has been removed from an edited show. They are kept intact as lifts.

LINED SCRIPT
The shooting script of the film onto which the script supervisor has noted all of the setups that were shot and what lines of dialog were included in each setup. The term is also used to denote the combination of the lined script and their facing page which contains take numbers, the length of the action, circled select takes, a description of each setup, camera roll number, sound roll number, lens number, and notes given on set for each take.

LOCKED
The point in the editing of a film when the picture editing is completed.

M

MASTER
The original footage that is shot either on film, tape, or digital media. It can also be the original edited master from which all copies are made.

MATCHBACK
A process for visual and audio replacement whereby higher resolution and better sound quality replaces the media with which the editor works.

MIXDOWN
Several audio tracks can be combined and mixed down to one track, retaining the original settings on each track.

MUSIC AND SOUND EFFECTS SPOTTING
When the film is cut, the composer and music editor will come and view the show with the editor, director, and producer and decide where music should be added. Similarly, the sound effects supervisor and his crew will view the film with the editor, director, and producer, and discuss the sound design. ADR is discussed and spotted.

MUSIC CODES
A timecode (in digital) or code number (on film) that is applied to the dailies in addition to the already existing timecode and key code. This music code enables the editor to find sync easily during a music sequence.

MX
Music.

N

NEEDLE DROP
A tune or piece of music that can be purchased and licensed for use in a film and most often has lyrics.

NONDROP FRAME TIMECODE
Timecode in which each frame is given a continuous and successive timecode number. As a result, the code does not exactly represent real time. The mismatch amounts to an 18-frame overrun every 10 minutes.

O

ONLINE

The process of editing the original master tapes into the final viewing tape at a high enough resolution to be broadcast quality. The final tape is called the final *edited master.*

OUTPUT

The process of transferring the film from an editing machine to a videotape or DVD for viewing.

P

PICKUP SHOT

When a shot has been made on the set and the director wishes to redo part of the take, the redo is called a pickup shot because only a portion of the take is redone. It is often designated with a PU after the take number on the slate. A pickup could also be shot at a later date. These are often done by the second unit.

PILOT AND 12

The network green light order for the pilot plus 12 more episodes.

PLAYBACK

A musical recording played back to the actors to which they lip sync on the set to maintain the same musical performance or dancing sync from take to take. Film playback is previously edited or stock footage that will play on a monitor or computer screen during the shoot.

PLAYBACK DAYS

The day on which the production will shoot scenes that contain visual or audio playback.

POPPING THE TRACKS

The process of marking up the frame in which the slate claps on a roll of dailies track. When this is done, you can sync them up with an already marked set of picture takes where you see the slate clap. Also called *marking the tracks.*

POSTLAP

In an L-shaped cut (when the audio is not cut at the same place as the film), this is when the audio continues after the picture edit.

PRELAP

In an L-shaped cut, this is when the incoming audio precedes the picture edit.

Q

QUICKTIME

A program written by Apple that allows Macs and PCs to compress, edit, and play back movies (with picture and sound). Some of the nonlinear editing systems are designed to use or create QuickTime (QT) movies.

R

RECORD SIDE

The interface on the Avid editing system that allows you to record and save your cuts. It is called the Canvas in Final Cut Pro.

RESOLUTION
The amount of detail in a digital picture image. When there is more compression, there is less resolution.

RUNOUTS
The 30 or more seconds of excess leader or fill that is put at the ends of a show.

S

SHOOTING SCHEDULES
Prepared by the production office, this schedule tells what scenes are going to be shot on which days, which actors will be required, the location, and any other relevant information that needs to be shared concerning that day's shoot.

SLIDE THE MUSIC
The ability on the time line to move the music forward or backward to find exactly where you would like to place it.

SOURCE SIDE
The interface on the Avid editing system that allows you to view your dailies and mark your selected clips for editing. It is called the Viewer in Final Cut Pro.

SPOT
A term used to view the final cut of a show and to determine where music or sound effects need to be added or where it should begin and end.

STANDARDS AND PRACTICES
The name of a department at a television network that is responsible for monitoring the language, violence, or sexual content of the program that airs. Also referred to as Broadcast Standards and Practices (or BS&P). This department is also responsible for the technical quality that is required for broadcast.

STOCK SHOTS
Also called *stock footage*. Often a production is not able to shoot certain shots, so it obtains the shots from other sources, such as stock libraries. The libraries sell hard-to-obtain shots, such as a volcano erupting. Stock footage can also be a collection of shots that have been sourced from a production and used repeatedly on a show over a period of seasons. These stock shots are used to establish a location, among other things.

STRIKE
Making a print of the film, such as to *strike a print*.

STRIPE
Applying sound to tape or film is called to *stripe a tape*.

SUBCLIP
A portion of a selected shot that can be removed as a separate clip and stored and edited.

SUBTITLE
Writing that appears at the bottom of the screen. It is often used to translate films into a different language, translate inaudible dialog, or identify location (country, city, building) or year.

T

TECH SUPPORT
A service usually provided by equipment suppliers who help with any technical problems you experience with their hardware.

TECHS
The people who are available to answer questions and help with technical problems.

TELECINE
A process that takes a film image and converts it into a video or digital image. It normally uses the 3:2 *pulldown* process.

TEMP SCORE
Music used during the editing process that is temporary and will be replaced by a composer's score and licensed needle drops.

TIME LINE
The display of the edited film and sound on an electronic editing machine.

TIMECODE
Electronic code numbers, also called *SMPTE code*, used on videotape and digital editing workstations for identification. It is also used to sync tapes to one another or to another machine. It comes in two forms: drop frame and nondrop frame.

TIMINGS
Measurements of a sequence or sequences in a cut show.

TITLES
Words that are shown on a screen with or without a picture behind them. There are Main titles, Opening Credit titles, and End Credit titles that give credit to the crew. See *subtitle*.

TRADES
Any paper or journal that deals with film business news, such as the *The Hollywood Reporter* and *Variety*.

TRIM MODE
A setting on the editing system that allows you to fix edits and adjust your shots by trimming the head or tail or by adding or subtracting frames. Also referred to as splice mode.

TRT
Total running time. The length of your film from the first frame of picture to the final fade out.

U

USER SETTINGS
Personal preferences that can be saved on your machine.

V

VAM
Video assembled master. It is the tape or DVD of the online, and is also referred to as the assembly master or edited master.

VFX OR VIZFX
Visual effects.

VOICE-OVER
A recording of a voice of an actor who does not appear on the screen.

W

WILD LINE
A line of dialog that is recorded without picture to replace a line with sound issues. It could also be a line of dialog that is recorded without picture to be used as added information in a scene.

Index

Index

Index

Index

Index

Index

Index

visual effects (VFX), 31
    for director's cut, 82
    preparing VFX notes, 91–92
VO. *See* voice-over (VO) narration
VO bin, 103–104
voice mail messages, 150
voice-over (VO) narration, 101
    folder for (reality shows), 116

W

Wall, Angus, 203
wall continuity, 17, 21t, 23–26, 24f. *See also* continuity;
    scene timings

watching dailies, 64–65
wild lines, 46, 139–140
wild tracks, 52
word of mouth. *See* networking
work, finding. *See* finding jobs
work clothes and appearance, 147, 153
work history (resumes), 11
work space synchronization, 112
working from home, 200, 201
writing numbers, practicing, 157

Z

Z bins (project window), 40, 40f, 41–42